Shakespeare's Globe

From 1997 Shakespeare's Globe flourished once more on London's South Bank after an absence of four hundred years. The playhouse is now a major attraction for theatregoers, scholars, tourists, teachers and students of all ages, who come to experience Shakespeare's plays and those of his contemporaries performed in their original conditions.

The team of artists and education specialists who made this happen come together here to reflect on their ten-year experiment. Principal actors, designers, musicians and Globe Education staff engage with international scholars in a lively debate about the impact of this extraordinary building. Featuring an in-depth interview with former Artistic Director Mark Rylance and a contribution from Patrick Spottiswoode, Founder and Director of Globe Education, the book highlights the complex relationship between designer, composer, actor and audience that gives energy to this thriving Shakespearean centre.

CHRISTIE CARSON is Senior Lecturer in the Department of English at Royal Holloway, University of London.

FARAH KARIM-COOPER is Lecturer in Globe Education, oversees all research activities at Shakespeare's Globe and chairs the Globe Architecture Research Group.

SHAKESPEARE'S GLOBE: A THEATRICAL EXPERIMENT

Edited by

CHRISTIE CARSON

and

FARAH KARIM-COOPER

CAMBRIDGE
UNIVERSITY PRESS

CAMBRIDGE
UNIVERSITY PRESS

University Printing House, Cambridge CB2 8BS, United Kingdom

One Liberty Plaza, 20th Floor, New York, NY 10006, USA

477 Williamstown Road, Port Melbourne, VIC 3207, Australia

314-321, 3rd Floor, Plot 3, Splendor Forum, Jasola District Centre, New Delhi-110025, India

79 Anson Road, #06-04/06, Singapore 079906

Cambridge University Press is part of the University of Cambridge.

It furthers the University's mission by disseminating knowledge in the pursuit of education, learning and research at the highest international levels of excellence.

www.cambridge.org
Information on this title: www.cambridge.org/9780521701662

© Cambridge University Press 2008

First published 2008
6th printing 2015

A catalogue record for this publication is available from the British Library

Library of Congress Cataloging in Publication data
Shakespeare's Globe : a theatrical experiment / edited by Christie Carson and Farah Karim-Cooper.
    p.   cm.
Includes bibliographical references and index.
ISBN 978-0-521-87778-7 (hardcopy) – ISBN 978-0-521-70166-2 (pbk.)
1. Shakespeare, William, 1564–1616 – Dramatic production.   2. Shakespeare, William, 1564–1616 – Stage history – 1950–   3. Shakespeare, William, 1564–1616 – Stage history – England – London.   4. Globe Theatre (London, England : 1996–)
5. Theater – England – London – History – 20th century.   6. Theater – Production and direction – History – 20th century.   I. Carson, Christie.
II. Karim-Cooper, Farah.
PR3106.S53   2008
792.9'5 – dc22   2008031329

ISBN 978-0-521-87778-7 Hardback
ISBN 978-0-521-70166-2 Paperback

CONTENTS

ILLUSTRATIONS

COLOUR PLATES

CHRISTIE CARSON is Senior Lecturer in the Department of English at Royal Holloway University of London. Before moving into the English Department she worked as an Institutional Research Fellow in the Department of Drama and Theatre at Royal Holloway and was Director of the Centre of Multimedia Performance History from 1996 to 2003. She is the co-editor of *The Cambridge King Lear CD-ROM: Text and Performance Archive* (Cambridge, 2000) and the Principle Investigator of the AHRB-funded research project *Designing Shakespeare: an Audio-Visual Archive, 1960–2000*, which documents the performance history of Shakespeare in Stratford and London. She has published widely on the subject of contemporary performance and the influence of digital technology on audience interaction and research practices, including articles for *Shakespeare Survey* and *Performance Research*.

FARAH KARIM-COOPER, as Lecturer in Globe Education, oversees all research activities at Shakespeare's Globe and chairs the Globe Architecture Research Group. She is also a Visiting Research Fellow of King's College London and co-convenes the Globe/King's MA in Shakespearean Studies: Text and Playhouse. In addition to publishing articles and essays in books, her first monograph *Cosmetics in Shakespearean and Renaissance Drama* was published in 2006.

FIONA BANKS is Head of Learning for Globe Education at Shakespeare's Globe, where she leads Globe Education's programmes, projects and resources for young people and teachers. Much of her time is devoted to the training and development of Globe Education's team of practitioners – actors and directors who bring their knowledge of playing Shakespeare to over 100,000 students each year, through workshops, lectures, performances, video conferences and outreach programmes. Originally a teacher, Fiona's key area of interest and research is in the role of the arts in schools and the potential for creative approaches to learning across the school curriculum. She teaches an MA in Performing Arts in the Classroom with King's College London and is currently developing a MEd module with Cambridge University, Understanding Shakespeare through Performance.

TIM CARROLL is the former Associate Theatre Director at Shakespeare's Globe, where he directed Augustine's Oak (1999), The Two Noble Kinsmen (2000), Macbeth (2001), Twelfth Night (at Middle Temple Hall and Shakespeare's Globe, 2002), The Golden Ass (2002), Richard II (2003), Dido, Queen of Carthage (2003), Romeo and Juliet (2004) and The Tempest (2005). He began his career with the English Shakespeare Company, and was Associate Director of the Northcott Theatre, Exeter. In 2004 he directed The Tempest for Teatro São Luiz, Lisbon. Tim has given lectures and talks nationally and internationally about theatre, directing and his work at the Globe.

PAUL CHAHIDI has an MA in Arabic and Persian from Trinity College, Cambridge. He trained at the Central School of Speech and Drama. He has been in several Globe productions, including Twelfth Night (2002), Macbeth (2001), The Two Noble Kinsmen (2000), Augustine's Oak and The Comedy of Errors (1999). Other theatre includes Rhinoceros and The Arsonists at the Royal Court, As You Like It, The American Pilot, Cymbeline, The Devil is an Ass, Julius Caesar, A Midsummer Night's Dream, The Merry Wives the

Musical, *The Taming of the Shrew*, *Tamer Tamed*, *Woyzeck* (all RSC); *Faustus* (Northampton), *Engaged* (Orange Tree), *Arabian Nights* (Young Vic), *Misalliance* (Clwyd) and *All's Well that Ends Well* (Oxford Stage Co.).

RALPH ALAN COHEN is the Founding Executive Director of the American Shakespeare Center and was the project leader for the Blackfriars Playhouse in Staunton, Virginia. He designed the Mary Baldwin College Master of Letters and Fine Arts programme in Shakespeare in Performance. He has directed 22 productions of the plays of Shakespeare and his contemporaries. He is the author of *ShakesFear and How to Cure It* (2007), the co-editor of *Your Five Gallants* in *The Complete Works of Thomas Middleton* (2008); and was guest editor of two teaching editions of *Shakespeare Quarterly*. In 1987 he was a first recipient of Virginia's Outstanding Faculty Award.

ALAN C. DESSEN is Peter G. Phialas Professor (Emeritus) at the University of North Carolina, Chapel Hill, and is the author of eight books, four of them with Cambridge University Press: *Elizabethan Stage Conventions and Modern Interpreters* (1984); *Recovering Shakespeare's Theatrical Vocabulary* (1995); *Rescripting Shakespeare* (2002); and, co-authored with Leslie Thomson, *A Dictionary of Stage Directions in English Drama, 1580–1642*. In 2005 he gave the annual British Academy Shakespeare lecture. Since 1994 he has been editor or co-editor of the 'Shakespeare Performed' section of *Shakespeare Quarterly*.

ANDREW GURR is Professor Emeritus at the University of Reading. He has published several books and many articles about the Shakespearean period, and has edited six plays by Shakespeare and his contemporaries. His most noted books are *The Shakespearean Stage 1574–1642*, now in its third edition (Cambridge University Press, 1992), *Playgoing in Shakespeare's London*, now also in a third edition (Cambridge University Press, 2004), *The Shakespearean Playing Companies* (1996), and most recently, *The Shakespeare Company, 1594–1642* (Cambridge University Press, 2004). Professor Gurr was Director of Research 1995–2002, is on the Globe Architecture Research Group and continues to act as an academic advisor to Shakespeare's Globe.

FRANKLIN J. HILDY is Professor and Director of Graduate Studies in the Department of Theatre at the University of Maryland. He is author of *Shakespeare at the Maddermarket* (1986), editor of *New Issues in the Reconstruction of Shakespeare's Theatre* (1990), co-author, with Oscar G. Brockett of four editions of *History of the Theatre* and over fifty articles on a wide range of topics, including the history of efforts to reconstruct the theatres of Shakespeare's day. He has served as an advisor to Shakespeare's Globe, London since 1984 and has been a consultant on numerous reconstruction attempts in the United States.

DAVID LINDLEY is Professor of Renaissance Literature at Leeds University. He has written on the Court Masque, on the scandalous story of Frances Howard, and more recently has edited Shakespeare's *The Tempest* for the New Cambridge Shakespeare, and has published a stage history of the play's performances at Stratford. His latest book is a study of *Shakespeare and Music* for the Arden Critical Companions series.

WILLIAM LYONS specialises in the research and performance of music from the twelfth to the seventeenth centuries and is a player of early woodwind instruments. He teaches on the Medieval and Renaissance Studies programme at the Guildhall School of Music and Drama and the Royal College of Music, and is a member of the acclaimed early music ensemble, The Dufay Collective. At the Globe, William has arranged, composed and directed music for numerous productions as well as playing for shows and acting as a historical consultant. He has also worked as composer and historical advisor for film, radio and television.

KEITH McGOWAN studied trombone with George Maxted and early music interpretation with Bernard Thomas. While studying music and Russian at the University of Nottingham and the Leningrad Institute of Theatre, Music and Cinematography he became fascinated by the sound and social history of early wind music. His association with Shakespeare's Globe began in the opening season as a musician in *Henry V*, and Keith has since directed music on a number of productions, including *Twelfth Night* (2002) and *Measure for Measure* (2004–5). He has also led sessions for Globe Education undergraduates on early music.

GORDON McMULLAN is Professor of Shakespeare and Early Modern Drama in the Department of English, King's College London. His publications include *The Politics of Unease in the Plays of John Fletcher* (1994), the Arden Shakespeare edition of *Henry VIII* (2000) and *Shakespeare and the Idea of Late Writing: Authorship in the Proximity of Death* (Cambridge University Press, 2007). He has also edited or co-edited four collections of essays, the most recent of which is *Reading the Medieval in Early Modern England* (Cambridge University Press, 2007). He is a general editor of Arden Early Modern Drama. He initiated the MA in Shakespearean Studies: Text and Playhouse that is collaboratively taught by King's College London and Globe Education.

MARK RYLANCE was Artistic Director of Shakespeare's Globe from 1995 to 2005. Mark trained at RADA under Hugh Cruttwell and at the Chrysalis Theatre School, Balham, with Barbara Bridgmont. He is the Co-Artistic Director of the London Theatre of Imagination and a member of the creative ensemble, Phoebus Cart, an Associate Actor of the Royal Shakespeare Company, an Honorary Bencher of the Middle Temple Hall and Chairman of the Shakespearean Authorship Trust. Mark acted in many plays at the Globe, beginning with *Othello* at the Bear Gardens in 1985, then *The Tempest* on the site of the reconstruction in 1991, and ending with *The Tempest* in 2005. His seventeen roles included Henry V, Richard II, Hamlet, Cleopatra, the Golden Ass, Olivia, the Duke in *Measure for Measure*, Proteus and Bassanio. He only directed one production himself during his tenure, *Julius Caesar*, in 1999. In 2007, he was the co-recipient with Claire van Kampen and Jenny Tiramani of the Sam Wanamaker Award for pioneering work that has contributed to the understanding and enjoyment of Shakespeare. More recently, in 2007, he wrote and acted in the successful play, *The BIG Secret Live 'I am Shakespeare' Webcam Daytime Chatroom Show*, at the Chichester Festival Theatre.

PATRICK SPOTTISWOODE joined Shakespeare's Globe in 1984 and became founding Director, Globe Education in 1989. Globe Education's twenty-three full-time staff provide lectures, workshops, courses and productions for over 100,000 people at the Globe every year and for many more through outreach and distance learning. Projects other than those referred to in this book include an International *Hamlet* Project involving 10,000 school students from Denmark, Germany, the UK and Poland, the commissioning of thirty-seven poets to revisit Wordsworth's 'Composed upon Westminster Bridge' for the poem's two-hundredth anniversary; translations of Spanish and Italian plays, Globe Quartos, Occasional Research Papers and Globe Folios. Patrick has been a visiting professor at Washington University, St Louis; Course Director for undergraduate courses at the Globe for several US universities; and co-convenor of conferences including Shakespeare and Martyrdom, at the Globe, and Shakespeare in Venice, in Venice.

JENNY TIRAMANI is an independent theatre designer and dress historian. She was Director of Theatre Design at Shakespeare's Globe Theatre from its opening in 1997 until 2005. In 2003 she received the Laurence Olivier Award for Best Costume Design for the all-male Globe production of *Twelfth Night*, and she was the co-recipient with Mark Rylance and Claire van Kampen of the 2007 Sam Wanamaker Award for her contribution to Shakespeare. Many of her theatre designs have been produced in the UK and abroad. She has given papers on the history of dress, theatre architecture and design practices in the time of Shakespeare at conferences and institutions such as the National Portrait Gallery, Royal Holloway University of London and the Society of British Theatre Designers. Her published works include articles in *Costume*, the Costume Society's journal, and she completed Janet Arnold's book, *Patterns of Fashion; The Cut and Construction of Linen Shirts, Smocks, Neckwear, Headwear and Accessories for Men and Women c.1540–1660* (2008).

CLAIRE VAN KAMPEN trained at the Royal College of Music. In 1986 she joined the Royal Shakespeare Company and the Royal National Theatre, the first female musical director with both companies. She has since developed an international career as a composer, writing and playing for theatre, television and film soundtracks as well as producing music for Shakespeare's plays in both the UK and the USA. In 1990 she co-founded the theatre company Phoebus Cart with Mark Rylance and their production of Shakespeare's *The Tempest* was performed in the foundations of Shakespeare's Globe in 1991. From 1997 to 2005 she was Director of Theatre Music at Shakespeare's Globe, creating both period and contemporary music for thirty of the Globe's productions. Claire also lectures to undergraduates, MA students and visiting scholars for Globe Education's programmes. Claire is a frequent broadcaster on BBC Radio 3 and has been a guest on many radio and television programmes worldwide.

YOLANDA VAZQUEZ has been a freelance Globe Education Practitioner since 2003 and works across all age ranges including MA and undergraduate students and international outreach. Recently, Yolanda was part of the team that created training for all English secondary consultants on behalf of the Department for Children, Schools and Families. Yolanda's acting roles at Shakespeare's Globe include Bertha in *Augustine's Oak*, Adriana in *The Comedy of Errors* (both in 1999), Hippolyta in *The Two Noble Kinsmen* (2000), Queen Elizabeth in *Richard III*, Hortensio in *The Taming of the Shrew* (both in 2003), Beatrice in *Much Ado About Nothing* (2004) and Hermione in *The Winter's Tale* (2005). Some of her other theatre work includes *A Midsummer Night's Dream* (RSC); *Six Characters Looking for an Author* (Young Vic); *Hedda Gabler* (ACT); *The Relapse* (Glasgow Citizens'/Thelma Holt); *She Wolf* (Glasgow Citizens' Studio); *Richard II*, *Two Shakespearean Actors*, *The Last Days of Don Juan* (RSC); *Romeo and Juliet* (Northampton).

JAMES WALLACE is an actor, and trained at the Central School for Speech and Drama 1990–3. He has also taught on the classical acting course at Central School and at the Globe. James has co-ordinated over thirty staged readings for the *Read not Dead* programme and has directed scenes for undergraduate performances in Globe Education's higher education courses.

MARTIN WHITE is Professor of Theatre at the University of Bristol. His research on the lesser-known playwrights of the early modern professional theatre is conducted through both practice-led and traditional forms of research. He has directed over fifty productions. He advises the Royal Shakespeare Company and until 2007 chaired the Architecture Research Group at Shakespeare's Globe. His publications include *Middleton and Tourneur* (1992); *Renaissance Drama in Action* (1998); 'Working Wonders: Mark Rylance at the New Globe', in *Extraordinary Actors* (2004); *The Roman Actor* by Philip Massinger (Revels Plays, 2007); and *The Chamber of Demonstrations* (2007), an interactive DVD exploring early modern theatre practice.

FOREWORD

Andrew Gurr

When we were working on the evidence for the design of the original Globe in order to identify the shape and materials needed to realise Sam Wanamaker's vision, we did sometimes discuss whether the end-product of our labours would work as a modern theatre. None of us seriously believed that it might attract big crowds. The most clear-sighted objective any of us had was to get the replica of Shakespeare's Globe as right as we could, so that we could then see what might be done with it. At a different time and in different books I had suggested that Elizabethan playgoers probably behaved more like a football crowd than modern theatre audiences, but none of us had any idea that the novelty of groundlings round the stage would transform the experience of modern playgoing in the way it has done since the first performances at the new Globe in 1996.

The greatest single benefit of the Wanamaker project was that it drew together a huge assembly of expertise, from theatre-history scholars to architects to historians of English vernacular building. It was a truly international enterprise, too. Besides Sam from the USA, the architect Theo Crosby was from South Africa, John Orrell was an Englishman resident in Canada, and I was from New Zealand. We all shared the same fascination with London that first drew Shakespeare to the city. We worked to complete most of the first step in the enterprise over a decade ago. In the ten years since it opened the Globe has used the skilled actors, directors and students of theatre to see how the old type of theatre might still work. The result has been to show that it works in a wholly fresh and invigorating way, a way that has told us a lot that is exciting about Shakespeare and his contemporaries. This book is a record of these first ten years, and what they have accomplished.

Underpinning all the work, and Sam's own vision, was and still is the assumption that Shakespeare as player and co-owner of his company's two theatres always knew exactly what he was doing. Therefore, the theory goes, a fresh approach to the original staging of his plays through the surviving play-texts should be able to show us a lot more of his practical genius than we have discovered through the last century or so. To establish that required digging into the state of theatre in Shakespeare's own time. It means not only creating a version of his own physical workplace but uncovering the stories behind his two theatres, finding out why his company from the outset wanted different summer and winter venues, and how they used them. Shakespeare invested 10 per cent of his own savings in the Globe, a theatre already old-fashioned when he helped build it in 1599, and nine years later when Richard Burbage finally secured the Blackfriars indoor playhouse to use for his company he took a similar share in it. From then on, as they had planned from the outset in 1594, the Shakespeare company was the outstanding theatre company of its own day and indeed of any time. For nearly fifty years it played with wonderful extravagance and indeed arrogance, leaving one of its playhouses empty each season while using the other, at a time when London suffered from an extreme shortage of playhouses.

Reproducing the full set of conditions under which Shakespeare produced his plays is impossible now, as we are often told. This book acknowledges that problem in several places. Now we have a version of what the Globe might have been like in 1599, in the same materials and therefore offering similar acoustics (though before the final painting and carvings were applied to the interior, as Martin White says in chapter 13, 'Research and the Globe'). Since then we have experienced the staging of several plays in what is now called OP (versions of what might have been the 'original practices'). And playgoers have flocked to this new/old theatre to experience the shock of the old.

The effect on actors and audience of open-air playing, where large crowds make themselves into visible and active participants in the event, has been the biggest revelation of the whole project so far. This book registers some of the ways in which so many people have navigated through what Claire van Kampen calls in chapter 6 the 'turbulent seas of mistrust' (see p. 79) to find out what they can from it all. They have evoked, quite rightly, many reservations about the discoveries that have been made and about what might be found in the future. It is vital to keep these reservations in mind as you read these accounts.

Perhaps the most weighty doubt of all is the obvious distance between playgoers then and modern audiences. Here is just one instance of that gulf. It shows itself in the difference between the performance conditions in Shakespeare's years and those of today in the minds of the audiences for whom George Chapman wrote his first comedy, *The Blind Beggar of Alexandria*, in 1595. He, and the Admiral's Men led by the greatest actor of his day, Edward Alleyn, knew exactly what they were doing. When they staged the play, the Admiral's had been set up a year before along with the Shakespeare company, the Chamberlain's Men. The two companies shared the exclusive right to perform at the Theatre and the Rose in the London suburbs, where they were free from the Lord Mayor's hostility. This meant that Londoners had only the two playhouses and the two companies to go to if they wanted to see a play. By late 1595 both companies were fully aware that their audiences were seeing the same faces on stage each day playing a different role, creating a problem of overfamiliarity. They had seen Alleyn as Hieronimo in Kyd's *Spanish Tragedy*, and as Tamburlaine, Faustus and Barabbas in Marlowe's great plays. So what Chapman did was create a farce using multiple disguises so that the audience could watch Alleyn posing as parodies of his own characters from other plays. He starts the play disguised as the Blind Beggar who is really Cleanthes, Egypt's banished general returned in secret to Alexandria. He also disguises himself as Leon, a usurer with a bottle-nose like Barabbas in *The Jew of Malta*, and as Count Hermes, a braggart who rants lines from *Tamburlaine*. In these four roles Alleyn spoke more than a third of all the lines in the play. The Barabbas and Tamburlaine-like figures allowed him to burlesque his own famous roles as a 'fustian king', the term he self-mockingly called himself in a letter to his wife in 1593. As the blind prophet he prophesies to three court ladies how they will meet their future husbands. Then in turn as Cleanthes, Leon and Hermes he meets and marries all three.

The play is a hilarious farce for which modern readers simply lack the experience to identify the parodied characters, let alone Alleyn's own self-mockery. The late Millar MacLure, for instance, said regretfully of the play that modern readers 'will have cause to reflect grimly (as every reader of minor Elizabethan drama must) on the curious tastes of our ancestors'. Unless you could recognise the false nose that Alleyn wore for *The Jew of Malta* and already knew his resonant lines spoken as Tamburlaine, and unless your playgoing was confined to the plays of the only two companies then permitted to perform in the vicinity of London, there is no way you could make sense of, let alone enjoy, Chapman's rollicking farce. We cannot now share the information the first playgoers had at the staging of these plays. Language is our most obvious loss – we proudly entitle the standees (an oddly American term for such a positive posture) in the yard with the name 'groundlings', ignoring the scorn that Hamlet packed into the word when he invented it to describe the gapers at his feet. In his time a groundling was a small fish, a loach with a huge sucker for a mouth that enabled it to feed off the algae from the stones at a river's bottom. As a pretend prince he might be expected to scorn the gapers staring up at him from the yard. Richard Burbage, playing that prince for the first time, is told how the boy companies have dislodged the adult players from the city. He grieves for the players, as we hear, but the original audiences would have known very well that the landlord of the boy company then playing at the Blackfriars and profiting from their success was Burbage himself. Lacking that information now, we are alienated from the thrill and comedy of the immediate moment on the original stage.

That is one enormous task the Globe's actors still have to confront. But in the first ten years' working with the Globe great progress has been made towards a more thoroughgoing reconstruction of Shakespearean playing conditions, and more is to come. Just as the Shakespeare company started at their one old-fashioned outdoor theatre and later added to it seasonal playing with their indoor theatre, so the addition of a version of the Blackfriars should allow Shakespeare's Globe to copy the original company with performances all the year round. The versatility and mobility of the original company, happy to transport its plays from one venue to another at the drop of a purse, is a challenge to creative theatre work now; that was one of the standard expectations then. Taking plays like The Tempest and The Winter's Tale indoors after a summer at the Globe, or starting them indoors and then taking them into the daylight, offers rich new possibilities that should teach us more about the principles and the practices of Shakespearean staging.

The Oxford English Dictionary says that the word 'maverick', used by Patrick Spottiswoode about the Globe project, was originally the name of a Texas rancher who neglected to brand his calves. The word was subsequently picked up to define a thief, anyone who stole and then branded such calves. While resisting any suggestion that the Globe is an illegal activity, the idea that it might be thought of as a not-yet branded calf ready to grow into a mighty bull does have its appeal.

ACKNOWLEDGEMENTS

The editors have a long list of people to thank. First and foremost we would like to thank Sarah Stanton for her tireless support, patience and energy for the project.

At Shakespeare's Globe, thank you to: Patrick Spottiswoode, Dominic Dromgoole, Andrew Macnair, Fiona Banks, Christopher Stafford, Deborah Callan, Madeline Knights, Alexandra Massey, Susie Walker, Crispin Hunt, Johanna Elworthy, Kieron Kirkland, Adrienne Gillam, Ros Aitken, Victoria Northwood, Sarah Dustagheer, Gwilym Jones, Claire Daniel, Penelope Woods, Sophie Leighton-Kelly, Maya Gabrielle-Talbot, Sally Preston, Nick Budden, Stacey Gregg, Lotte Buchan, Eva Koch-Schulte, Paul Williams, Peter Kyle and Nicholas Robins.

Thank you also to those who supported the book and provided guidance: Mark Rylance, Claire van Kampen, Jennifer Tiramani, Graeme Wallace, Gordon McMullan, Ann Thompson, Ewan Fernie, Ben Knights and Robert Hampson. In particular we would like to thank Andrew Gurr for his generous gift of time and understanding.

The editors would like to thank Shakespeare's Globe for its support and assistance in gathering and reproducing all illustrations. Thank you also to Shakespeare's Globe Library and Archive for research support and guidance.

We would like to thank the CAPITAL Centre at the University of Warwick, in particular, Carol Rutter, Susan Brock, Tony Howard, Paul Prescott and Jonathan Bate for their support for the reproduction of colour illustrations, which has enabled us to demonstrate vividly the visual aesthetic of the work at Shakespeare's Globe.

Christie Carson would personally like to thank Jane Gawthrope, Brett Lucas, Nicole King, Jonathan Gibson, Farah Karim-Cooper, Ewan Fernie, Elaine McGirr, Jennifer Neville, Douglas Cowie, Lynne, Mark, Anna and Cameron Rickards, Pam and Mark Sanderson and Doris, Jim and Gillian Carlisle. Christie would like to dedicate this book with thanks to Neil and Edwina Carson and Alan, Ruth and Ted King.

Farah Karim-Cooper would personally like to thank Jerry Cooper, Sabreena Cooper, Captain F. A. Karim, Fawzia Karim, Charles Cooper, Barbara Cooper, Christie Carson, Geraldine Morris, Olivia Jennings, Chris Stafford, J. (Shammy) Karim, Reshad Karim, Dana Warden. Farah would like to dedicate this book to Captain F. A. Karim, Fawzia Karim and Carol Ann Compton Clements.

The editors would like to acknowledge Sam Wanamaker, whose guiding principles are at the centre of this volume. We would like to think he would have contributed a chapter had he been alive to see the outcomes of his vision.

INTRODUCTION

Christie Carson and Farah Karim-Cooper

Globe performativity enables a direct expression of the Shakespearean past and its articulation in the present.[1] (W. B. Worthen)

New Globe productions have emphasised and valorised the popular elements of the plays and of the play-going experience, both of which have become too gentrified and 'cultured' . . .

The 'construction of the audience' as 'playful, popular and participatory' . . . has been designed to offer an historical and personal experience of authenticity.[2] (Rob Conkie)

Scholarly discussions on the Globe have proliferated in the last five to six years with several book-length studies finding their way into university presses. This discursive activity demonstrates the growing interest in Shakespeare's Globe as a site for intense critical enquiry. What these quotations show is the capacity for Globe productions, through an interaction with audiences, to produce a variety of complex meanings. Scholars have attempted to identify particular 'Globe conventions'[3] and interpretive strategies such as the spatial intimacy of the actor/ audience relationship, the responses such proximities produce and the dominant style or aesthetic of the productions that has emerged in the first ten years of the theatre's work (regarded critically as an attempt at 'authenticity', which Rob Conkie's study, cited above, focuses on at length). Some of these conventions are highlighted in academic reviews of plays, such as those in *Shakespeare Bulletin*, written by scholars with backgrounds in either performance studies, theatre history or literary studies. Academic reviews, distinguishable from theatre reviews, are important and critically rigorous exercises, but are discussions inevitably focusing on a particular production or a season of productions, so are unable to provide a thorough understanding of the developmental nature of performance practices at the Globe. Ways of writing/talking about the Globe have undoubtedly developed from the early architectural discussions to encompass more complex, theoretical analyses of the theatre's current practices and social position, as well as the meaning-making processes of the Renaissance period.

Mark Rylance as Artistic Director of the Globe Theatre during this developmental period has been very aware of the relationship initially established between the Globe and the academic community:

Those in the academic community who had supported the project, long before many in the theatre world were able to see what Sam [Wanamaker] saw, were able to celebrate all of their careful research which ensured that this was the most considered reconstruction possible in 1997. Subsequent discoveries made while playing in the space in later years would lead us to revise several of the Globe's features.[4]

Rylance's respectful awareness of the early scholarly investment in the space is coupled with his assertion of a distinct shift in terms of who is responsible for making the 'discoveries' on the Globe stage. Rylance suggests that it is the theatre practitioners who have played an increasingly significant part in determining how the architectural features will develop, using their practice as a body of research. The editors of this volume see this shift as crucial to, but also a part of, the ongoing debate or dialogue about Shakespeare's Globe and the role of scholarly work within it.

Before setting out what this book aims to do, it is important to situate this study within a wider discourse on Shakespeare's Globe. Critical work addressing the Globe project has developed in three stages: beginning with the active involvement of scholars in research into reconstruction and projected aims; followed by early responses to theatrical experiments as well as attempts to usefully document this work; and culminating in a critical engagement with the new theatre practices developed, including the increased role of the audience and an analysis of the social positioning of this theatre within a theatrical and broader cultural context. It should be noted that to date there has been virtually no critical engagement with the idea that Shakespeare's Globe acts as a combined centre for education, research and theatre.

Scholarly debate on the Globe began as a historical discourse focused on playhouse architecture, staging practices and documentary evidence for the purpose of reconstruction. Emerging from this debate is a number of very valuable compilations of scholarly papers given at conferences on the reconstruction project. As early as 1979, scholars were gathering and publishing papers considering the uses and dynamic potential of the proposed reconstructed Globe. Very early on in this discussion, John Russell Brown uses the term 'experiment' in his essay 'Modern Uses for a Globe Theatre', acknowledging the exploratory nature of the project from the outset: 'we would have the Globe, but we would still have to learn to use it; we would have to explore, experiment, and create'.[5] Brown's use of the pronoun 'we' intriguingly suggests not only exploration but a close, collaborative relationship between the scholar and the actor. Did Brown imagine a scenario in which the scholar would sit and observe the players, guiding and instructing them in early modern staging practices? There is no question that he saw the process as uniquely collaborative: 'we shall have to exchange views . . . we shall have to collaborate in many kinds of practical work'.[6] He recommends that not only the Globe's architecture be replicated as accurately as possible, but also the conditions of playing, including the 'close backstage quarters of the Globe . . . in order that we may know what it is like for an actor to step out of that busy, thriving, darkened world onto the empty platform'.[7] The beginning of this debate therefore established the centrality of two key principles: the experimental approach and the collaboration of scholars and practitioners. However, the feasibility and desirability of such conditions from a modern actor's point of view was not taken into consideration in these early discussions. At this point it is the scholars setting up the expectations, and what emerges is the expression of a desire for first-hand involvement by scholars in the theatrical experiments.

In Franklin J. Hildy's edited collection, *New Issues in the Reconstruction of Shakespeare's Theatre: Proceedings of the Conference Held at the University of Georgia*, essays by Alan Dessen and Hugh Richmond set forth the academic expectations by the early 1990s when the project was becoming a reality. These conversations continued to situate the reconstructed Globe as a 'laboratory' or 'testing ground where actors and scholars working together can investigate how Elizabethan plays could or would have been staged'.[8] Like the scholars in the 1970s, Dessen's optimism about the collaborative endeavours of scholars and practitioners working together is coupled with a seriousness of intent, giving grave importance to the future experiments into Elizabethan staging. Dessen argues that 'if the processes that underlie the use of the new Globe (whether mental, physical, or commercial) are tainted from the outset, the results of any tests or experiments will also be compromised or contaminated'.[9] Again such expectations demonstrate a remarkable ambition for the scholar him or herself to be involved *directly* in the process of theatre-making.[10]

Similarly, Hugh Richmond highlights the notion of the scholar as integral to experimentation on the Globe stage. While recognising the impossibility of an absolute 'reconstitution' of the 1599 Globe, Richmond nevertheless sees the potential in 'a close approximation', which may be 'all that is needed for many effective performance experiments'.[11] Richmond also predicts that the Globe will have difficulty transposing 'devices' that originate in the Globe's 'theatrical environment'.[12] By the time his essay was written, it was clear that the reconstruction itself would be a 'close approximation' or 'best guess' (to use Andrew Gurr's phrase), rather than the early romantic dream of an exact replica that was arguably one of the driving forces behind the scholarly support for the project. With this in mind, Richmond carefully argues for an investigation into how modern 'production techniques' could be 'modified advantageously by the broad conventions of Elizabethan staging rather than by an attempt at universal duplication of the circumstantial conditions provided by any single Elizabethan theatre'.[13]

Once the theatre was built and performances were produced on the stage for the first time, early responses to the experiments began to assert problems with the building itself as well as demonstrate the difficulties inherent in the somewhat naively anticipated, collaborative dialogue between actors and academics. Initially, the structural features of the building were called into question by critics such as Paul Nelsen, who asks:

(1) What authoritative, or at least significantly persuasive evidence is there to validate the presence of pillars at the first Globe; (2) if stage posts were an integral part of the 1599 Globe's architecture, where might they have been located?[14]

Enquiries such as this increased the sense that the building itself was becoming more of an unreliable marker of early modern playhouse architecture. Added to the concerns of unfaithful replication of the architecture were concerns about the use of the space. Lois Potter's review of the 1998 season questioned not the structural features of the stage but rather the modern theatre professional's ability to use it:

The directors and actors do need to play to the audience on the sides of the stage, not just to those out front; some of the actors do indeed need to improve their delivery; and there is no excuse for freezing the important bits of action between the pillars.[15]

Potter in her critical review suggests that in the late 1990s when the Globe began its theatrical experiments the gap between 'original practices' and modern practices in the theatre was vast. Once the theatre was in operation the intimate relationship imagined between the scholar and the stage disappeared and the debate between the practical imperatives of the space – 'what works' – and the theoretical imperatives – of 'what ought to work' or at least 'what ought to be tried' – emerged.

Scholars working at the Globe were encouraged to describe rather than to engage in debate with the practical experiments. Pauline Kiernan's *Staging Shakespeare at the New Globe* (1999) is a culmination of her work as a post-doctoral fellow in Andrew Gurr's Research department at the Globe in the late 1990s. Her analysis of staging practices at the Globe has no interrogative tone and so is a departure from the theoretical essays that take into account the compatibility of the modern actor and the Globe's architecture. Her work on the Globe *Research Bulletins*, in which she documents the early experiments by recording the discussions at rehearsal and interviews with the cast members, is enlarged in her book as she takes into account the 'experiments' conducted in the first season. More objectively critical perhaps is Cynthia Marshall's essay in *Shakespeare Quarterly* (2000), which takes into account the audience as part of the performance. She argues that the Globe is a 'radical theatre space', suggesting that accounts of the theatrical experiments to date are reluctant to consider the impact of the audience on the meanings produced by the productions. Discussing the Globe's production of Henry V (1997), she argues that it 'worked, primarily through auditory interactions, to animate the audience'.[16]

The role of the audience in the production of meaning at the Globe Theatre has become of increasing interest to scholars as the practical experiments on the stage have developed. Critical enquiries that include the involvement of the audience provide a more thorough reflection on the all-encompassing experience of seeing a play at the Globe. Chantal Schutz, also formerly of Globe Research, suggests that by 2001 audiences were beginning to respond in new ways to Globe performances:

At the Globe, a new dynamic is created: audience attitude oscillates between the uninhibited enthusiasm of football matches and the dilettante snobbery of classical concerts, but with the added dimension of self-consciousness born from its idea of what Elizabethan audiences may have been like; it results in something completely new.[17]

Catherine Silverstone's analysis of the 1997 production of Henry V points out that 'spectators are certainly encouraged to play along ... presumably in an effort to simulate the imagined experience of early modern playgoing'. But she registers too an anxiety on the part of the Globe about appropriate audience behaviour. She cites the findings from the Workshop Season in which it was discovered that many groundlings would sit in the yard; 'this behaviour was not sanctioned by the theatre management who wanted the yard audience to stand. So before performances in the Prologue Season the yard was sprinkled with water to encourage standing'.[18] Commenting on the Globe's early teething problems with regard to audience expectations, Silverstone argues that the Globe's combined use of radical encouragement and 'disciplinary measures' to regulate the behaviour of the audience forces the spectators to 'exhibit a range of responses from complicity to resistance'.[19]

W. B. Worthen's theoretical analysis of a phenomenon he terms 'Globe performativity' might be seen as the culmination of this period of increasingly distanced critical engagement. Continuing a critical narrative that highlights the unique participatory nature of the audiences, Worthen argues that the multifaceted nature of Shakespeare's Globe as a tourist site, an icon and as a theatre, characterises 'the distinctive force of Globe performativity, which arises not merely from the play performed there but in the embodied expectations, enactment, and experience of the Globe's performers – actors and audience'.[20] Worthen's argument that the audience at the Globe also performs suggests that, by 2003, the codes of conduct for audiences were well established. He refers to the 'groundling groupies' as having 'developed their own rituals, behaviour that is readily played by the actors on stage'.[21] What this more recent criticism reveals primarily is the gulf that increasingly exists between the actor and the academic. Thus, over the period of critical engagement with this theatre the position of the academic has shifted, from the early enthusiastic and romantic participation of the scholar, to the involvement of the scholar as chronicler, to the placement of the scholar outside the experimental process as an 'objective', critical observer, standing in the yard and watching his or her fellow-spectators as well as the performers on the stage.

What this volume aims to do is to re-establish a dialogue between the scholar and the practitioner, juxtaposing their observations and discoveries of the first ten years of the Globe's performance practice. By doing so we hope to narrow the gap that has increasingly divided these two approaches. The first aim, then, of this volume, which is addressed in Part I, is to document the material conditions and theoretical parameters of production at Shakespeare's Globe and in particular to analyse the premises of cultural materialism and apply them to the theatre of Shakespeare's period. In Part II we hope to demonstrate that experiment-led thinking did not confine itself to theatrical practice at the Globe by highlighting the significant interventions that Globe Education has made, not only in Shakespeare studies but in educational practice nationwide. The Globe project began both as an educational and a theatrical endeavour and often criticism loses sight of how these two creative bodies were designed to work alongside each other. In order to suggest a critical way forward, Part III of this volume will return to the early principles that united scholars and theatre practitioners by attempting to review the lessons learned through practical experimentation over the entire developmental period of the first decade of the theatre's operation.

Therefore, this volume poses three separate but related questions. First, what can a practical approach to the cultural production of the Renaissance period contribute to an understanding of that period for scholars and audiences? Second, what can an experimental approach to learning tell us about our own creative practice as teachers and researchers? And finally, what have we learned in concrete terms from the coming together of Shakespeare's plays and the Globe's architecture in the present period? In order to address the opposing forces of the literary push of the reader into the period, and the dramatic pull of the text towards a present audience, we have brought together a wide range of the participants in the project. The body of experience and expertise that Shakespeare's Globe encapsulates is unprecedented. This volume hopes to replicate the engaged debate that daily enlivens the Globe centre when a range of experts gather to discuss the aims and outcomes of this endeavour. Rather than flattening opposing positions, we have set up a structure that highlights differences in approach in order to propose a new kind of criticism that can incorporate a more complex understanding of the results of the theatrical and educational experiments the Globe has generated.

There is a great deal of ground to cover and this volume will certainly not attempt to present an exhaustive account of the findings of this theatre. It will also not attempt to dissolve the 'fifth wall' that Hunter and Lichtenfels say stands between academics and practitioners. Rather, this study will attempt to make that divide more transparent on the assumption that greater understanding of working practices may help to lead to more productive collaboration.[22] Given that Shakespeare's Globe was set up as both a theatre and an education centre, with experimentation at the heart, it seems essential to write up the experiment. Scientific vocabulary has been derided by Paul Menzer when describing this project but this criticism, like many of the project, seems to be generated by a misunderstanding of the methods of theatre practitioners by literary scholars.[23] The methods of theatrical experimentation are not taken from the science laboratory but from centuries of theatrical practice. The workshop, the staged reading, the rehearsal process, the design process, all have established methods that take a creative approach to the practical, yet critical, problem of developing a theatrical interpretation of the plays. To negate this history of practice by eliding it, as funding bodies have, with the scientific method, is to misunderstand the tradition that is under discussion.

This volume aims to tackle a range of similar popular misconceptions about this project. Too many assessments of the work have been singular in their aims, drawing conclusions about the project as a whole from a viewing of individual performances of a particular production or several productions within one season. In order to introduce a more rigorous approach to criticism of this work it is essential to provide adequate detail regarding the principles which have guided the work. It is also necessary to compare the outcomes of this project with the intentions of its creators, rather than with critics' preconceptions and idealised theoretical projections. Shakespeare's Globe is not the only reconstructed Renaissance theatre and it is not the only theatre to have an educational component. What makes this centre unique, however, is its location and its educational work, as well as the extended applied approach taken over the first ten years of operation to 'original practices' productions. Recent scholarship, educational practice and contemporary theatre trends have all influenced the way this project was undertaken. It seems sensible, therefore, to gather together scholars, educators and practitioners to make an assessment of the work thus far in order to think positively about the nature of future critical work.

The book considers the first decade of activity in the Globe Theatre, spanning the entirety of Mark Rylance's reign as Artistic Director. Occasional reference is made to the first two years of Dominic Dromgoole's work as Artistic Director primarily as a marker of the possibility and the actuality of change. The period under discussion has been dominated by a single artistic team. The primary subject of this analysis is the extended collaborative research project that came out of the work of Director of Design Jenny Tiramani, Music Director Claire van Kampen and Artistic Director Mark Rylance. Their combined approach to 'original practices' has helped to define a new generation of scholarship on this subject. As Dominic Dromgoole has noted, there may never again be a coming together of three such talented and dedicated practitioners to work in a rigorous way over an extended period of time within such an extraordinary building; 'like any good artistic aesthetic or movement, it was a result of the coincidence of very extraordinary personalities at a particular moment in their lives . . . and beyond that a broad consensus in the academic community. And such things are very rare and very special when they happen.'[24] The question which arises out of this statement must be: is the specific expertise and experience developed by these theatre artists crucial to experimentation in 'original practices' at the Globe? This study will try to address this and other questions about the development in critical thinking about 'original practices' as a scholarly tool by providing an analysis of this experiment in a way that will both reassess the history of the Globe Theatre to date and structure further debate.

Therefore, this book aims to influence the way writing on this subject is formulated in the future. It is essential to acknowledge that Shakespeare's Globe is many things to many people. The work of the exhibition space is beyond the scope of this book and will not be addressed here. The work of Globe Education will be described in a way that relates specifically to the relationship between theatre practice, learning and research. The view presented is particular and is focused almost entirely on the development of a critical debate between theatre artists and scholars from different disciplines, who can all learn from the experimentation that has taken place and can help to direct the experimentation of the future. Two additional questions which arise from this study must be: who can claim ownership of the outcomes of the first period of experimentation and who will direct the future of those experiments?

While it is essential to acknowledge differences of approach, there remain a number of areas where theatre practitioners and literary and dramatic scholars can easily agree. In fact, one of the key outcomes of this experimental process has been to create a greater understanding between practitioners, educators and academics of their respective methodological approaches, something which will become apparent in the essays included in this volume. The key area of agreement is about the direct relationship between the texts of the plays and the architecture of the building. Performed in their natural environment, stripped of technology, these plays present fundamental questions to practitioners and scholars alike. Standard acting training becomes inadequate, even detrimental, in this space. The role of the director in the modern theatre is entirely undermined in this quite uncontrollable environment. Similarly, editorial practices are faced by real challenges when the underlying assumptions of those practices are tested on this stage. The practitioners who have dedicated themselves to working in this space have also dedicated themselves to relearning their craft in order to address the demands of this building. Audiences, similarly, have come to understand the physical and intellectual commitment that is required to participate fully in a performance at the Globe Theatre. It seems that criticism has some way to go to replicate the kind of rethinking that engaging in a collaborative way with the Globe Theatre requires.

The Globe Theatre has been a disappointment to many scholars. It has not told them what they wanted it to and it has not involved them as they had hoped. But some of the initial visions of recreating a historical moment through the harmonious collaboration of practitioner and scholar must be seen to be a romantic ideal. Instead, what this theatre has offered up to the scholarly community is a real understanding of the possibilities of practical experiments that are historically and critically informed. This theatre has in many important ways highlighted the limitations of current approaches to performance, teaching practices, literary criticism and editorial practice. Theatrical, educational and scholarly practices are in a period of transition. The work of these seemingly separate professions is increasingly beginning to overlap and inform one another. Similarly, the disparate disciplines of theatre history, literary and performance criticism have come to influence each other within the Academy over the decade under discussion. This book is part of that process of integration of approaches and therefore does not propose any scientific distance or objectivity. The collection conscientiously includes the practitioners and the scholars who have been most involved in the Globe's developmental process in order to illustrate the kinds of criticism that are possible when the experiments are addressed from a position of real understanding. Scholars who do not have a direct involvement with Shakespeare's Globe, but are perhaps no less invested in these changing means of understanding our critical position, have also been included. What we hope to illustrate is that an informed criticism is necessary in order to reflect the complexity of the original aims of the project and the developmental nature of its outcomes.

In order to provide an opportunity to engage with what has undoubtedly been a fairly closed debate, this book both documents the process as recorded by those involved and tries to move the critical debate about the work forward. The aim is to acknowledge the rigour of the approach taken but also the necessary selectivity of that approach. If we can move away from complaints about what cannot be recreated in the space it will be possible to gain from the very real lessons that have been learned. By highlighting our misconceptions about the period, the experiments may be producing profoundly important outcomes.

Possibly the most productive experiment to take place in terms of the discoveries of 'original practices' was the movement of *Twelfth Night* from Middle Temple Hall to the Globe Theatre. This comparative approach allowed for a re-examination of the findings of the experiments that were based in only one of these spaces. The fact that Shakespeare's Globe is planning to build an indoor theatre, while the Blackfriars Theatre in Staunton, Virginia, is planning to build a replica Globe, says quite a bit about the desirability and potential of such practical experiments. A comparative approach to space has been matched by an understanding of a practical contextual exploration of the work of other writers of the period, the potential of which has been rigorously explored through Patrick Spottiswoode's *Read Not Dead* programme. The Globe centre as a whole has moved towards an immersive contextual model for the work of Shakespeare, building up a picture of all of the activity that surrounded this iconic playwright.

Beyond any judgements about the quality of any particular performance presented at the Globe it must be acknowledged that a body of experience and a pool of expertise about the period exists in connection with this centre which is unparalleled. The *Lively Action* and *Read Not Dead* programmes, for example, have developed a group of theatre and Globe Education Practitioners with an extensive familiarity with the language as well as the social and theatrical conventions of the period that has not been replicated elsewhere. To demonstrate the wide range of non-Shakespearean drama that has been staged by Globe Education, we have included a comprehensive list in the Appendices detailing the year, play, playwright and co-ordinator of each of the *Read Not Dead* staged readings. An initial engagement of this kind with the period has often led the co-ordinators and actors involved in the project to want to learn more, which has helped them to articulate and document their own discoveries in more formal ways than previously – James Wallace's chapter in this volume acts as a concrete example of this. As a result, a movement towards understanding and appreciation can be witnessed on either side of the increasingly transparent dividing 'fifth wall'.

In order to convey a sense of the full range of activity but also the level of expertise involved at Shakespeare's Globe, this book has been carefully structured to document first the practical and theoretical parameters of the 'original practices' project, then the work undertaken by Globe Education and finally the practical outcomes of the discoveries on the stage that might help to inform future scholarship. The work of scholars is interwoven with the accounts of the educators and practitioners in order to place the work of this theatre in a wider context both practically and critically. To provide a context for this specific case study of practical experimentation Franklin J. Hildy, whose involvement with the Globe project spans three decades, begins the volume with an overview of the history of reconstruction. Part I of the book then details the four key areas involved in the 'original practices' project: stage action, stage appearance, music and sound and the actor/audience relationship, juxtaposing practitioners and scholars discussing each topic. Part II provides an account of the work in Globe Education, contextualising and mapping out the department's experiments in public programming, learning and academic research. Part III concludes the volume's analysis of 'original practices' by documenting the practical results of the experiments on the stage through the accounts of the Director of Music and two musicians, the work of the Artistic Director and two seasoned Globe actors. To end this section Ralph Alan Cohen provides what he calls a 'rule book' for directors working in reconstructed spaces of this kind, drawn from his experience not only as an academic but also as the Artistic Director of the Blackfriars Theatre in Virginia. All of the essays collected together for this volume help to foreground the usefulness of combining practical and theoretical approaches to reach a greater understanding of the plays and the period by the most productive means available to us.

The volume ends with a conclusion addressing not only the questions raised in this introduction, but also larger issues surrounding the status and future of Shakespeare's Globe in the educational and theatrical landscapes. A series of appendices follows that includes: a list of other Globe projects internationally, a draft of an un-official Artistic Policy (as seen through the imaginations of the Artistic Committee of 1988) and Alan Dessen's 'Ten Commandments' for use of the space, devised in 1990. The first of these documents provides further context for the work of this theatre. The other two documents, created at the instigation of the project, illustrate the ways in which the desires of the practitioners and scholars both intersected and diverged in the initial stages of development, but they also convey a great sense of optimism and potential. The aims of the Artistic Policy are, of necessity, grounded in practical concerns, while the aims of the scholars are more speculative. To facilitate future study, and to indicate the level of real co-operation that this volume has achieved between practitioners and scholars, a list of the entire production history of Shakespeare's Globe Theatre has been developed with the theatre artists that introduces a new and more rigorous categorisation of the approach taken to each production. This document, like the ones that precede it, is a testament to optimism but it is one that is now grounded in greater understanding of diverging methods of working. The volume as a whole must be seen as a practical example of the kind of integrated and informed criticism that the editors are advocating. It examines broadly the range of activities that takes place in the Education and Theatre departments, while focusing more narrowly on particular working methods and ground-breaking experiments, in particular the 'original practices' project and the *Read Not Dead* readings. It is the premise of this collection and the belief of its editors that if criticism of the theatrical experiments at the Globe more generally could accommodate the conflicting, and at times contradictory, pulls of the past and the present, of the literary and the performative, of the speculative and the practical, then the profoundly important outcomes of the activities at Shakespeare's Globe might be more widely understood and appreciated.

NOTES

1 W. B. Worthen, *Shakespeare and the Force of Modern Performance* (Cambridge University Press, 2003), p. 103.

2 Rob Conkie, *The Globe Theatre Project: Shakespeare and Authenticity* (Edwin Mellen Press, 2006), pp. 252 and 45.

3 Lois Potter, 'A Stage where Every Man Must Play a Part?', *Shakespeare Quarterly* 50, 1 (Spring 1999), 80.

4 Mark Rylance, *Play – A Recollection in Pictures and Words of the First Five Years of Play at Shakespeare's Globe Theatre*. Photographs: Sheila Burnett, Donald Cooper, Richard Kolina, John Tramper (London: Shakespeare's Globe, 2003), p. 15.

5 John Russell Brown, 'Modern Uses for a Globe Theatre', in *The Third Globe: Symposium for the Reconstruction of the Globe Playhouse*, ed. C. Walter Hodges, S. Schoenbaum and Leonard Leane (Detroit: Wayne State University Press, 1981), p. 17.

6 *Ibid.*, p. 18.

7 *Ibid.*, p. 20.

8 Alan Dessen, '"Taint Not Thy Mind . . . ": Problems and Pitfalls in Staging Plays at the New Globe', in *New Issues in the Reconstruction of Shakespeare's Theatre: Proceedings of the Conference Held at the University of Georgia February 16–18, 1990*, ed. Franklin J. Hildy (New York: Peter Lang, 1990), p. 135.

9 *Ibid.*, p. 136.

10 The Ten Commandments for the Globe that Dessen fashions derive from this essay and are cited in Appendix 3.

11 Hugh Richmond, 'Techniques for Reconstituting Elizabethan Staging', in *New Issues in the Reconstruction of Shakespeare's Theatre*, p. 159.

12 *Ibid.*, p. 162.

13 *Ibid.*

14 Paul Nelsen, 'Positing Pillars at the Globe', *Shakespeare Quarterly* 48, 3 (Autumn 1997), 326.

15 Potter, 'A Stage', p. 81.

16 Cynthia Marshall, 'Sight and Sound: Two Models of Shakespearean Subjectivity on the British Stage', *Shakespeare Quarterly* 51, 3 (Autumn 2000), 354.

17 Chantal Schutz, 'Music at the New Globe', *Early Modern Literary Studies*, special issue 8 (May 2001), 34.

18 Catherine Silverstone, 'Shakespeare Live: Reproducing Shakespeare at the New Globe', *Textual Practice* 19, 1 (2005), 43.

19 *Ibid.*, p. 44.

20 Worthen, *Shakespeare*, p. 84.

21 *Ibid.*, p. 100.

22 Lynette Hunter and Peter Lichtenfels, eds., *Shakespeare, Language and the Stage: The Fifth Wall: Approaches to Shakespeare from Criticism, Performance and Theatre Studies*, Arden Shakespeare (London: Thomson Learning 2005).

23 Paul Menzer, 'Afterword: Discovery Spaces? Research at the Globe and Blackfriars', in *Inside Shakespeare: Essays on the Blackfriars Stage*, ed. Paul Menzer (Selinsgrove: Susquehanna University Press, 2006), p. 224. Also see the introduction to Part II for further discussion of this issue.

24 Dominic Dromgoole, interview with the editors, 24 May 2007.

CHAPTER ONE

THE 'ESSENCE OF GLOBENESS': AUTHENTICITY, AND THE SEARCH FOR SHAKESPEARE'S STAGECRAFT

Franklin J. Hildy

In May 2007, ten years after the official opening of Shakespeare's Globe, Howard Brenton made this observation about the experience of seeing a play there for the *Guardian*: 'seeing the scenes flow one against the other in something like their natural habitat, I marvelled at Shakespeare's stagecraft... With an exact mastery he sweeps one scene off and another on, twisting action around the pillars of the stage. The Globe reveals Shakespeare to us in a way no other "new" theatre has.'[1] Whether Brenton was aware of it or not, this was precisely what many of those who had worked on this project had always believed it was capable of doing. Two weeks later, Susannah Clapp, writing for the *Observer*, provided a further vindication of these efforts by noting: 'In the past 10 years, the stage has gained, in the Globe, a space which has shown at a stroke how a Shakespeare play can be a popular event.' This too had long been one of the goals of those who have, over the past 150 years, wanted to see a playhouse of Shakespeare's day recreated. Clapp goes on to say: 'In the past five years, it has responded more incisively to current events than either movies or television.'[2] If this is indeed the case, it is one of the many reasons why the theatres of Shakespeare's day were so successful. For those involved this is exactly the sort of discovery we hoped we would make from the Globe experiment.

My real involvement in the Globe project dates to 1984,[3] when, following the 'Shakespeare's Globe Reborn' conference held at Northwestern University, Sam Wanamaker asked me to establish a Southeastern Regional Center for what was then the Shakespeare Globe Center of North America. Over the years I have been fascinated not only by the twists and turns in the development of the project but by the rich history that led to its creation. This history, I believe, can be traced back to at least 1765 when Edward Capell, seventh editor of the works of Shakespeare, ended his introduction to those volumes with the suggestion that if we are to fully understand Shakespeare's plays, 'the stage he appear'd upon, its form, dressing, actors should be enquir'd into, as every one of those circumstances had some considerable effect upon what he compos'd for it'.[4] This was the first articulation of the notion that there is a relationship between the way a playwright constructs a play and the physical conditions of theatrical performance that exist during that playwright's career. The obvious implication was that you cannot fully understand one without an understanding of the other. Volumes have been written about why this is a naive notion.[5] It is certainly possible, for example, that the flow of scenes Brenton observed has nothing to do with Shakespeare's actual stagecraft and everything to do with what we want that stagecraft to have been. But the success of Shakespeare's Globe suggests that history can indeed be used to make important contributions to the present, even if it is only to help us see something about ourselves.

Shakespeare's Globe, as a specific project, began in 1969 when Sam Wanamaker first read that the Greater London Council was considering a major urban renewal initiative for the Borough of Southwark. By October 1970 he was ready to propose a large-scale development plan that extended from London Bridge to Blackfriars Bridge, and included what I like to call an 'essence of Globeness' theatre as its centrepiece.[6] Before the year was out, however, that centrepiece had changed to an 'authentic reconstruction' of Shakespeare's Globe and over the next twenty years, while the overall scale of the project was shrunk to a more realistic size, that authenticity became increasingly uncompromising. This was not because those involved had any illusions that perfect authenticity was possible, but because it forced a level of discipline on the project that had never been attempted before. Previous attempts to reconstruct the theatre started with the assumption that concessions had to be made to modern tastes, modern notions of audience comfort and modern building codes. Such concessions became excuses for not attempting to identify, let alone answer, the important questions.

Shakespeare's Globe was designed with the assumption that no such concessions were acceptable. As a result, only those which were unavoidable, like accommodations for fire safety concerns, were made. This is not to suggest that the result was a project that is error free, and no one involved with it ever assumed that it would be. Debates over the proper decoration of the house have left the Globe unfinished for more than ten years. The layout of the lower galleries is currently being re-examined because, of all the options allowed by the historical evidence, the one that was chosen when the theatre was designed twenty years ago no longer seems to have been the best one. These and many other such issues are reviewed and corrected on a regular basis. The shape of the stage and location of the stage columns are among the myriad details that may one day also require an adjustment. Of greater concern is that when the archaeology report, conducted on the excavations on the foundations of the first Globe in 1989, is released by the Museum of London, it will suggest that Shakespeare's Globe was built larger than the archaeology will support. This is probably not correctable but the implications of this can be explained in the exhibition. All of these issues serve as an important validation for the project, which was, after all, intended to advance our knowledge about the theatre of Shakespeare's day. Because of its steadfast dedication to the idea of authenticity this theatre has actually identified its own flaws, giving us a new understanding of what issues are important and why. But to fully understand the significance of the project, it is necessary to look at the history that brought us to this point.

REVIVING SHAKESPEARE'S STAGECRAFT

There are fewer than six degrees of separation between the opening of Shakespeare's Globe in 1997, and the events of 1897 when William Poel, one of England's first modern directors, made the first known drawings of what the Globe theatre may have looked like and proposed to the London County Council that they build it near the original site of Shakespeare's playhouse.[7] By this time Poel had been attempting to recapture Shakespeare's stagecraft for over sixteen years. He was motivated, he said, by his disappointment in contemporary productions of Shakespeare's plays.[8] Editors of Shakespeare had long been helping their readers by indicating a physical location for each scene in a given play and of course they described those scenes in terms of the time of the story. By 1830, 'pictorial illustration', also known as 'antiquarianism', had followed the editors' lead by actually attempting to provide sets to illustrate each of these scenic locations in performance. Inevitably, this forced some reorganisation of the texts and/or the cutting of entire scenes in order to reduce the number of changes required. Poel found that this practice distorted the carefully plotted sweep of action in the plays. Poel also deplored the tradition of star performers who often 'adjusted' play-texts in order to allow them to show off their particular talents. This too resulted in cuts that altered the structure Shakespeare had so carefully crafted. Yet even with all these cuts, the plays were slow because of the time required to change sets and deliver lines in an overly ponderous manner that destroyed the momentum of the plays. Antiquarianism, therefore, became Poel's nemesis and he set himself the task of saving Shakespeare from it by attempting to recover the original stagecraft for which the plays had been created.

Over the years, he, and those who followed him, came to exaggerate the negative impact of traditional performance on Shakespeare's work and it must be said that many of the productions they most disparaged were highly regarded by others. But Poel's complaints were not unique. In 1877 the French critic Théodore de Banville had pleaded for a new theatre 'where a single action continues without interruption in quite different locales'[9] and others were calling for similar changes. This was exactly what Poel believed Shakespearean stagecraft had originally done and he saw the recovery of that stagecraft as an avant-garde undertaking. 'Some people have called me an archaeologist', he told the *Daily Chronicle* on 3 September 1913, 'but I am not. I am really a modernist. My original aim was just to find out some means of acting Shakespeare naturally and appealingly from the full text as in a modern drama.'[10] The 'means' he found became known as the Elizabethan Revival.

Poel started his revival with *Hamlet* in 1881, but it was not until he became an instructor for the Shakespeare Reading Society in 1897 that his work received significant attention. In 1888 the famous Swan drawing, still the only known contemporary drawing of the interior of an Elizabethan open-air playhouse, was discovered. Two years later Poel saw the Jocza Savits production of *King Lear* (1890) performed on a 'classical stage' at the Shakespeare theatre in Munich.[11] These events made him realise the extent to which his own work was lacking the appropriate stage environment.[12] In 1893 he introduced his 'Fortune fit-up', thereby staking claim to the authority of the Fortune contract, which, since its publication in 1790, has been the most highly regarded document relating to Elizabethan theatre architecture. In actuality his movable stage was based on the more sceptically received Swan drawing, discovered five years earlier. At the back of the stage was a balcony flanked by two doors (at stage level), as shown in the Swan drawing. Below the balcony was a 'discovery space' (or inner stage)[13] which is not shown in that drawing but was adopted by nearly everyone who wrote about Elizabethan theatres after A. H. Paget laid out the case for it in 1891.[14] When the Swan drawing was published by Karl Gaedertz, he argued that the stage posts it features so prominently provided a mid-stage location for curtains that could be closed to facilitate scene changes. Poel adopted this practice, using costumed stage hands to open and close the curtains, in spite of the obvious objection that a large part of the audience in those polygonal playhouses of Shakespeare's day would have been looking at the stage from the sides.

Poel developed a system for staging that allowed unlocalised or outdoor scenes to occur in front of the stage posts, while indoor or otherwise localised scenes could be staged on the middle stage (behind the posts), within the inner stage or on the balcony. The curtains associated with the middle stage, inner stage and balcony could be opened and closed so that the action never had to be delayed to bring on large properties. There were many flaws with this system. But this stage design was remarkably effective in the hands of Nugent Monck, who had been Poel's regular stage manager for 1900–8 and went on to be his foremost proponent in England. Monck staged all of Shakespeare's plays and about five hundred others of all types at his Maddermarket Theatre in Norwich, which in 1921 became the first recreation of an indoor Elizabethan playhouse in the world. His work influenced a long list of directors during the years between the wars.

Another of Poel's followers, B. Iden Payne, modified Poel's methods to work on proscenium arch stages. Payne had worked with Poel in 1908 and 1910 and went on to become his foremost proponent in the United States. As Payne noted, what Poel's system taught a generation of directors was first, that 'the fundamental quality of a Shakespearean performance should be the complete fluidity of action' and second, that 'something approximating to the main features of the Elizabethan theatre (as usually understood) is not only the most suitable but is even essential if the desire of the director is not self-exploitation but an honest determination to make the plays come to life for a modern audience'. Much of the debate ever since has been over exactly what the 'main features' of the Elizabethan stage were, and how much 'approximating' was necessary or useful in the attempt to recover Shakespeare's dramaturgy. Directors like Payne had come to believe that Shakespeare's dramaturgy was to be seen 'in the allocation of the different portions of the stage to the scenes as they unfold'.[15] For them all that was important was the essence of the layout of an Elizabethan stage. Payne taught this system across America but gradually it came to be recognised that the extensive use of curtains was little more than a clever modification of the Victorian use of tabs. One of the important contributions of Shakespeare's Globe has been to demonstrate that these curtains are not necessary.

While Poel was a leader in these explorations, he was not alone. Just two years after Poel introduced his 'fit-up', Harvard University built an 'Elizabethan stage' for a production of Jonson's *Epicoene* in 1895. This stage was undeniably based on the Swan drawing, so it had no 'inner stage' or even a central opening. There were also no curtains between the posts, which were square, rather than round as shown in the drawing.[16] In 1904, George Pierce Baker had this stage remounted and set up in the 1,000-seat Sanders Theatre building on the Harvard campus. He calls this a 'wholly independent' experiment from the Poel 'fit-up' but his alterations included expanding the square stage of the Swan drawing into a rectangle,[17] adding curtains between the posts and creating an inner stage. He also used costumed actors, as Poel had done, to serve as an Elizabethan audience in the yard (where they seem to have stood) and in the stage boxes. Poel had built his stage to test (some would say legitimise) his own theories. Baker, by contrast, was experimenting with the theories of others.

For those whose outlook on Elizabethan playhouse reconstructions was influenced by the Elizabethan Revival or Baker's alternative to it, it has been a disappointment that Shakespeare's Globe has limited its testing of competing ideas about Shakespearean stagecraft to a few post-season productions by the Original Shakespeare Company, directed by Patrick Tucker. The 'original practices' productions developed by Mark Rylance, Claire van Kampen and Jenny Tiramani have held the promise of creating a coherent approach to the staging of plays at Shakespeare's Globe, but the promise of this approach has not yet been fully realised. This may be due to an overreaction to the constant accusation of 'museum theatre' that has plagued such projects since Poel's day. It is time for the fear of this phrase to be abandoned at Shakespeare's Globe. Given that museums are places where world class authorities share their expertise with the general public in exciting and dynamic ways, 'museum theatre' should be a term theatre companies strive to embrace.

DEGREES OF AUTHENTICITY

Poel's 1897 reconstruction drawing of the Globe playhouse was the first of its kind. This drawing became the basis for the first known model of the Globe which went on display in 1902. This model, in turn, inspired the first nearly full-scale reconstruction of the Globe which was built as part of the 'Merry England' (or 'Shakespeare's England') Exhibition at Earl's Court, London, in 1912.[18] The architect for this project was Edwin Lutyens, one of the pre-eminent architects of the day. Poel's plan had called for a twenty-four-sided building with a diameter of 80 foot, surrounded by a one-storey walkway 4 foot wide, thus making its total diameter 88 foot. The only known photographs of the 1912 Globe show what looks to be a twelve-sided building subdivided into twenty-four bays. But the theatre looks much smaller than the Poel model, probably under 70 foot in diameter including the lower walkway. Inside, the stage did not extend to the middle of the yard, a feature Poel found objectionable.[19] But this is the only reconstruction prior to Shakespeare's Globe to use all three galleries for audience seating. Half-hour performances of excerpts from plays by Shakespeare, Marlowe and Fletcher were held daily in this theatre, at 3:30, 5:30 and 9:00 p.m. so artificial lighting must have been involved. Building this Globe was the idea of an American, Mrs George Cornwallis West, the former Lady Randolph Churchill who was the Brooklyn-born Jennie Jerome, mother of Winston Churchill. It was intended to raise money to build a permanent reconstruction in Southwark in time for the tercentenary of Shakespeare's death in 1916, but by the time that date arrived all of Europe was embroiled in the Great War. So this first Globe reconstruction was not an extension of the 'space as laboratory' approach that Poel's 'fit-up' and the Harvard experiment had been. Instead, this project attempted to combine the public interest in Shakespeare with public interest in history, for other purposes. As a consequence it linked all future Globe reconstructions to the ideas of 'cultural tourism', 'museum theatre' and 'Disneyland', all ideas used to disparage Shakespeare's Globe – which was, after all, also proposed by an American.

Among the many visitors to the 1912 Globe was O. S. E. Keating, who twenty-two years later became the general manager of another 'Merry England' exhibition, this one built for the second season of the 1933–4 World's Fair in Chicago, entitled 'A Century of Progress'. When Thomas Wood Stevens proposed a Globe theatre as part of this venture, Keating became its most avid supporter.[20] Stevens had impeccable credentials for bringing Shakespeare to the masses. He had written and staged over forty pageants, including some of the most popular ones of the time. Stevens had also created and chaired the first degree-granting programme in theatre and had recently completed a theatre history text. In addition he had been the founding artistic director of Chicago's famed Goodman Theatre. Stevens was not, however, particularly experienced with Shakespeare so he turned to his long-time colleague, B. Iden Payne, to help with the concept for the Globe reconstruction and to provide the appropriate staging methods to be used in it. The actual design, however, was carried out by Chicago architect Henry Hoskins, who stretched the square described in the Fortune contract into an elongated octagon (see figure 1).[21] Inside was a yard[22] that was surrounded by three levels of galleries, the upper one of which was fake. The stage was small, thrusting just 16 foot into the audience. It measured 16 foot across the front and tapered out to 25 foot where it intersected the frame. It then tapered back along the lines of the frame to a discovery space,[23] surmounted by a similarly sized balcony.[24] Like Poel's 'fit-up' stage this experiment used curtains between the stage posts as these were necessary to the staging approach they borrowed from Payne. We know from the work done at Shakespeare's Globe that by making the Chicago Globe so small – it seated just over four hundred – they lost the critical mass of audience needed to make the dynamics of Elizabethan theatre-architecture work. By seating the audience in the yard they prevented the space from generating the kind of energy and excitement we now know these buildings were capable of producing. By not having a third gallery audience, they unknowingly removed one of the key components of such a space. And by elongating the shape they made the space as frontal as if they had simply used a standard auditorium with a balcony. The addition of a roof over the yard was also a major drawback to the authenticity they claimed for this building. The Chicago Globe, then, was in many ways a step backward from the Earl's Court Globe. But the presence of the actors in the same volume of space as the audience, with no proscenium-arch frame, and no front curtain, gave many people a new realisation of what theatre could be. In spite of the theatre's failings, over 400,000 people saw productions in this space and for many of these it changed their perception of Shakespeare for ever.[25] One of these people was Sam Wanamaker who, in building Shakespeare's Globe Theatre, has in turn changed the perceptions of a whole new generation.

With the assistance of B. Iden Payne and Theodore Viehman, Stevens undertook the task of cutting plays that generally took around two hours to perform, even with Poel's method of rapid delivery, down to thirty to forty-five minutes.[26] The company performed these streamlined scripts seven times a day from the end of May to October 1934. The Globe Company then moved to San Diego for the 1935

1 Old Globe Theatre, Century of Progress International Exhibition – World's Fair, 1933–4, Chicago, Illinois

California Pacific International Exhibition, where a slightly larger Globe, based on the Chicago model (but seating 560), was designed for them by architect George Vernon Russell. This time, at least, there was no roof over the yard although, sadly, one was added later. The Globe company was invited back for the 1936 season but were already scheduled to transfer to the Texas Centennial Exposition in Dallas where a third Globe, again based on the Chicago model, had been designed for them by architect Hans Oberhammer. The solution to this problem was to create a replacement company, the Fortune company, for the second San Diego season. A third company, the Blackfriars company, also had to be created for the 1936 season because yet another Globe, this one designed by architect James William Thomas, had been built for them at the Great Lakes Exposition in Cleveland, Ohio (see figure 2). Among the members of the Blackfriars company in Cleveland was Sam Wanamaker.

Over a three-year period at the height of the Great Depression, then, these three companies staged eighteen plays by Shakespeare, plus Marlowe's *Doctor Faustus*, in 5,000 performances seen by over 2 million people either at the Globe reconstructions built in Chicago, San Diego, Dallas and Cleveland, or on tours, several of which were sponsored by the Federal Theatre Project.[27] In 1939 an attempt was made to franchise the 'Thomas Wood Stevens Globe' when the entire 'Merry England' village from Chicago was recreated at the New York City's World Fair, 'The World of Tomorrow'. Neither Stevens nor Payne were directly involved in this project. Instead, Margaret Webster, a well-known actress and the premier woman director in New York at the time, was hired to produce the same four plays that had opened the Chicago Globe five years earlier, in her own streamlined versions.

2 1936 Old Globe Theatre, Great Lakes Exhibition, 1936–7, Cleveland, Ohio

Webster had just directed two seasons of Shakespeare for the Maurice Evans Company and her nearly five-hour-long, full-text production of Hamlet was the talk of Broadway. Yet this Globe was a failure. Its failure was attributed to underfunding, bad weather and the fickleness of the New York audience. But the truth is Margaret Webster had a limited vision of what constituted a modern approach to Shakespeare and no real sympathy for, or understanding of, the Elizabethan Revival. For the rest of her career she criticised what she derisively referred to as 'Globolators', without demonstrating that she had any real understanding of their goals or methods.[28]

SHAKESPEARE'S GLOBE AND THE 'ESSENCE OF GLOBENESS'

These Globes of the Great Depression were inspired by the rhetoric of William Poel and his Elizabethan Revival but it seems fair to say that they were given legitimacy by the inclusion of an Elizabethan theatre in the Folger Shakespeare Library when it opened in 1932. Their success inspired the creation of the Oregon Shakespeare Festival (1935) and the San Diego Shakespeare Festival at the Old Globe Theatre

(1949). Those organisations, in turn, inspired the more than 150 such Shakespeare Festivals that exist across the United States and Canada today, including those which claim a relationship to the 1599 Globe like the Stratford Festival Theatre in Ontario, Canada (1953), the Utah Shakespeare Festival (1961) and the Globe of the Great Southwest in Odessa, Texas (1965). But it would be hard to argue that they had any greater legacy than the inspiration they gave to the young Sam Wanamaker, which eventually led to his single-minded dedication to the creation of Shakespeare's Globe in London. From its inception, Wanamaker's project stimulated imaginations and caused a remarkable number of theatres to be built, most along the 'essence of Globeness' lines that attempted to combine what was being learned about the form of the Elizabethan theatres with the benefits of modern theatre design, especially in the area of stage lighting. No fewer than eighteen Globe Theatre projects worldwide followed,[29] some of which were under consideration before the Wanamaker Globe was announced. Not all of these theatres still exist, and this number does not include the numerous proposed projects which have not been built.

The complex heritage of Shakespeare's Globe explains a great deal about the diversity of goals it has had, a diversity that has provided endless ammunition for its critics. From Poel, the Globe inherited the notion that this could be a laboratory for the exploration of Shakespeare's dramaturgy. From the Folger the Globe inherited the notion that such projects have an educational responsibility. And from the Stevens Globes it inherited the belief that it could make Shakespeare popular, offering an alternative to the established theatre of its time. Remarkably, Shakespeare's Globe has tried to do all these things and has succeeded beyond the expectations any of us had for it.

There is, of course, no right way to do Shakespeare and even the most ardent supporters of the Elizabethan Revival would not have wanted to see all English Renaissance plays done exclusively in the revival style. But I have long argued that Shakespeare's Globe offers us an opportunity to learn how to 'translate' Shakespeare for a modern audience. The Elizabethan Revival was based on the assumption that the Age of Shakespeare was, by any measure, one of the most successful periods theatre has ever experienced. There may be important lessons to be learned from a meticulous examination of the stagecraft that made it work. Theatre is a collaborative art form that draws on the work of many artists, from the artist of language (the playwright), to the artists of sound and movement (the actors) to the visual artists of architecture, art, design, sculpture and fashion. What happens when you want to translate a piece of classical theatre for a modern audience? There is a language of performance involved that transcends the language of words. Is it possible to translate this language in any meaningful way if one has never studied the original performance language and come to an understanding of its grammar and syntax? Shakespeare's Globe offers the opportunity for a new generation of directors to learn the theatrical language of the age of Shakespeare and learning that language will make it possible to translate the plays more effectively for audiences in the twenty-first century.

NOTES

1 Howard Brenton, 'Playing to the Crowd', *Guardian*, Saturday 12 May 2007.

2 Susannah Clapp, 'Theatre Has Moved on – whatever We Critics Think', *Observer*, Sunday 20 May 2007.

3 My own experience with Shakespeare's Globe goes back to August of 1973 when I first visited the theatre tent on the site of the current Globe complex. It carried through my graduate school years when J. L. Styan and Robert I. Schneideman, major early supporters of the project, were my mentors.

4 Edward Capell, *Mr. William Shakespeare, His Comedies, Histories, and Tragedies* (London: 1790; New York: AMS Press, 1968), p. 74. I have previously written about this history in 'Reconstructing Shakespeare's Theatre', *New Issues in the Reconstruction of Shakespeare's Theatre: Proceedings of the Conference Held at the University of Georgia February 16–18, 1990*, ed. Franklin J. Hildy. New York: Peter Lang, 1990), pp. 1–37, and 'Why Elizabethan Spaces?', *Elizabethan Performances in North American Spaces: Theatre Symposium* 12 (2004), 98–120.

5 See Jonas Barish, 'Is there "Authenticity" in Theatrical Performance?', *Modern Language Review* 89 (1994), 817–31, for a good example of this. A good sampling of other criticisms can be found in W. B. Worthen, 'Reconstructing the Globe, Constructing Ourselves', *Shakespeare and the Globe: Shakespeare Survey* 52 (1999), pp. 33–45.

6 The curators of 'Reinventing the Globe: a Shakespearean Theater for the 21st Century' at the National Building Museum in Washington DC (January to August 2007) borrowed this phrase for part of the historic background section I helped them create. For a review of that project see Jeremy Kahn, 'Imagining and Reimagining the Globe', *New York Times* 13 January 2007, A1 and A21.

7 Martin White, 'William Poel's Globe', *Theatre Notebook* 53, 3 (1999), 148.

8 *Ibid.*

9 Quoted in Marvin Carlson, *Theories of the Theatre*, expanded edition (Ithaca: Cornell University Press, 1993), p. 288.

10 Ropert Speaight, *William Poel and the Elizabethan Revival* (London: Heinemann, 1954), p. 90.

11 Theatre professionals throughout Europe were interested in this process of recapturing pre-proscenium production methods. This included not only Poel in England and Savits in Germany, but also Nikolai Evreinov in Russia, W. B. Yeats in Ireland, and both André Antoine and Aurélien Lugné-Poe in France, just to name a few of the more prominent practitioners. Much of the work of the revivalists is covered in Dennis Kennedy, *Looking At Shakespeare* (Cambridge University Press, 1993), pp. 25–42, but for the attempt by Yeats to bring medieval drama to the Abbey Theatre see my *Shakespeare at the Maddermarket* (Ann Arbor: UMI Research, 1986), pp. 18–24; for Evreinov and the Ancient Theatre in St Petersburg see Spencer Golub, *Evreinov: The Theatre of Paradox and Transformation* (Ann Arbor: UMI Research, 1984), pp. 107–43; and for Antoine's work with French drama see Oscar Gross Brockett and Robert R. Findlay, *Century of Innovation: A History of European and American Theatre and Drama Since 1870*, 2nd edition (Englewood Cliffs, NJ: Prentice-Hall, 1991), p. 111.

12 Jill L. Levenson, 'The Recovery of the Elizabethan Stage', *The Elizabethan Theatre* 9 (1986), 215–16.

13 The 'Fortune fit-up' stage was 30 foot wide by 19 foot deep. The 5 foot depth of the inner stage made the overall stage depth 24 foot. Stage columns, 18 foot tall, standing about 14 foot apart, supported a fake penthouse roof over the central portion of the stage, dividing the stage depth in half.

14 A. H. Paget, 'The Elizabethan Playhouses', *Transactions of the Leicester Literary and Philosophical Society* (London: 1891), pp. 237–50.

15 B. Iden Payne, 'Shakespeare at Work in his Theatre', *Educational Theatre Journal* 19, 3, Shakespearean Production (October 1967), 327 and 329.

16 This stage was the basis for the design of another one used at the Berkeley Lyceum in New York City, in 1902.

17 The stage was 40 foot by 20 foot.

18 The most complete report on the Globe of 1912 is Marion F. O'Connor's, 'Theatre of the Empire: "Shakespeare's England" at Earl's Court, 1912', in *Shakespeare Reproduced: The Text in History and Ideology*, ed. Jean E. Howard and Marion F. O'Connor (New York: Methuen, 1987), pp. 68–98. See also Ralph G. Martin, *Jennie, Lady Randolph Churchill, the Dramatic Years, 1885–1921*, vol. 11 (New York: Signet, 1970), p. 316. For Poel's negative reaction to the Earl's Court Globe see William Poel, *Shakespeare in the Theatre* (London: Sidgwick and Jackson, 1913), pp. 208–12.

19 The size and stage arrangement that made this building out of step with the ideas about the Globe that were then current made it remarkably close in design to what was found in the archaeology of the first Rose playhouse of 1587.

20 Rosemary Kegl, '"[W]rapping Togas over Elizabethan Garb": Tabloid Shakespeare and the 1934 Chicago World's Fair', *Renaissance Drama* new series 28 (1997), 73–97.

21 The 80 foot square described in the Fortune contract became a 55 foot wide by 70 foot long elongated octagon that was 32 foot high.

22 The yard measured just 36 foot by 42 foot.

23 The discovery space was 14 foot wide by 7 foot 6 inches deep.

24 Hildy, 'Reconstructing Shakespeare's Theatre', pp. 27 and 63–4.

25 See Donna Rose Feldman, 'An Historical Study of Thomas Wood Stevens' Globe Theatre Company, 1934–1937' (PhD dissertation: University of Iowa, 1953). Additional information on the Chicago Globe can be found in Rosemary Kegl, '"[W]rapping Togas over Elizabethan Garb"', pp. 73–97.

26 Over three years the Globe companies performed edited versions of: *The Taming of the Shrew*, *The Comedy of Errors* (arranged by B. Iden Payne), *A Midsummer Night's Dream* (arranged by Theodore Viehman), *Julius Caesar*, *All's Well that Ends Well*, *As You Like It* (B. Iden Payne), *Doctor Faustus*, *Macbeth*, *King Lear*, *Twelfth Night*, *Much Ado About Nothing*, *Hamlet*, *The Winter's Tale*, *The Merry Wives of Windsor*, *Henry VIII*, *The Tempest*, *The Two Gentlemen of Verona*, *The Life and Death of Falstaff* and *Romeo and Juliet*. The * indicates texts that are still available from Samuel French.

27 Melvin R. White, 'Thomas Wood Stevens: Creative Pioneer', *Educational Theatre Journal* 3, 4 (December 1951), 290. (Note, the article says nineteen plays but one was *Doctor Faustus*.) The Federal Theatre Project was an attempt by the government of the United States to ensure work for theatre artists during the Great Depression. It operated from 1935 to 1939 with

production companies in over thirty-three cities across the United States. It is often said to have been the closest the United States has ever been to having a national theatre.

28 If she even knew that her great-grandfather, Benjamin Webster, had been one of the very first to experiment with reviving Shakespeare's stagecraft when he produced *The Taming of the Shrew* at the Haymarket Theatre, London, in 1844, with a minimalist set designed by J. R. Planché, she does not seem to have taken any pride in that fact.

29 A full list of the International Globe Theatre projects after 1970 is given in Appendix 1.

PART I

THE 'ORIGINAL PRACTICES' PROJECT

INTRODUCTION

Christie Carson

Franklin J. Hildy's chapter provides a sensitive account of the history of reconstruction as well as a clear articulation of the reasons behind this movement. His chapter indicates the extent to which this 150-year process has always involved the collaboration of theatre historians, architects and theatre practitioners. While in some cases the building followed and at other times it led the theories of historians, the understanding of the plays has been continually enlivened by the process of reconstruction. The longevity of this process, as well as its prevalence worldwide, must be acknowledged in order to place the experimentation undertaken at Shakespeare's Globe in its proper scholarly and theatrical context. The recognition from the outset that authenticity is not wholly achievable does not negate the attempts to work towards an understanding of 'original practices' as influenced by architecture through the redefinitions of stage craft and actor/audience relationship that this building requires. As Hildy points out, the Globe Theatre has achieved in a number of ways what reconstruction has been aiming towards for the past 150 years: not authenticity but a practical space for experimentation that is informed by scholarly concerns about the period.

This section of the book aims to present the practical and theoretical parameters of the 'original practices' experiments that have been conducted on the Globe stage over the first ten years of its existence. Each essay presents a 'situated overview', to take John Joughin's term,[1] in order to present a wide range of responses to the space and the work that has gone on in it which reflects an active engagement in the process, in the case of the practitioners, and an active engagement with the ideas and scholarship around the practices of the period, in the case of scholars. This section draws together the most knowledgeable representatives available to discuss each of four areas from quite different perspectives. Practitioners and academics have been asked to reflect on four different areas of the theatrical experience:

stage action, stage appearance, music and sound and the actor/audience relationship. The essays addressing each topic demonstrate differences in approach and fundamental incompatibilities but they also highlight productive intersections of practice and theory. While practitioners and scholars can and have worked productively together both in this theatre and in this volume, their central aims and the outcomes of their work remain different. In essence, the volume has been designed to mimic the theatrical process of creation in that it allows each contributor to speak to his or her area of expertise in order to provide an integrated debate of the highest quality.

STAGE ACTION

In the first pair of essays looking at stage action, director Tim Carroll sets the tone of this section of the book by pointing out the absurdity of looking for 'realism' or 'authenticity' in the theatrical event, which is so obviously and joyously dependent on the imagination. Carroll provides an animated discussion of the role of the audience in the Globe Theatre, and gives useful examples of the way this theatre differs from other modern theatre spaces in its ability to involve the audience in a communal reaction to the coming together of words, actions and whatever the outdoor environment chooses to throw at the performance. Carroll's position is that the theatre is a place for the collective imagination of the audience to work; it is not a space for discovering realistic or authentic practice but rather a place to discover an engaged audience response in the present moment.

In contrast to Carroll's chapter, which addresses primarily the concerns of theatre practitioners and audiences in the space, Alan Dessen poses some difficult questions from his ample experience and expertise both as a theatre historian and as a member of the Globe's audience. Dessen's influential papers at the 1984 Northwestern Conference and the 1990 International Conference on the Globe and Rose Theatres helped to shape our thinking about what theatrical experimentation might achieve before the theatre was built. However, in this piece what Dessen addresses head on is what he calls 'theatrical essentialism' or the tendency to raise the importance of an engaged audience response today above the opportunity to experiment with an 'original' audience response. Dessen draws on a range of examples from the thirty productions he has seen at the Globe to illustrate stage practices that are not historically accurate, not as a form of chastisement but as a way of questioning the boundaries of an 'original practices' (OP) approach executed in a commercial theatre. This essay interrogates both those productions that conscientiously followed an OP aesthetic and those that did not in order to illustrate the kind of ideas that are overlooked in an environment that must, by necessity, sell enough tickets to carry on. A key point in Dessen's argument is that important visual signals are lost on an audience untrained in the visual culture of the period. He asks whether it is really possible to create 'original practices' of action when the responses to that action will inevitably be so different. Dessen argues that there are enormous limitations in the experiments conducted because the audience is untrained.

These two essays point out both the extraordinary new opportunities provided by the Globe Theatre for a current Shakespearean audience, and the limitations of reproducing an 'original' or 'authentic' response in that audience. This dialogue usefully points out the need for a clarification of the principles and practices of the 'original practices' project as defined by the creative team of Jenny Tiramani, Claire van Kampen and Mark Rylance. As both Carroll and Dessen point out, there is a clear distinction between those productions that had as an aim the discovery of 'original practices' and those that, to use Mark Rylance's term, were 'free-hand'.[2] The articulation of the approach to design, music and acting follows in the accounts of the three key participants in this collaborative research project. These are interwoven with the work of critics in each case to illustrate how the work of this specific project can usefully open up a debate around larger theoretical questions about the role of practice-based research in scholarship.

STAGE APPEARANCE

In the first chapter in this subsection the complex question of recreating a Renaissance visual aesthetic, as well as a sympathetic relationship between actor, audience and theatre building, is usefully addressed by Jenny Tiramani. This chapter also makes clear that while a rigorous approach was taken to 'original practices' the approach was, by necessity, selective rather than comprehensive. Tiramani also points out the way that critical responses to the project as a whole tended to focus on the visual when assessing the success of 'original practices'. Her extensive experiments in early modern stage and costume design have involved an exploration of a range of theatre spaces as well as audience arrangements and lighting states. The combination of costume and stage design with gesture, movement, cosmetics, sound, lighting and audience response have illuminated aspects of the plays that have been generally overlooked. Tiramani highlights the fact that while we have access to evidence of a variety of kinds to assess the visual representation of the plays and the period there is little evidence regarding the use of the costumes and objects on stage in action.

Farah Karim-Cooper picks up this point about the use of material culture on stage in the essay which follows. She points out the way that cultural materialist criticism has focused on the interaction between objects and people in the daily life of the period but that the relationship between those practices and the practices of the stage is hard to pin down. She documents her own research work on cosmetics to illustrate the kinds of sources that can be found from the period as well as the useful ways that practical experimentation can help to enhance that knowledge. Karim-Cooper's work advising practitioners on productions at the Globe Theatre has impressed upon her the importance of combining speculation about practices taken from documentation from the period with experimentation that tests those theories on stage.

MUSIC AND SOUND

In the first chapter in the subsection on music and sound Claire van Kampen, as Director of Music at Shakespeare's Globe, consolidates Tiramani's work on design with evidence of a similarly rigorous, yet exploratory, approach to aural texture. Working collaboratively with directors, actors, musicians and audiences, van Kampen points out how difficult it has been to recreate an 'authentic' aural environment for the productions but marvels at the extent to which audiences have become informed of the concerns of the period as a collective group. Van Kampen usefully refers to 'historically informed experimentation' which has come up with interesting results, particularly in terms of moving from the indoor space of Middle Temple to the Globe Theatre. The area of sound and music has been involved in reconstruction for many years through the early music movement; however, as van Kampen points out, this work has not been integrated into the theatre of this period before. As a result modern theatre audiences are much more accustomed to inauthentic music that is used in a filmic way to produce an emotional effect. She questions the viability of drawing these two approaches together and suggests that a new audience must be trained to understand the aural expectations of the period, integrating music in the plays in new ways.

In David Lindley's essay, which follows, he points out the limitations of 'histor- ically informed' performance, while at the same time holding on to a belief in the importance of a contextualised understanding of dramatic texts. He questions van Kampen's notion of training a new audience, based on the assumption that it is impossible to train an audience to hear with pre-electronic ears. In critical terms Lindley sees the necessity of finding a middle ground between presentist critics, who believe the texts must be experienced in the present moment, and historicist critics, who want to re-experience the texts in their own period. The creative tension he sees between these two critical positions articulates to a large degree the kind of complex criticism that the volume advocates. The larger question he addresses about the need for a pragmatic approach to critical ideas on this subject presents a particularly welcome addition to this debate.

THE ACTOR/AUDIENCE RELATIONSHIP

The final subsection of this part of the book addresses views about the actor/audience relationship. It begins with an interview with Mark Rylance in which he provides an account of the principles that guided his work and articulates how he tried to fulfil the expectations and aims of the project's founder, Sam Wanamaker. These principles were combined with a desire to make new discoveries in the building. The very real difficulties that the architecture poses in terms of traditional acting and directing practices were met in his time as Artistic Director by a renewed commitment to work towards 'original practices' through collaborative exploration. The very real demands of the audiences and the building as a tourist centre at times were at odds with the serious approach taken to recreating the period. The tension Rylance describes between the demands of the original scholarly project, the audience and the building itself paints a picture of genuine exploration and discovery under difficult circumstances.

In the final chapter of the section I highlight the way in which the Globe Theatre has been drawn, at times unwillingly, into a debate about the social position of Shakespeare. I examine the way that this theatre is hailed as accessible for a wide range of audiences and question what definition of accessibility is being employed in this debate. Throughout this section of the book both practitioners and scholars return again and again to the idea that the Globe Theatre audience is unique. I try to examine that assertion by placing the development of the Globe Theatre within the movement in the theatre more generally towards a more participatory model, something that can be traced from the early 1960s both in terms of theatre buildings and in terms of critical responses to the work on stage.

In raising the question in this final chapter of what makes the audience at the Globe Theatre special, I present the notion that it is the positioning of Shakespeare as a populist dramatist supporting a commercial theatre rather than as an elite artist holding up the subsidised theatre. This difference in approach is largely, I argue, a cultural difference. The American free-trade model of Shakespeare at the Globe is juxtaposed critically against the British public-service model at the Royal Shakespeare Company. The Globe model in many ways undermines the previously held truths of the cultural-capital model represented by the RSC. While I argue that placing these two theatres in opposition is in many ways unhelpful and to a large extent simplifies the issues at stake, this seeming battle also speaks very clearly to anxieties about an Americanisation of British culture. The period of the Globe Theatre's practical experiment in 'original practices' drew on not just a particular gathering of artists that is unlikely to be repeated, it also embodied a particular social moment when history, culture and national identity were very much in flux in Britain. Shakespeare has always taken on a central place in that debate and therefore Shakespeare's Globe in many ways became the eye of a particularly interesting storm during the period under examination. The building's ability to silently question assumptions about performance and scholarship was met by a commitment to re-examine those assumptions in order to challenge and change them, in some cases, and to move towards retrenchment in others. This section of the book illustrates a range of responses, all of which acknowledge, to varying degrees, the need for a reassessment not only of the current critical approaches to this theatre but also of the role of theatre in our society, based on the practical evidence presented by this enlivened alternative.

NOTES

1 John Joughin, 'Shakespeare now: an Editorial Statement', *Shakespeare* 1, 1 (June 2005), 7.
2 See Mark Rylance, 'Research, Materials, Craft: Principles of Performance at Shakespeare's Globe', p. 105.

STAGE ACTION

3 Timothy Walker as Malvolio in *Twelfth Night* (2002), Shakespeare's Globe

CHAPTER TWO

'PRACTISING BEHAVIOUR TO HIS OWN SHADOW'

Tim Carroll

IMAGINATION IN THE THEATRE

In Act 2 scene 5 of *Twelfth Night*, Maria runs in and says, 'Get ye all three into the box-tree' (2.5.13).[1] Malvolio, the steward, is approaching. So Toby, Fabian and Andrew Aguecheek all jump into or behind some sort of foliage, where they wait to see if Malvolio will fall for the trick that they have prepared for him. The trick is of course a letter, written by Maria but meant to look as though it comes from the Lady Olivia, with whom they suspect Malvolio is in love. The letter contains various hints that it might be from Olivia and is intended to suggest to Malvolio that he carry out a series of rather ludicrous, cryptic instructions, like wearing yellow stockings.

Now, if this were real life, what would the people hiding in the 'box-tree' really expect to see? They might well expect to see Malvolio come in and find the letter. If they are lucky, they might watch while he reads it, and then he will move on, perhaps with a smile on his face, perhaps looking angry. Realistically, that is all they can expect. But of course that would be very boring on stage. Somehow, they need to see more than that. They need to see his reactions to the letter, what he really makes of it, and, almost more importantly, before that, they need to see the state of inflated egotistical fantasising that will make Malvolio such a willing gull.

Maria says he has been 'yonder i' the sun practising behaviour to his own shadow this half hour' (2.5.14–15). The point of this, I am sure, is to justify to us the fact that Malvolio is about to come on and do something that otherwise would seem very strange: he is going to talk to nobody at full volume. Now, in real life, we do of course fantasise from time to time. And yes, we might occasionally do so out loud. We might even, for whatever reason, read out a letter on our own, and it is even possible that we could be spied on by other people as we do so. But the combination of all these things? And the fact that the three people listening in are having a perfectly audible conversation among themselves while they do it? There is only one place where this could really happen, and that is on stage.

The whole situation is so unrealistic that I had a disagreement with one of my colleagues at the Globe, who said, 'You have the box-tree too close to Malvolio.' He said, 'Surely they should be in the musicians' gallery, where it is easier to believe that Malvolio would not hear them.' I said, 'Wherever we put them, it is impossible to *believe* that Malvolio would not hear them. It's a game.' And this, I think, is why Maria says he has been 'practising behaviour to his own shadow': not to make us believe what we are about to see, but to ask us to be complicit in accepting something which is literally unbelievable. But it does not just do that: it also prepares us to play the role we will be required to play in the scene. Maria's words tell us that when Malvolio comes on stage he will be indulging in the mental pastime, familiar to anyone, of self-glorifying fantasy. So we know that our task is to be the imaginary audience that admires this fantasy Malvolio. The following scene may, therefore, be strictly impossible, but on a psychological level it contains profound truth.

The same goes for all the other implausible features of this marvellous scene. The 'reality' of the situation is sketched in for us in a very playful way by the writer, simply by having Fabian repeatedly say to the others, 'Please be quiet, shut up or he'll hear you' ('O peace, peace, peace, now, now' (2.5.51)). We know, of course, that he has heard them already. We know that it is an actor who has learned his lines. These lines simply give us a marker to say, all right, it is that sort of tense situation when you might be detected. We also know that he probably would not read out loud. He is an educated man. He does not have to move his lips while he reads, let alone speak. Sir Toby prays that the spirit of fooling will 'intimate reading aloud to him' (2.5.75–6). In other words, he quite openly tells the audience, 'I know, it is daft, isn't it? There is no way he would read this aloud, but let's hope he does.' And what happens? He reads aloud. Of all the scenes I directed at the Globe, this may be my favourite, because it could only happen in a play. Good theatre is not an imitation of anything, it is 'the thing itself' (*King Lear* 3.4.95).

THE ROOFLESS GLOBE

In my time at the Globe, my approach to Shakespeare has been radically affected by the theatre building itself. And when I ask myself why it has had such a profound effect on me and my work, I realise that it almost all comes down to the fact that the Globe has no roof. This seemingly simple piece of historical accuracy has two crucial consequences. The first is that the audience and the actor are in the same light. (This made such a defining difference that we never seriously considered lighting evening shows any way other than the way we did, that is to say, trying to replicate the shared light of the afternoon.) The second is that it introduces into every performance an element of inevitable unpredictability.

To begin with the latter: directors, by and large, like to control everything. We may not all be egomaniacs, but I do not think we would become directors if we were not control freaks. And yet for me the most exciting thing about the Globe has been the fact that I *could not* control everything. There are certain things that the architecture of the Globe, especially its rooflessness, remove from one's control. The most obvious one is the weather. Now, I would be lying if I said this was always a blessing. Often it was a real pain. But just occasionally it would feel as though the gods were on our side. I can recall many very serendipitous moments, such as the first time we did *The Tempest* in 2000 (Lenka Udovicki's production), when Prospero broke his staff and the moment was greeted with a great thunderclap. This was only the most striking of many such happy accidents. At other times the weather came to our aid whether it liked it or not: when Trinculo talked about 'yond black cloud, yond huge one' (2.2.20) we found, strangely, that it worked just as well whether there was such a cloud or whether the sky was completely blue; two different jokes, two different kinds of joke, both delightful.

Then there were the aeroplanes. It seems, unfortunately, that most pilots use the Thames to guide themselves down to Heathrow, so they go right past (over) the Globe. Usually, this is just boring and irritating, but just occasionally it has potential, such as when Gonzalo in *The Tempest* (my 2005 production this time) was imagining his perfect commonwealth. A plane flew overhead. He watched it ruefully and then said that in his perfect state we would have no 'need of any engine' (2.1.161).

Even such a commonplace and frivolous thing as a pigeon can make something wonderful happen. I will never forget what Jasper Britton did one day as Macbeth (2001). During one performance, just after Macbeth had learned that his wife had died, a pigeon landed on the stage just in front of him. It was, of course, completely incongruous. Some people in the audience giggled nervously: surely this was going to spoil the moment. But did it? No. Jasper, being the remarkable actor he is, immediately saw his opportunity. He looked at the pigeon as though its landing merely summed up the undignified absurdity of life. Then, when the pigeon began to walk along the front of the stage, it was as though this made a strange thought occur to Macbeth. He said 'Life's but a walking shadow, a poor player / That struts and frets his hour upon the stage' (*Macbeth* 5.5.23–4) and then he waited till the pigeon flew off before saying 'And then is heard no more' (25).

The sound that came from the audience in response to this moment was very interesting. Many of them gasped, others laughed. But the laughter was not, as one might imagine, a dismissive or empty response. One of the most important lessons I learned at the Globe is that laughter from an audience does not necessarily mean, 'We simply found that funny and we do not think anything serious could have happened.' This is what some of our critics, in their shallow way, assumed was happening when the audience laughed at the 'wrong' things. But in this case, and in many others, it meant something much more profound. It meant that they had shared with Jasper a moment of beautiful revelation, vouchsafed by the beauty of chance. At that moment I felt very proud of him and of the audience.

THE GLOBE AUDIENCE

Perhaps the most unpredictable element of all in the Globe is the audience itself. Again, I think it is because there is no roof. Because they are in the same light as us, their own reactions are much more significant (and somehow volatile) than in a dark theatre. An actor cannot go out on to that stage and give a soliloquy without speaking directly to the audience. It would be perverse: they are clearly in the same place as the actor. And when an actor is so openly talking to the audience, the possibility has to be there that the audience will answer him back. The audience does not do it very often, but just occasionally, something interesting happens, such as in Barry Kyle's 2001 production of *King Lear* when Edmund was wondering aloud which of Goneril or Regan he should take as his mistress (and of course wondering aloud means asking the audience). Someone shouted out 'have them both'. Michael Gould's response to this was a facial gesture that was unmistakable: 'That's not a bad idea.' Almost more interesting is when the potential is there for the audience to respond, but it remains unrealised. For instance, in *Hamlet*, when Mark Rylance said, 'Am I a coward?' (2.2.548). There was no doubt that he was really asking the audience. He went on: 'Who calls me villain?' (549). Now, this was quite a scary moment, because in the audience I was thinking 'Well, he has got a rapier and a dagger, so if I say "I do" I would probably regret it.' This may explain why the audience always remained silent at that point (thus perfectly setting up the line, ''Swounds, I should take it' (553)). Even without explicit intervention, the audience's presence lent the situation an electric charge which I doubt it has in most productions.

In both the *King Lear* and the *Hamlet* examples it is clear that the audience is being used as a very special kind of listener. And this is an important point: the audience members are not passive recipients; they are the most versatile scene partner in the world. The audience can be the character's best friend in the bar listening to a dirty joke, or it can be the stern grandfather passing judgement on the character's behaviour. The Jailer's Daughter in *The Two Noble Kinsmen* sometimes talks to the audience as though it was simply her best friend and she is asking for advice. In other soliloquies, without informing the audience that she has changed its role, she turns the audience into the disapproving society telling her to return to hearth and home. When John of Gaunt, in the 2003 Globe production of *Richard II*, talked about the betrayal of the country he loved, he made the audience for a while the

40

whole of England. It was not a very comfortable experience, because there was a sense that as an audience member you were not excluded from the accusation: if England has been betrayed, who let it happen? The fact that the audience could all look across to each other in the same space meant that we really had to consider the least comfortable answer.

Even if the audience is in a friendly relationship with the actor, such as when Viola is talking to it, a key component of that role is resistance. Actors often say they find soliloquies difficult because they have nothing to bounce off. They talk of having to generate the energy for a soliloquy. To which I say, in the Globe you do not have to generate anything. It is already out there, in the audience. The presence of the audience says, in effect, 'We are quite prepared to think, and even (in your imagination) say, anything that you need us to.' In other words, 'We will hold any misconception or prejudice that will give you a reason to speak.' So the audience can silently say to Viola, 'You know about that ring, don't you?' To which she can respond, '[No!] I left no ring with her' (*Twelfth Night* 2.2.15). When Richard II is in prison, the audience may be thinking, 'Well, of course, a spoiled brat like you – you must be banging your head against the wall, wailing and complaining to the gods.' And he says, '[No, actually,] I have been studying how I may compare this prison where I live unto the world' (*Richard II* 5.5.1–2). In fact, every statement that an actor makes on stage is – or can be thought of as – some kind of correction or contradiction, and the Globe audience is, it seems to me, peculiarly skilled at providing what the actor needs to trigger such responses.

The audience is not only capable of being different people at different times. It can even be different people at the same time – as indeed it is, because the auditorium is divided into such different parts. Mark Rylance often said that he thought of the theatre as being like a body: the people in the yard as the stomach, the source of the appetite; the people in the lower and middle galleries as the heart, intent on the emotions of the piece; and the people in the top galleries as the mind, looking down from their Olympian height and appreciating the wit of the play. There may be some truth in this. Even socially, there is a certain plausibility about it, because the groundlings only pay five pounds and therefore they know that they can go to the pub when they get bored. This means they may need to be entertained with dirty jokes and visual effects (what Hamlet calls 'inexplicable dumb shows' (*Hamlet* 3.2.10)), rather more than the people in the middle gallery, who have paid thirty pounds and are determined to follow through the story and see what happens to the characters. The people in the top, meanwhile, often buy restricted-view tickets, from which one might conclude that they are passionate Shakespeare lovers who do not have much money (perhaps they are academics); they would be interested in the wit and the language of it. This means the actor can decide to address him or herself to a different part of the audience, depending on what kind of person he thinks he is appealing to. When we did *Macbeth* in 2001, the Witches were a kind of satanic cabaret, which appealed very much to the audience in the yard. Lady Macbeth, meanwhile, was clearly racked by feelings of guilt (even before she did anything) and was often looking to the upper galleries and the middle galleries, as if it might be her parents who were judging her. *Twelfth Night*, on the other hand, made use of the (largely imaginary) social distinctions of the space: Feste is fundamentally a creature of the yard, even though some of his more witty jokes might have to be thrown up to the top galleries because only the scholars up there would get them; whereas Malvolio would much rather only talk to the expensive seats, because that is his natural milieu, but of course he keeps being dragged down to the level of these groundlings who will insist on reading dirty meanings into everything he says.

Whether or not there is any social or spiritual truth in the above theories and observations, it is an observable fact that in the Globe one can get several different reactions from the audience all at the same time. It can easily happen that the yard can be laughing while the watchers in the gallery sit stony-faced. It never struck me that one group was more right than the other; I drew a different moral from the phenomenon. To me it proved that the whole notion of consistency of mood (about which critics get very worked up), has no significance in Shakespeare – or at least no intrinsic value. I think he puts tragedy and comedy right up against each other, even into the same moment, and leaves the audience members to take their pick as to which they are more interested in. This is something that distressed Voltaire and it distresses critics now. Those journalists who were offended by my *Macbeth* (which is to say most of them) often singled out our treatment of the Witches. They felt that it was disastrous to turn them into such shameless entertainers. Maybe I should have pointed out to them that the first references to *Macbeth* we have come from the diary of Simon Forman (1611), who saw a performance and singled out for praise the Witches' *singing and dancing*.[2] I think we might have been nearer to an 'authentic' experience than even we realised.

'THE TEMPEST'

In my last season at the Globe I tried to bring together everything I had learned to *The Tempest*. It seemed to me that what I had learned more than anything there was that, if you ask the audience members to use their imagination, they will. They really can cope with anything – a lot more, at any rate, than most critics. Thus, the very opening of our *Tempest* had Mark Rylance as Prospero creating a storm at sea using just a chessboard and some chess-pieces. All the voices were his. Prospero then (in keeping with the show's Jungian inspiration) split into three and we saw his alter egos: Ariel his imaginative faculty, and Caliban his instinct. Those three actors then played every part in the play. This did, of course, put enormous demands not only on the audience members' imagination but on their ability to comprehend. What struck me, in the responses we had, was that people who already knew the play tended to say to me, 'Well, I understood it, of course I did, but I am sure if I had not known the play I would not have.' Whereas people who did not know the play at all tended just to say, 'Sure, I got it.' This rather confirmed my growing suspicion: the Globe audience's willingness and imagination may in fact be infinite. We certainly never found its limit.

The Tempest opened with three women, in modern clothes, climbing on to the stage from the yard and literally dragging Prospero out from the tiring house. This was, from one point of view, a way of enacting the way that the audience's desire to know the story drags the actors out on stage to perform it. More fundamentally, the fact that these women (who had a major role in the show) were in modern dress, while the three actors who were to speak the text were Jacobean, was an attempt to make explicit the relationship between the long-past text and the contemporary people who gather to watch it. A more comical version of this was in Act 3 scene 3, when the Lords see a banquet being brought towards them by strange creatures. After a lot of experimenting, we decided to make these strange creatures the groundlings themselves, the people standing in the yard. So Gonzalo went over and took their nuts and chocolate from them, as though accepting gifts from them. And then, to add insult to injury, he said that they had wonderfully good manners, even 'though they are of monstrous shape' (3.3.31). I suppose to a Jacobean lord the people standing in the yard these days would look absolutely bizarre.

The production attempted to exploit the audience's ability to play so many different roles. When Miranda looked out towards the audience at the beginning, somehow it became the sea in which the ship was being wrecked. For Gonzalo the audience was the island's topography: 'how lush and lusty the grass looks' (2.1.52) – though as far as Antonio and Sebastian were concerned, the ground was 'tawny' (55). The characters could not even agree as to whether the audience looked good or not. As we had found that different areas of the theatre had different responses, so Ariel generally found himself drawn to talk to the upper gallery, while Caliban addressed himself to the yard.

The element of unpredictability could not be omitted even if we wished it to be: in one performance, when Prospero, in the last scene, said 'I have hope to see the nuptial / Of these our dear-beloved solemnised' (5.1.12–13) a baby in the arms of one of the audience members cried out. Mark registered this cry as indicative of what might be hoped for from the nuptials, and then gave his own personal counterpoint to this person at the beginning of his life: 'And thence retire me to my Milan where / Every third thought shall be my grave' (5.1.14–15).

During one of our last performances the audience's ability to play the role required of it merged seamlessly with the weather's ability to intervene unpredictably. Mark had developed the habit of using the audience to be the 'elves of hills, brooks, standing lakes and groves' (5.1.33) whom he summons to bring the play to its climax. When, that night, it began to spit with rain just as he prepared to speak, it was as though his invocations were summoning those spirits both within the audience and in the drops of rain that gently fell. This felt like a very blessed moment, as it fused the elements that had made possible any and every piece of magic that had happened in ten years at the Globe. It was through the audience's imagination, as well as through the chance intervention of the elements, that we had 'bedimmed the noon tide sun' (The Tempest 5.1.42), or 'to the rattling thunder . . . given fire' (44–5). It had even proved possible, thanks to the audience's ability to dream, to bring the ghost of Hamlet's father on stage: 'graves at my command / Have waked their sleepers, oped, and let'em forth / By my so potent art' (The Tempest 5.1.50).

At a moment like this it did not matter whether one saw The Tempest as Shakespeare's farewell to the stage, or Prospero's farewell to his art, or even Mark Rylance's farewell to the Globe. The important message was that, if anything has happened here, whether by chance or design, it is the audience's imagination that has made it possible. Nothing else could have done it. After all, it has not been real: it is all an insubstantial pageant that will, like the great globe itself, fade and leave not a rack behind. So the only way any of it will work is if the audience plays along with the performers. That, for me, is really what the Epilogue in The Tempest is about. It says, 'Gentle breath of yours my sails / Must fill, or else my project fails' (Epilogue 11–12). People assume that this 'breath' refers to the audience cheering as it applauds, but it need not be. It could simply be the breath of inspiration, the divine flatus of imagination. And the audience will give that to the performers as long as they ask for it with sufficient humility. This is what Prospero means, I think, when he says that he hopes to be relieved by prayer, 'Which pierces so, that it assaults Mercy itself, and frees all faults' (Epilogue 17–18).

NOTES

1 This chapter is based on a talk given at the University Ca' Foscari, Venice, at the Paper Bullets of the Brain symposium, May 2005. The title is a quotation from Twelfth Night (2.5.14–15), The Norton Shakespeare, ed. Stephen Greenblatt et al. (London, and New York: W. W. Norton, 1997). All subsequent references are to this edition.
2 Simon Forman, Bocke of Plaies (London: 1611).

CHAPTER THREE

'ORIGINAL PRACTICES' AT THE GLOBE: A THEATRE HISTORIAN'S VIEW

Alan C. Dessen

In recent years the term 'original practices' (hereafter designated as OP)[1] has been invoked not only in London's Bankside Globe but also in several theatrical venues in North America – most notably by the American Shakespeare Company in Staunton, Virginia, and the Atlanta Tavern Theatre in Atlanta, Georgia. The on-stage practices linked to the term, however, can vary widely, for few common denominators are to be found among the practitioners. In Atlanta, according to artistic director Jeff Watkins, OP translates into fast-paced productions with 'a unit set of an Elizabethan design; Renaissance or Medieval costumes; live music on acoustic instruments; organic sound; a culturally diverse ensemble of sixteen to twenty-two actors, dancers and/or musicians'; and in general terms 'a conviction that communion of actor and audience through poetry is the essence of theater'. In Staunton, artistic director Ralph Alan Cohen's 'production principles' for productions at his reconstructed Blackfriars Theatre are (1) 'universal lighting' (there is no variation of illumination in this venue so that, as at the Globe, the players and playgoers are always in the same light); (2) doubling of some roles (given a cast of thirteen or fewer); (3) no sets; (4) period costumes; (5) reduced length of some scripts; and (6) acoustic music. At this venue, moreover, not only is a seated audience on three sides, but up to a dozen playgoers may be seated on the stage (as at the original Blackfriars) and thereby be targeted by the actors (e.g., for comic business; see colour plate 8).

In a significant majority of the roughly thirty productions I have seen at the Bankside Globe between 1997 and 2005, directors have not sought to conform to OP (as has also been true of many productions at the Staunton Blackfriars). Admittedly, some OP features are a permanent part of the London venue – in particular, 'universal lighting' but also the configuration of stage, standees and seated playgoers on three (and sometimes four) sides. Moreover, some historical practices have been definite strengths at the Globe, especially period dress (thanks to the efforts of Jenny Tiramani) and period music. Several productions have involved

45

all-male casts, starting with *Henry V* (1997) and including *Julius Caesar* and *Antony and Cleopatra* (1999); *Twelfth Night* (2002); and *Richard II* and *Edward II* (2003).

My focus in this essay, however, is on what I term the original theatrical vocabulary – the language of the theatre shared by the playwrights, players and playgoers at the first and second Globe – elements of which do not correspond to standard stage practice today. Ay, there's the rub. Even at a historical reconstruction of the Globe or Blackfriars, exactly what does (or can) OP mean when applied to a production mounted with directors, actors, designers, publicists and playgoers from the 1990s or early 2000s?

To raise such a question is to move into the murky area in which theatre history and commercial theatre overlap. For a variety of reasons, the findings of theatre historians have had little impact on today's productions, even at a 'historical' site such as the Bankside Globe. Most significant is the presence of a director (a figure not a part of Shakespeare's company) who provides a controlling point of view that can trump OP concerns. A major reason for the resistance of directors, actors and other theatre professionals to historical scholarship is what I term *theatrical essentialism*. Proponents assume that, regardless of other changes in language, culture and social practice, a basic core of truths about theatrical practice persists and can therefore be best understood by those in the theatre community regardless of the findings (and strictures) of scholars and other laymen.

A representative example is the argument, advanced by Sir Peter Hall and others, that no theatrical professional, then or now, would construct a Globe stage with the two posts supporting the canopy or 'heavens' as positioned in the Bankside reconstruction because such a configuration interferes with sightlines and impedes the flow of the action.[2] To an essentialist, building upon long-established reflexes, such an objection seems self-evident. The theatre historian, however, can respond with a question: was the ability to see all the events on stage from a good vantage point prized as highly then as it is now? Those playgoers seated in some of the most expensive seats at the original Globe (in the area above and behind the stage) could not see tableaux or other special effects presented in the discovery space. In addition, Tiffany Stern has provided evidence that playgoers, whether in the yard or in the galleries, felt free to move when they could not see something on stage.[3] Other forms of essentialism or transhistorical meanings regularly applied to Shakespeare's plays (e.g., about 'human nature') have long been under attack in the scholarly community, but the theatrical strain remains deeply embedded in workaday activities and thinking, as have assumptions about 'character' and psychological or narrative realism.

Along with essentialism, the other major theatrical reflex that conflicts with 'historical' findings at the Globe and comparable sites can be summed up as: 'If you have it, use it.' As already noted, a director at the Bankside Globe or Staunton

Blackfriars does not have access to variable lighting, so that all the scenes must be played in the same illumination (as befits an OP approach). Nonetheless, a theatre historian can cite other staging practices in recent productions that have appealed to theatrical professionals but cannot be documented from the period in question.

Consider how the yard, that area populated by the standees (or groundlings) between the platform stage and the rear doors, has been used at the Globe as a playing area. Most common among the plentiful examples are entrances and exits, as in the 1997 *Winter's Tale* where Autolycus made his first entrance (4.3) thrusting his way through the standees; the 2000 *Tempest* where Ariel made her final exit to freedom through the yard; or the 1999 *Antony and Cleopatra* where a drunken Lepidus was borne away through the groundlings (2.7). More elaborate effects include Act 1 of the 1997 *The Maid's Tragedy*, where the masque was presented on the stage but the king watched it from a throne set up in the yard, and the 2003 *Richard III*, where in 3.7 Richard and Buckingham on the stage sought the support of the Mayor placed on a stand facing the stage amidst the groundlings (I being one of them). In a programme note for his 2001 *King Lear* Barry Kyle stated: 'Since this season at the Globe is not about original practices, we have taken a freer approach to what follows', an approach that, among other things, sought 'to explore the vigour of the yard'. He therefore placed a pole in the midst of the standees, which Edmund climbed to deliver his 1.2 soliloquy and which Edgar scaled for his 2.3 speech in which he announces his decision to become Poor Tom.

Particularly elaborate were director Lucy Bailey's choices in her 1998 *As You Like It*, which started with a pre-show that used a singer in the yard and a dumb show on the stage to tell the audience about Sir Rowland de Boys and his sons, and then used this area for several key scenes including the wrestling in 1.2, Rosalind observing Phebe and Silvius in 3.5 and the celebration of the killing of the deer in 4.2. A programme note announced: 'The steps at the front of the stage are not a known original feature of the Globe but part of an experiment in the use of the space.' These bleacher-like wooden steps facilitated actors' ascents and descents and therefore made entrances and exits through the yard smoother. Especially effective was the *exeunt* of Duke Senior and his lords through one door at the back of the yard to end the first Arden scene (2.1) and, after a rapid change of costume, an immediate re-entry of the same actors as Duke Frederick and his lords through another yard door.

As a playgoer I enjoyed many of Bailey's effects – although seated in the lower gallery I was unable to see Orlando's winning ploy in the wrestling (a moment I find significant). Similarly, Richard's wooing of the Mayor and citizens (in a production also directed by Barry Kyle) was a rousing success, as we citizens were encouraged to approve, applaud and eventually to join in with cries of 'God save King Richard.'

This approach provided a strong sense of participation in an 'event' (an effect often sought in renditions of the orations in the Forum scene of *Julius Caesar*) but still struck me as problematic in that 'we' knew the truth about Richard's nature and plans (and moments earlier had seen what happened to Hastings) as opposed to an on-stage crowd that could be deceived or intimidated. Similarly, Kyle's placing Edgar in the yard undercut a potentially meaningful sequence (2.2–2.4) wherein Kent in the stocks is juxtaposed on stage with Edgar in flight, a juxtaposition that encourages a playgoer to see an analogy between them.[4] The narrative, however, places the two figures in two distinctly different places (Kent in the courtyard of a castle, Edgar emerging from 'the happy hollow of a tree' (2.3.2)), so that directors wedded to 'geographical realism' regularly resist this moment, often by using variable lighting to black out Kent during Edgar's speech that constitutes 2.3 in most modern editions. Kyle had no such control over the illumination at the Globe, but, thanks to his use of the yard, he could place Edgar at some distance from Kent. What for me is the most distinctive OP moment in this script was therefore sidestepped at the Globe in 2001.

Here is the dilemma. To use the yard is often to set up some theatrically exciting effects (as in Bailey's *As You Like It* and Kyle's *Richard III*). On the other hand, as a theatre historian I am aware that no evidence exists that the yard was used for entrances, exits, processions or special effects at the first or second Globe.[5] Silence is not evidence, but, given what we know about acting companies, stages and audiences then, the absence of such a practice does make sense (e.g., the high value they placed on costumes would preclude close physical contact with the groundlings).[6] However, in the real world of today's professional theatre the 'if you have it, use it' approach will prevail regardless of comments from disgruntled academics.

Use of the yard and disagreement about the positioning of the posts provide two examples of the collision between historical evidence and OP as understood at the Globe. Another example is provided by the presentation of specific locales or 'places' on this non-representational stage that lacks today's sets and the potential implications of such choices. The many courtroom scenes in this period include the indictment of Hermione in *The Winter's Tale* where she is directed to enter '*as to her trial*' (3.2.10).[7] Evidence from a range of plays indicates that the accused figure would have been positioned at a 'bar' and thereby isolated from others on stage in a fashion that may prefigure or parallel her reappearance '*like a statue*' (5.3.19) in the final moments. That property, however, was not included in the 2005 Globe production. Similarly, the presence of potted plants in the garden scene of *Richard II* (2003) or, more significantly, the on-stage fountain and arbours in *Much Ado About Nothing* (2004) made a difference to the co-ordinates of those central moments, as did a large table that stayed on stage for a sequence of scenes in *Twelfth Night* (2002).

Note the anomaly here. In OP terms, evidence does survive about the presence of a bar in courtroom scenes,[8] but that property was not introduced for the relevant moments in The Merchant of Venice (1998) or The Winter's Tale at the new Globe. In contrast, even in announced OP productions directors regularly provide large properties (tables, greenery, fountains) deemed appropriate for a given locale or atmosphere. The concern with appropriate-to-the-period features such as costume, music and casting (in the case of all-male companies) does not necessarily extend to areas where today's reflexes may not mesh well with the historical evidence. For example, thanks to the presence of the elaborate fountain in the 2004 Much Ado, the observers or eavesdroppers in 2.3, 3.1 and 3.3 did not make use of the stage posts – as opposed to the Duke in Measure for Measure, 3.1 (2004) who was positioned there to eavesdrop on Isabella and Claudio – and the interval in this Much Ado came later than usual (after 3.3, the first Dogberry scene) so that the fountain could be removed, another non-OP feature.

What then is or should be the role of the theatre historian in discussions of the use of the yard, large properties or analogous choices? Such practices may not be Historically Correct (HC as opposed to PC), but directors would not make such choices – at the Globe, in Stratford-upon-Avon, at Ashland, Oregon – were there not gains to be achieved. Rather, the issue for me remains: what, if anything, is diminished, blurred or lost in such choices? What is the price tag? Wherein lie the trade-offs? I am sympathetic to the problems faced by theatre artists in their attempt to draw in and hold on to paying customers who lack scholarly glosses and cultural contexts. Nonetheless, as teacher, playgoer and theatre historian my basic question remains: in moving from script to stage at the Globe or elsewhere, what role can or should be played by our knowledge of the original stage conventions or staging conditions? To what extent are such features as much a part of the 'language' of the scripts as the words and metre? The theatre historian may provide some windows into the past, but, to revert to the question regularly raised by my undergraduates, so what?

Consider some test cases where potentially meaningful effects in the original scripts may be blurred or lost owing to interpretive reflexes linked to theatrical essentialism or an 'if you have it, use it' approach. My examples fall under the broad umbrella of 'imagery' as understood as images for the playgoer's as well as the reader's eye. What happens to performances or performance criticism when X that was a significant, even italicised factor for the original playgoers disappears today?

First, consider references to keys in widely varying contexts in Measure for Measure. In Isabella's first scene 'Francisca, a nun' tells her 'Turn you the key' so as to let Lucio enter (1.4.0, 8). This key need not have been visible (the phrase could be a way of saying 'open the door'), but, along with the two women's costume, a key that does or does not allow a man to enter is a useful signal for setting up 'a convent' on the

Globe stage. The presence of keys is clearest in 4.1 when Isabella displays two keys given her by Angelo to facilitate their assignation. His garden, she reveals, has a vineyard with 'a planched gate, / That makes his opening with this bigger key. / This other doth command a little door, / Which from the vineyard to the garden leads' (4.1.30–3). As opposed to the convent key in 1.4, these two keys are associated with lust and stealth. Finally, the Duke, pretending to rebuke the Provost for beheading Claudio, states: 'For which I do discharge you of your office; / Give up your keys' (5.1.461–2), a comment that suggests that the Provost, like other stage jailers, was identified throughout the play (not merely in the final moments) by a visible set of keys.[9]

To note the presence of keys in three different contexts is not to offer a major reinterpretation of this complex play. Nonetheless, a network of visible (and hence readily linked) images may have been available to the original playgoers, a network easily missed (and nearly invisible) today. Should the one 'nunnery' scene (1.4) somehow be linked to the series of 'prison' scenes in terms of liberty versus restraint or some other set of associations? Why call attention to Angelo's keys in 4.1 if not to heighten some kind of linkage? Since 'place' often is generated by costume signals, relevant too is the question: how is Isabella costumed after 1.4? Does she continue to wear a wimple or some equivalent so as to carry with her a sense of the convent or has she shed any such visible link? Are such questions tangential in an already highly problematic play or do they call attention to signposts that have dropped out of sight?

Consider next three separate and apparently discrete scenes in *Romeo and Juliet*: (1) the first appearance of Friar Laurence (2.3); (2) Juliet's visit to the friar's cell in which she is given the potion (4.1); and (3) Romeo's seeking out of the apothecary (5.1). The first is often designated in our editions as *in a garden* or *in a field* because the friar enters '*with a basket*' (2.3.0) and talks about gathering weeds and flowers; the second is designated as the friar's cell as established by the dialogue; the third is placed in the streets of Mantua outside the apothecary's shop. But in those original productions on a bare stage with no set, all the first scene requires is an actor with a basket from which he pulls a single flower; the second and third require only vials of potion or poison that are given to Juliet and Romeo. Those vials could be picked up from a table (but then a table would have to be discovered or thrust on to the stage) or pulled out of a pocket or, to underscore imagistic continuity, pulled out of a basket carried by the friar or apothecary.

A reader or playgoer wedded to geographical realism will see no connections among the place where the friar gathers flowers and weeds, the cell where he provides the potion, and the shop where the apothecary provides poison. Moreover, both theatrical essentialism and 'if you have it, use it' reflexes cry out for some form of on-stage representation of garden, cell and street. However, in the original *as [if] in* staging (*as in a garden, as in a cell, as in front of a shop*) the links among the three moments need not be overly subtle (something to be teased out after many readings) but could be italicised. In the first of these scenes Friar Laurence notes that within the same flower (taken from his basket) 'Poison hath residence and medicine power' and links these two opposites or options to 'grace and rude will' within humankind (2.3.24–30). A playgoer who then sees two subsequent moments that strongly echo this speech is encouraged to make connections and think about issues central to the play. To impose upon this sequence a later anachronistic sense of place-locale may then blur some potentially meaningful links that could enhance that playgoer's sense of the choices made by the two title figures, choices linked visibly to two contrasting basket-bearing suppliers of vials. Here something of importance can be lost in translation.

Consider finally a sequence of scenes in *Coriolanus*. In 2.1 Coriolanus returns in triumph from the Volscian wars to be greeted in public; 2.2 moves the narrative to the Senate; 2.3 takes Coriolanus in his gown of humility into the streets to seek the voices of the plebeians; 3.1 moves back to the Senate for a major confrontation between Coriolanus and his enemies within Rome. As is the norm throughout the period, the Folio stage directions – with one notable exception – provide no information about 'place' and offer nothing equivalent to the locale headings to be found in many editions today. That exception is found in the first of the two Senate scenes: '*Enter two Officers, to lay Cushions, as it were, in the Capitol*' (2.2.0). The locale for this scene is clearly 'the Capitol', but that 'place' is to be created by the dialogue, by the costumes of first the officers, then the senators, and by the laying down of cushions, an action that initially defines the theatrical space. Such '*as it were, in*' thinking in turn makes possible a quick (and efficient) switch to 'the street' in 2.3 for the gown of humility scene and then a switch back to 'the Capitol' in 3.1. For the theatre historian this *as [if] in* technique typifies the narrative flexibility of Shakespeare's chameleon stage.

Such a Jacobean approach to 'in the Capitol' can in turn heighten images blurred or eclipsed today – in this instance the *cushion*. In the second Senate scene an angry Coriolanus tells the senators that if they give in to the commoners, 'Let them have cushions by you. You are plebeians / If they be senators' (3.1.100–1). For me, this line suggests that the cushions, although not cited again in a stage direction, were a visible presence here as well as in the earlier Senate scene. Later in the play Aufidius notes the title figure's inability to move 'from th' casque to th' cushion' (4.7.43), from war-generalship (as symbolised by the warrior's casque or helmet) to peace-politics (as symbolised by the cushion). These two passages and, more important, the larger process being described are much clearer if the playgoer has seen the

Capitol or the Senate defined on stage not by furniture or a set but by the laying down of cushions.[10] Two dialogue references are easily missed, but these properties may have had a strong theatrical presence in the first performances of this script, especially if the tumult occasioned by Coriolanus' conflict with the tribunes and plebeians in 3.1 involved disruption of the cushions.

To extrapolate further, consider the potential effect of casques and cushions in the play's complex final scene. The Folio calls for three groups for this final confrontation: Aufidius and his conspirators who actually commit the murder; the commoners who enter with Coriolanus ('Enter Coriolanus marching with Drum and Colours, the Commoners being with him' (5.6.69)); and the Volscian lords. As I understand Shakespeare's strategy here, this final scene sets before us in a Volscian city the same elements (lords, conspirators, commoners) that Coriolanus had faced in Rome between 2.1 and 3.3 (patricians, tribunes, plebeians), a confrontation that, despite the support of one group (the patricians), had led to his banishment, his 'I banish you', and his 'There is a world elsewhere' (3.3.120–35). To include the same elements in the final scene in the Volscian city, again, with one of the groups – the lords of the city – supportive, is to act out the obvious fact that there is no world elsewhere, that the hero's second confrontation with such a city leads to a second defeat, this time resulting in his death – and an ignominious death for the conquering war machine of Act 1. Admittedly, such a parallel is hard to realise today for a playgoer unfamiliar with this daunting script, but here is where attention to the original stage practice can be fruitful. Imagine a Coriolanus in armour and bearing a casque-helmet who twice confronts the Roman senators seated on their cushions (2.2, 3.1) only to be banished from Rome. What if this casque-bearing figure appears again in the play's final moments to confront the Volscian lords also seated on their cushions? As in the second Roman senate scene (3.1), those cushions could be disturbed when Aufidius and his fellow conspirators, cheered on by the same commoners (who moments earlier had cheered Coriolanus), kill him.

In calling attention to keys, vials and cushions my goal is not to defend my readings (which are meant to be suggestive rather than conclusive) but to flesh out what may have been heightened images for the original playgoers. The near mystical expectations linked to the construction of the new Globe in the 1990s (a version of 'if you build it he will come') may have faded – so that to the sceptic OP claims may seem only a marketing tool for 'museum theatre' – but my question remains: are we today with our superior know-how and technology missing images or linkages that would have been obvious, even italicised to the original playgoers? Can a sense of OP that extends beyond period costume and music expand rather than constrict our approach to the surviving playscripts? Whose plays are they, anyhow?

NOTES

1 For purposes of this essay I will use this abbreviation, though, in a wider context, it can easily be confused with a related term, 'original pronunciation'.

2 For a discussion of the controversy over the placement of the posts at the new Globe see Paul Nelsen, 'Positing Pillars at the Globe', *Shakespeare Quarterly* 48, 3 (Autumn 1997), 324–35.

3 Tiffany Stern, '"You That Walk i'th Galleries": Standing and Walking in the Galleries of the Globe Theatre', *Shakespeare Quarterly* 51 (Summer 2000), 211–16.

4 For a discussion of both the Kent/Edgar juxtaposition and the comparable situation in *As You Like It* 2.5, 2.6 and 2.7, see my *Elizabethan Stage Conventions and Modern Interpreters* (Cambridge University Press, 1984), pp. 101–4.

5 Earlier scholars had argued that the stage direction *passing over the stage* involved use of the yard, but such signals are now read as signals for movement from one stage door to another. See the 'pass, passing, passage' entry in Alan C. Dessen and Leslie Thomson, *A Dictionary of Stage Directions in English Drama, 1580–1642* (Cambridge University Press, 1999).

6 Today's playgoers are likely to be better behaved than their Elizabethan/Jacobean counter-parts and perhaps more amenable to actors in their midst. Moreover, Richard Burbage and his fellows would probably not have risked damage to their costumes on which they placed a very high value. E.g., a 1614 agreement between Philip Henslowe and actor Robert Dawes spells out various fines for absenteeism, lateness and drunkenness; the fine for removing a costume from the playhouse was forty times greater than the fine for missing a rehearsal. See Neil Carson, *A Companion to Henslowe's Diary* (Cambridge University Press, 1988), pp. 73–4.

7 Citations from Shakespeare's plays are from the revised Riverside edition, ed. G. Blakemore Evans (Boston and New York: Houghton Mifflin, 1997).

8 For a summary of the evidence about courtroom scenes see Alan C. Dessen, 'Recovering Elizabethan Theatrical Vocabulary: a Reconsideration of the Evidence', in *Textual and Theatrical Shakespeare: Questions of Evidence*, ed. Edward Pechter (University of Iowa Press, 1966), pp. 46–50 (44–65).

9 Various passages can be cited as context for such keys, whether discussions of liberty-restraint (e.g., 1.2.124–30), Angelo's 'devilish mercy' that Isabella describes to Claudio 'that will free your life, / But fetter you till death' (3.1.64–6), and even the 'strange picklock' (3.2.17) found by Elbow on Pompey. In prison Pompey is told that if he helps Abhorson, 'it shall redeem you from your gyves' (4.2.10–11), a line that suggests that Claudio and the other prisoners may be wearing fetters throughout.

10 For an illustration of King James in the House of Lords in 1614 that includes such cushions (or, more properly, *woolsacks*), see June Schlueter, 'Michael van Meer's *Album Amicorum*, with Illustrations of London, 1614–15', *Huntington Library Quarterly* 69 (2006), 301–13, figure 7. Schlueter translates the inscription in the left margin as 'Thus the King in England holds counsel in the gathering of the upper Parliament' and notes that 'The Lord Chancellor's seat, a woolsack, is in front, between the king and the clerk of the Parliament, and there are rows of judges, lawyers, bishops, earls, and barons' (p. 311).

STAGE APPEARANCE

CHAPTER FOUR

EXPLORING EARLY MODERN STAGE AND COSTUME DESIGN

Jenny Tiramani

This chapter will first endeavour to give a context for and define the role of so-called 'original practices' (OP) stage and costume design during the first ten years of Shakespeare's Globe. Following this, it will explain the principles adopted for the development of reconstructed Elizabethan clothing, properties and hangings of 'original practices' Globe productions, and then explore the various discoveries made by taking such work out of the Globe and performing these productions in other spaces. Using primary evidence from the past always requires an act of interpretation to produce a possible reconstruction from it. There is not enough evidence to definitively produce an 'original practices' production of *Henry V* with the amount of medieval clothing used (or not) in 1599, or one of *Romeo and Juliet* with the Italian flavour used (or not) in 1595. There are many possible early modern interpretations of the design for each play and every OP production we did in the first ten years at the Globe proposed a particular interpretation of the evidence we have.

FIRST IMPRESSIONS AND FIRST PRINCIPLES

As a designer coming to the unfinished Globe in 1996 my position and my relationship with the building was a unique one. There was an unfinished theatre, a clean slate, no precedents to live up to, and in the wider British theatre community there was no great expectation to live up to either. The project was viewed as a joke by some people, as a curiosity by others and as a tourist attraction by many. The theatre itself was extraordinary and unfamiliar, so everything we embarked on was by definition an experiment, because none of us had encountered a theatre like it. The Globe was intended by its originators to be a kind of laboratory in which to carry out experiments into Elizabethan and Jacobean playhouse production. To do this we found that we had to write our own rule book.

Over the first ten years, one of the strands of work I developed with Mark Rylance and Claire van Kampen was that of exploring certain stage conventions of late sixteenth-century theatre. The phrase 'original practices' was coined for this work in 2002 although, in hindsight, some productions staged between 1997 and 2000 have had this phrase attached to them as well. Because of the nature of the building, the public often assumed that any Shakespeare production presented there was 'how it would have been performed originally'. Although the public perception was that the Globe was doing 'original practices' performances all the time, a glance at the performance list in this book shows that the opposite was true – before 2003 these shows were the exception not the rule.

Appendix 4, which lists 'Shakespeare's Globe Productions', attempts to categorise the shows into various types but this clearly exposes the folly of any such attempt; I would suggest that it also nullifies the significance of terming any particular productions as 'original practices' because each and every production contained elements of the 'original practices' of Shakespeare's actors and also many practices that were not dreamed of four hundred years ago. Even those productions conceived as 'original practices' for the Globe cherry-picked particular 'original practices' elements to explore on stage, while rejecting others.

A production such as Hamlet in 2000 is listed as an 'original practices' production, and yet the musicians played modern music, in modern clothes, and there was a mixed-gender cast. The only 'original practices' feature of the production was that the actors were in Elizabethan dress and such categorisation reflects the widespread tendency today to define a theatre production by its visual appearance. Indeed, the majority of the categories used in the performance list refer to the nature of the dress worn. By exploring the categories of 'modern dress' and that of 'original practices' perhaps the true nature of the experiments conducted during the first ten years will emerge.

A MODERN AESTHETIC ON THE GLOBE STAGE

There is a large body of evidence concerning the costuming of plays in the early modern period, which suggests that much of the playing apparel of the late sixteenth-century actor was contemporary dress. This does not mean that actors in the late sixteenth century did not strive to give their productions a historical flavour, or an exotic style, but it was not possible for them to create a set of completely new, specifically designed costumes for every play in their repertoire, either financially or practically (see colour plate 1).

The critical aspect of productions at the Globe where the actors are wearing clothes from the same society as the audience is that of uniting everyone in the theatre, actors and audience, particularly in the daylight conditions of afternoon

1 Mark Rylance as the Duke of Vienna, *Measure for Measure* (2004), Hampton Court Palace

2 *Cymbeline* (2001), Shakespeare's Globe

3 *The Winter's Tale* (2005), Shakespeare's Globe

4 Hamlet, Teatro Olimpico, Vicenza (2000)

5 *Twelfth Night*, Middle Temple Hall (2002)

6 Guthrie Theatre, Minneapolis (2003)

7 Jig from *Much Ado About Nothing* (*Playing Shakespeare with Deutsche Bank*, 2007), Shakespeare's Globe

8 The interior of Blackfriars Playhouse, the American Shakespeare Center, Staunton, Virginia

performances. This unity would have been most apparent four hundred years ago between those members of the aristocracy sitting in the lords' rooms above the stage and the many aristocratic characters being played on stage below them, and also between the far fewer portrayals of 'the common man', such as the gravediggers in Hamlet, and the groundlings standing around the stage's edge. 'Modern dress' in this sense has rarely been attempted at the Globe, because, although it may be the most authentic 'original practice' in costuming, it brings its own problems in the Globe Theatre space. In Jack Shepherd's 1996 production of Two Gentlemen of Verona there was a commonality between the dress of actors and audience, but there was no connection between these people and the (unfinished) architecture of the theatre itself. The Globe has a large, impressive and powerful stage. There is therefore a danger of actors wearing twenty-first-century clothes appearing somewhat diminished, because most of our contemporary dress is understated, modest and often dowdy. An actor in Elizabethan dress wearing a tall hat, a crown or helmet, with a richly coloured gown or cloak literally takes up more physical space on stage, and it has often proved true that actors in these clothes assume a more powerful stage presence than their twenty-first-century dressed counterparts.

The two modern dress productions I designed for the Globe were Cymbeline in 2001 (see colour plate 2) and A Midsummer Night's Dream in 2002, both directed by Mike Alfreds. Having decided on modern cream silk shirts and trousers as the clothing worn by all eight performers in Cymbeline, the choice was made to neutralise the back wall of the stage, so that the stage would complement the simple, modern costumes. In other words, rather than dress the performers in clothes that would naturally blend with the aesthetic of the Elizabethan stage decoration, the stage decoration was changed to blend with the aesthetic style of the performers' costumes. This was achieved by covering the frons scenae (including the side doors and central discovery space) with wooden panels, textured and painted to look like plain, beige, plastered walls. The actors reached the stage by entering through the yard and then remained on stage throughout the performance. A similar desire to neutralise the stage decoration has repeatedly been demonstrated by directors and designers at the Globe. My own experience has been that far more theatre professionals are disturbed by the decoration of the Globe than members of the audience, who generally embrace the newness and strangeness of it. Designers today are more accustomed to starting with a clean slate, an empty space upon which they can impose their own aesthetic. Among the productions that have tried hard to proclaim an identity separate and different from that of the prevailing aesthetic of the Globe architecture itself is the 2001 production of King Lear, when the director and designer covered the two Globe stage pillars and the entire frons scenae in rough wooden palings.

In 1997 the stage area was constructed, carved and painted, according to the best evidence available. However, the audience galleries were not decorated. They remain as mainly plain oak scaffolds until the money is raised for their completion. The intention is to produce a stage and auditorium decorated to create a continuous, harmonious whole. While the stage area of the Globe is significantly more decorated than the rest of the interior, it gives a false impression of the decorated stage looking like a 'set design'. I suspect that this may be an added reason for the widespread obscuring of the stage by the various directors and designers who have so far worked on individual Globe productions.

Another contributing factor may have been that most designers working in Britain today are both set and costume designers – set design is hierarchically considered to be of a higher status than costume design, and most set budgets are considerably larger than costume budgets. From 1997 to 2005, Globe productions were budgeted in a radical reversal of this trend, with costume budgets exceeding those for set design, in the hope that this would encourage directors and designers to concentrate their storytelling choices on the dress of the performers, just as the players of the late sixteenth century did. However, the early modern concept of adding very little to the permanent look of the stage for a particular play is an alien concept to the twenty-first-century theatre designer. You might almost say that designers today would not feel they were contributing enough to the production unless they made a significant visual statement of their own. Sometimes the tension between the modern aesthetic expressed by a designer and the decoration of the Globe stage has been exciting, but it has often resulted in a confused, jumbled stage picture that was not helpful to the unfolding narrative of the play.

AN ELIZABETHAN OR JACOBEAN AESTHETIC ON THE GLOBE STAGE

The world of Elizabethan arts and crafts is one that is rich and strange to many of us today. The rejection of Latin and the subsequent flowering of the English language in the literature and drama of the second half of the sixteenth century were mirrored by a flowering of the decorative arts and crafts of the weaver, painter and carver. These have been expressed in the various decorative aspects of the architecture of the Globe interior: in a rich combination of *trompe l'œil* stone and marble effects on wood and the depictions of classical figures such as Thalia, Melpomene, Apollo and Mercury. Within this framework of entirely possible décor of the English Renaissance, characters clothed and behaving as if they are from an Elizabethan or Jacobean world seem entirely 'at home' on the Globe stage. This, for me, is one of the strongest arguments for staging some productions of early modern plays in this manner at the Globe.

At any period of history the prevailing aesthetic connects the architecture, furniture and clothing of its inhabitants. In the 1770s, when the panniers of women's court dress were at their widest, the doors of grand houses were designed wide enough to accommodate them. In the late sixteenth century, doorways rose in height as the compulsory hats of their inhabitants grew taller and taller. So when I first discussed the possibility of mounting productions in Elizabethan dress at the Globe with Mark Rylance in 1996, our starting point was the architecture of the new Globe and the way it had been researched, shaped and constructed. The following five points cover the principles we then followed over the first ten years, in our attempts to work in harmony with Shakespeare's stage world:

1 The Globe was built from materials available in 1600 – oak, lime plaster and thatch – and recorded surviving accounts of sixteenth-century theatre building. Therefore, our costumes would be made from materials available in 1600 – linen, wool, leather and silk – and the properties and hangings would also be made from materials available in the period. These costumes and props would relate to those listed in the inventories and wills of actors or mentioned in the plays of the early 1600s.

2 The construction methods used to build the Globe were also those of the early 1600s: for example, the oak timbers were joined with wooden pegs, and the paint pigments used to paint the theatre were those available in late sixteenth-century London. Therefore, we would construct the costumes by hand, in the way clothes were made in 1600.

3 The shape of the Globe was determined by archaeological, visual and written evidence from Shakespeare's time. Therefore, we would base the shapes of our clothes on the surviving patterns and garments of the early 1600s and increasingly we investigated the use of geometry and pattern-cutting methods of Elizabethan tailors.

4 The iconography used in the decoration of the Globe was chosen to depict the relationship between mortals and gods, from heaven to earth, in a manner seen in surviving buildings of the late sixteenth century. Therefore, for the decoration of hangings for the stage we sourced appropriate complementary iconography (see the description of the hangings used for *The Winter's Tale* below). The iconography of clothing was explored in a similar way, particularly with regard to the symbolic use of colour in the early modern period.

5 The use of the Globe space by the audience would be that of the early 1600s, the groundlings standing in the yard and audience sitting in the lord's rooms above the stage. Therefore, we would endeavour to help our actors understand the way in which Elizabethans wore their clothes and use them in the appropriate

manner, according to surviving evidence: for example, by wearing some form of hat or headgear at all times (unless mad or madly in love) and removing the hat in the presence of higher-status characters.

Materials, construction, shape, iconography and context: these simple principles – principles directly inspired by the building of the theatre itself – eventually offered a framework within which we could work on the costumes, properties and hangings for what became known as our 'original practices' productions. It was always my experience that the more rigorously these five principles were applied, the more exciting were the results on stage.

In a production such as *The Winter's Tale* in 2005 (see colour plate 3) where the clothes, furniture and hangings were all produced from primary evidence of the early seventeenth century, we sought a harmony between the specific elements made for the production and the permanent decoration of the theatre itself. We made hangings painted in the popular Jacobean 'grisaille' technique, using a monotone palette resembling carved stone. On the painted Globe stage, featuring a variety of *trompe l'œil* painted stone and marble, we hoped that the stage picture was integrated in such a way that it was not noticeable which elements were permanent and which were specially added for the play. The subject chosen for the hangings was the winged figure of Time on his chariot, a theme eminently suitable for this play, and one that would also be fitting (and therefore could be recycled) for a range of other plays concerned with the passing of time, such as *Pericles* or *King Lear*. Our painter used a surviving engraving in the Warburg Institute, *The Triumph of Time* by Georg Pencz, as his reference, just as an Elizabethan painter might have done.

The success of such a production depended on drawing the audience into the world of the play. Although their clothes of different periods divided the audience and actors, the Jacobean world created by the combination of the building itself and the design of the play was strong enough to pull the audience towards it; perhaps even into imagining that they were part of that world. However, not all aspects of this production of *The Winter's Tale* followed well-known practices of Shakespeare's theatre. There was a cast of both men and women, there was no bear (only a paw appeared from behind a hanging), and the character of Time appeared in a long black cloak looking far more human than the winged figure described in the play. In other words, the fantastical features of the play were rejected by the director, and a naturalistic version presented instead.

As described earlier, every so-called 'original practices' production chose to explore certain design features of Shakespeare's theatre, while rejecting many others. Whichever aesthetic was chosen for the productions described above, there were other lessons to learn concerning the combination of modern world/Elizabethan world, when Globe productions were taken to other venues, both modern and old, as described in the following section.

PLAYING GLOBE PRODUCTIONS IN OTHER SPACES

Several attempts were made, in the early years, to replicate the Globe stage when we were invited to take Globe productions abroad. The first was to take the 1996 modern-dress production of *Two Gentlemen of Verona* to the New Victory Theatre in New York. The result was a complicated mixture of styles – an Edwardian proscenium theatre with a Globe-based stage design and the actors (and some audience on stage) in modern dress. Many aspects of the New York production were very successful, although even with the lighting of the entire space, including the auditorium, there was still the inevitable separation of the stage and auditorium by the proscenium, which felt very much in conflict with the 'Globe experience', an experience we were eager to share with audiences abroad. The 1998 staging of *As You Like It* at the indoor Tokyo Globe, in Japan, went farther in taking the seats out of the stalls area so there was a groundling audience, but this was the last time a version of the Globe stage itself was attempted in the first ten years. It was decided that, I think rightly, it was simply not possible to give these audiences a satisfactory experience of what is crucially an outdoor playhouse. The next two productions to tour – *Cymbeline* to the Brooklyn Academy of Arts, New York, and *King Lear* to the Tokyo Globe, both in 2001, were staged on modern stage settings, with much less attempt to create a 'Globe experience'.

Instead, another approach to touring came out of an invitation to stage an 'original practices' production of *Twelfth Night* in the Middle Temple Hall in 2002. We had previously staged two existing Globe productions in the Teatro Olimpico, Vicenza (see colour plate 4), a surviving theatre of Shakespeare's time, built in 1585, and we found that, unsurprisingly, the plays worked well in a theatre contemporaneous with when they were written. However, *Twelfth Night* (see colour plate 5) was the first Globe production to be originated in a surviving Elizabethan playing space (the Hall was built c.1570) and one where a performance of the play was recorded in 1602. The production had an all-male cast, dressed in the fashions of the early seventeenth century, with music and dances of the period. Some rehearsals took place in the hall itself, with the actors in Elizabethan rehearsal clothes, and there was clearly a very strong relationship between our production and this building, even though there are many more recent features in the hall, including a large Van Dyck portrait of Charles I on horseback. Part of the reason for the great atmosphere there may be due to the fact that the Hall has been in continuous use for meals and entertainments by the lawyers of the Middle Temple for the last four hundred years. This was in great contrast to the Great Hall at Hampton Court, which felt more like a museum than a space for theatre, during the summer of 2004, when three Globe Shakespeare productions were played there.

Twelfth Night was performed at the Globe later in 2002 and we were then invited to tour the USA in 2003 with the production. The most pressing question for us was how to stage the production as a tour, where it would play in a variety of theatre and non-theatre spaces, all built in the twentieth century. What kind of environment would most suit this Elizabethan production that we had performed in both the original indoor space of the hall, and the reconstructed outdoor space of the Globe? We decided that, for the first time in ten years, we would try to reconstruct some elements of an early seventeenth-century indoor playing space. Having performed the play at Middle Temple, we felt that the strongest and most useful features for us to tour were versions of a hall screen and a wooden floor (see colour plate 6). Using the smaller, simpler screen at Wadham College, Oxford, and the deal floor of the Cartoon Gallery at Knole House in Kent as references, we built a touring kit that provided us with an upper level for musicians above the screen, two doors of entrance and a defined playing area, around which the audience were seated in different configurations, according to the shape and size of the venue, although usually in a layout similar to that used at Middle Temple Hall. The simplicity of this format proved remarkably flexible and intimate, giving an impression of an original performance in a minimal way. However, one illusive aspect of indoor performance remained largely undeveloped – that of the lighting. Knowing that the plays were originally lit by candlelight indoors, even on afternoon performances when such halls could be gloomy, we used a large standing candelabra placed near the screen at Middle Temple and on tour, as a gesture towards this, although we were only allowed to use electric candles and needed theatre lamps to provide the level of lighting expected and required by health and safety officers today.

Between this tour and the 2005 USA tour of the all-male 'original practices' production of Measure for Measure on the same 'screen and floor' setting, I took part in an experiment with real candlelight at Bristol University, in a reconstructed indoor playhouse based on the surviving Inigo Jones/Webb drawings. I was struck by the non-directional quality of the light given by candlelight alone and it remains the key aspect of early modern theatre design I would like to explore much further. For the Measure tour we added more candelabras, hanging over the stage, but electric candles do not give out the same kind of light as real ones so the lighting was never really close to the original playing conditions, and, sadly, the health and safety regulations forbade us from playing in candlelight as the actors originally did in the seventeenth century. The Bristol experiment showed that the reconstructed Globe clothes looked amazing in real candlelight, shimmering and glistening as the actors moved. The lighting levels of candles are of course much lower than those of natural daylight during the outdoor, afternoon performances at the Globe but the candlelight gives an overall, glowing, shared light to both actors and audience – just as daylight does – and this is a feature of early modern theatre design that is radically different from our own prevailing custom of lighting the actors on stage, while leaving the audience unlit. In the 'original practices' Globe productions discussed here, the fact that the players were being dressed as characters from the world of the author created no barrier between them and the audience, especially when they shared the same light. This 'shared light', whether in the afternoon daylight at the Globe, or the more artificially produced candlelight of indoor performances, provided the framework within which I believe audiences could enjoy joining the early modern world of Shakespeare's plays.

CONCLUSIONS

Throughout this chapter I have referred to 'we'. Experimentation in performance with a rigorous exploration of Shakespeare's own theatre practice was (and is) only possible through sustained collaboration over a number of years. The 'we' refers not only to the continuing collaboration between Mark Rylance, Claire van Kampen, Tim Carroll and myself, but also to the dedicated team of tailors, seamstresses, cordwainers, haberdashers, painters, wood-carvers, armourers and supervisors with whom I worked at the Globe. In the free-lance theatre culture of Britain today, this rare opportunity stands as an example of the benefits of sustained collaboration. It allowed us the boldness to try out different ideas and develop those that were most fruitful. It gave us the rare chance to keep learning about the early modern world and keep returning to explore it in more detail every year.

CHAPTER FIVE

COSMETICS ON THE GLOBE STAGE

Farah Karim-Cooper

In his essay, '*Poetaster*, the Author, and the Perils of Cultural Production', Alan Sinfield comments on the critical shift in meaning of 'materialism'. Once at the centre of Marxist discourse, the term 'materialism' in relation to the study of the early modern period now focuses more narrowly 'on the thinginess' of culture.[1] This type of study of the materials of culture entails an analysis of the semiotics of things inhabiting Renaissance domestic interiors, the commercial exchanges and the playhouses, including ingredients in food, medicine and cosmetics. Jonathan Gil Harris and Natasha Korda see a methodology that is 'returning to Marx's more dynamic labor-oriented theories of materiality', where the dynamic processes of material production are given equal weight with the objects themselves.[2]

Theatrical production is given prominence in this discourse because of its collaborative, material practices. Linked to this line of critical enquiry is the examination of stage properties, which emphasises the importance of this critical study to the history of Renaissance theatre in England. Gil Harris and Korda have argued that 'the objects of the early modern stage were often intended not merely to catch, but to overwhelm the eye by means of their real or apparent costliness, motion, and capacity to surprise'. While for years some theatre historians have insisted upon the 'bare stage' of early modern London, Gil Harris and Korda argue that this notion is a myth:

Eyewitness accounts of contemporary theatre goers, the play-scripts themselves, the inventories of tiring-house costumes and properties kept by theatrical companies and entrepreneurs, and even the writings of anti-theatricalist Puritan divines . . . furnish innumerable reminders that early modern London playgoers did not just *hear* plays; they also upheld the original, Greek root of 'theatre' – *theasthai*, meaning 'to watch'.[3]

The new Globe's aesthetic has been informed by this very notion. The Renaissance penchant for painted surfaces, classical motif, *trompe l'œil*, disguise and sumptuous

66

display characterises the visual experience of an 'original practices' production at the Globe that is neatly complemented by the ornately designed scenic façade of the stage. The culminating production of *Twelfth Night* at the Globe in 2002 demonstrated the illustrative power of Renaissance clothing and cosmetics, a subject that was particularly relevant to my research.

RESEARCHING MATERIAL CULTURE

An enquiry into sixteenth- and seventeenth-century material culture depends largely upon an extensive and detailed recovery of early printed texts and surviving manuscript documents. My research into cosmetics in English Renaissance culture relied upon a search through recipe manuals, conduct manuals, anti-theatrical tracts, inventories for household goods and revels accounts. Specifically, emblem books, woodcuts, portraits and surviving objects, such as cosmetics boxes and implements, helped to construct, though in a fragmented sense, an image of the Renaissance painted lady and her beautifying practices. The number of recipes for facial cosmetics, hair dyes, perfumes, depilatory creams and toothpaste, while useful, did little in helping to establish in concrete terms the textures and consistencies of the materials used to beautify the body in the early modern period. Archival research simply enabled a theoretical reconstruction of cosmetic usage in the period. Such research helped in determining the function of cosmetics culturally and aesthetically, and in theorising cosmetic materiality, but there is very little textual or pictorial evidence as to its use on the early modern stage and its practical application in the domestic sphere. Questions such as the following were crucial to constructing an argument about the importance of beautification in early modern culture: How did cosmetics look once applied to human skin? What was the relationship between aesthetic representations of women in portraits and the living canvases of boys' faces on stage and women's faces in the public sphere? How was makeup used on the early modern stage, both as a theatrical device and as a signifier of femininity?

As has already been established by various contributors to this volume, 'original practices' productions at Shakespeare's Globe are fraught with a variety of complex problems related to the impossibility of creating an 'authentic' theatrical encounter in the reconstructed space. Catherine Silverstone's account of Shakespeare at the Globe observes that 'even though those working at the Globe acknowledge that they cannot produce a fully authentic early modern theatre, the historical nature of the building, the effect it has on both actors and audiences, and the continued attempts to reproduce original staging practices, suggest that the Globe is, perhaps inevitably, riven with anxieties about the past and its (re)production today'.[4] Jenny Tiramani admits that no 'original practices' production has ever been exactly that, since there were modern practices involved in mounting those productions. Then what does 'original practices' mean in relation to early modern material culture and its representations on the stage?

The term 'original practices' takes into account the use of 'original objects', at least in their reproduced form. And 'objects' here refers to props, textiles, wigs and even the ingredients of which makeup bases consist, all items created according to the principles of construction originally established by Sam Wanamaker and then adopted by Tiramani in designing for the stage.[5] During the developmental phases of the project before the stage was built, academics like Andrew Gurr could see the benefits of what were originally termed 'authentic' productions.[6] To academics, the Globe project theoretically offered itself up as a laboratory, a place to test previously held notions about Shakespearean performance. Gurr argued in 1997 that 'the new Globe is no more than a test-tube, the basis for experiments aimed at getting a better idea of how Shakespeare expected his plays to be staged'.[7] While the theatre has proven itself to be much more than a 'test-tube' for academics, it has nevertheless been used for experiments where many discoveries about early modern playhouse practice have been and continue to be made. Significantly, the question of what would happen to a Shakespeare play in its original architectural configuration with a vertical audience is something that scholars have been forced to think about in more concrete terms. The impact that these playing conditions have on the meaning of the play can now be tested, analysed and interpreted. W. B. Worthen observes that the Globe 'reflects a desire to see performance releasing original Shakespearean meanings', and, yet, in many ways, what the reconstructed Globe has shown is the complexity of what might be considered to be 'original Shakespearean meanings'.[8]

This chapter will explore the Globe's choice to use white face-paint in their 2002 'original practices' production of *Twelfth Night* and it will consider the impact that such experiments can have on academic enquiries into early modern material history. Globe experiments with makeup in 2002 and again in 2005 when the company revived their 2004 production of *Measure for Measure*, with an all-male cast, have not necessarily answered my questions, but have instead helped to reshape my thinking and forced me to ask more focused questions about the practical application of cosmetics during the Renaissance period. What has remained inevitably frustrating, however, is that for obvious reasons there were key elements missing from the experiments: the white lead ingredient and boy actors. This absence of crucial ingredients imposed limitations upon the exercise, limitations that were already compounded by the lack of tangible evidence of *exactly* what ingredients were used in the stage makeup Elizabethan and Jacobean actors applied to their faces; like the building itself the ingredients comprising the makeup used in these Globe productions were a 'best guess'.

PAINTING FACES IN A POSTMODERN GLOBE

Acquainted with the work of Gurr and the Research department at the Globe, I contacted him in the hope that he would be able to point me towards theatrical inventories that revealed what cosmetics early modern actors used, how much they paid for them and how much they owned. As it turned out, there were no such documents, he revealed, but he led me to Tiramani, who asked me to come in to the Globe to see if perhaps I had anything she would find useful. I came laden with recipes, pictures, glossaries, and she showed me a few extracts from Hilliard's *Arte of Limning* (c. 1600) and shared with me her practice of reconstructing early modern clothes for Globe actors. It was the beginning of a relationship that would bring me back to the Globe in 2002 when the company decided to use white base foundation for the first time. This was an extraordinary thing to do, primarily because makeup of that type on the modern British stage is often associated with pantomime. The Globe had already been accused of being a 'museum theatre', a theme park, or a Shakespeare carnival. Cynthia Marshall argues that the Globe is above all a 'radical theater space', so a theatrical experiment that tested the impact painted white faces might have on a modern urban audience could be seen as appropriate.[9] But would a modern audience accept such a theatrical experiment? The *Twelfth Night* company in 2002 asked its audience to believe that thick white face-paint on grown men was a clear sign of femininity. A modern audience would not have access to the meanings that painted faces had in Elizabethan and Jacobean England or on the Renaissance stage, but clearly, through such experiments, the new Globe was shifting the established associations that white face-paint has with sophisticated forms of theatre, Kabuki and opera, as well as with clowns and pantomime. Curiously, however, the Globe was also drawing upon these associations to intensify the comic and symbolic effect of white makeup in the play. When Mark Rylance, who played Olivia, was asked about the use of makeup in this production, he remarked that:

the players loved hiding and revealing . . . It is part of great storytelling and it is also a part of most of the main characters, that they have something very hidden which everyone else is trying to figure out, until they reveal it at the right moment . . . the hiding of the face that makeup does . . . corresponds with the idea of hiding even Olivia's passion . . . behind a very controlled movement . . . They [the audience] understood very quickly and were drawn forward by the mystery of what was inside her.[10]

Rylance's interest was not only in what the painted faces of actors could tell us about Shakespearean stage practices, but, more profoundly, in the psychological impact that such practices had on the audience and on our understanding of what motivates the characters telling the story.

Before rehearsals for this production, I spoke to members of the Globe hair and makeup staff. They used as a base, white chalk, a substance that was indeed available in the period. However, most facial foundations in Shakespeare's day were made with a mixture of white lead and vinegar (a blend known as *ceruse*, which had been in use for centuries, dating back to ancient Rome). For obvious reasons, the Globe had to find a way of constructing 'authentically' made-up faces that produced the same visual texture of the white pigments used to paint contemporary Renaissance portraits. Although *ceruse* could have yielded slightly different results, the use of white pigment, chalk and almond oil created a teasingly similar effect. They used Moroccan clay mixed with oil to create a red, vermilion-like pigment to redden the lips and cheeks. Although some of the ingredients were not named in the Elizabethan recipe manuals, they would have probably been available in the period; therefore, these materials adhered to the principles upon which Tiramani was working and has outlined in the previous chapter.

While studying plays like Thomas Middleton's *The Lady's Tragedy*, 1611, in which a dead woman's face is painted (followed by a scene in which her spirit appears on stage simultaneously), I developed a multitude of theories as to how scenes such as this might be staged given that the makeup is crucial in the execution of the main plot. Makeup allows for all kinds of staging possibilities, and it was likely to be extremely useful to the Elizabethan and Jacobean theatre, which was highly dependent on *trompe l'œil*, disguise, cross-dressing and spectacle.

The Globe's 2002 production of *Twelfth Night* was originally designed for performances at Middle Temple Hall to celebrate the play's four-hundredth anniversary; 'to complement the setting and the occasion of the limited anniversary performances, the production aimed to explore "original practices", encompassing clothing, music, set and casting'.[11] This production was one of the Globe's finest according to critic Christopher Rawson, writing about the production on tour. Commenting on the use of male actors, Rawson observes:

you're always aware of the men beneath the skirts, but it matters less as the play progresses. They become their roles. The dynamics are very clear: director Tim Carroll's work is never gimmicky, with many comic details not immediately apparent in the text. A bonus to the all-male casting is that when Viola's twin brother appears, played by Rhys Meredith, the two really do look confusingly alike.[12]

Rawson later comments that the actors wore makeup, but was not discouraged by this particular Elizabethan reconstruction. In fact, the use of white makeup in *Twelfth Night* worked in a variety of ways, not to resolve, but to test some of the theories that I had developed about staging doubles (spirit and body, or twins). Viola played by Michael Brown and Sebastian played by Rhys Meredith were convincing in their representation of identicality, not merely because of the costumes that they wore

4 Michael Brown and Rhys Meredith as the twins in *Twelfth Night* (2002), Shakespeare's Globe

and the gestures that they used, but also because of the pale mask of white makeup on their faces (see figure 4). The effects of their identicality were created not just by wearing identical costumes, but also by the application of a white facial makeup base; it was dizzying, particularly when one twin was exiting just as another was entering the stage. Designer Tiramani had chosen to use a subtle application on their faces to contrast with the bold, thick, white texture on Rylance's Olivia (see figure 5). Olivia's face – a mask of white makeup – gestured towards the notoriously painted face of Queen Elizabeth I. Her face in contemporary portraits was painted with the same materials found in her cosmetics, which is why Elizabethans spoke about 'face-painting'. The thick mask of face-paint also, as Rylance intended, enhanced Olivia's unwillingness to emerge from hiding – she reveals her face behind her veil, but what is there is still a mask; she remains hidden. When Viola suggests to her that her face is 'excellently done, if God did all' (1.5.207),[13] she slyly accuses Olivia of using makeup. When Rylance's Olivia protests that her beauty is natural, the audience at the Globe exploded with laughter, not only recognising the irony of such a remark coming from such a heavily painted lady, but also the irony of the actuality of the performance: that a male actor lies underneath the layers of costume, gesture and makeup. Thus makeup on the early modern stage and

5 Mark Rylance as Olivia, *Twelfth Night* (2002), Shakespeare's Globe

the current Globe stage is a metatheatrical device, gesturing towards the veneer of performance and the audience's willing participation in such theatrical deceptions. The use of makeup on Cesario/Viola and Sebastian allowed the audience to believe in the identicality of the twins. The costumes and wigs simply added to this effect; however, it was the makeup that actually concretised this particular device. But not all critics were convinced by the credibility of the effects of makeup. In his critical discussion of the production at Middle Temple Hall, David Nicol felt that some of the characters were too otherworldly:

With their strange haircuts (very short at the front, very long at the back), their faces caked in make-up, and their skinny legs sticking from voluminous trunks, the siblings looked like bizarre life-forms from an alien zoo rather than attractive, androgynous young humans.[14]

Nicol admits later, however, that the performance did receive a standing ovation. Perhaps the actors in thick period makeup and reconstructed early seventeenth-century clothing did look 'bizarre', but it was because the Globe company was in the early stages of orientating their audience to the imagery and aesthetic of the English Renaissance, an aesthetic that has come to be expected of Globe performances.

When Worthen argues that the Globe stages 'an anxious performance of the past in the present', he suggests that 'original practices' productions are somehow conscious of their limited possibilities:

The alien subject of the Shakespearean stage may be recoverable as an object of scholarship . . . but must remain remote from any modern performance practice: we no longer have the social structure, theatrical instruments, or performative conventions to lend those alien beings their true force on stage.[15]

While part of this statement is true, it is not necessarily the case that the 'alien subject of the Shakespearean stage' has to remain remote, in fact the unique reciprocity between actor and audience imposed by the architectural configuration that Worthen himself writes eloquently about not only invites the alien subjects of the Shakespearean theatre into the space, but also forces a modern audience to confront the past through a renegotiation of current theatrical conventions. The use of early modern makeup practices impacts upon a modern audience by asking it to construct new associations, at least in a Shakespearean theatrical context, with the white, painted face.

The results of the makeup experiment at the Globe, in Rylance's words, are that 'makeup also helps enormously in the Globe space where the light is quite strange . . . the makeup helps on a practical level'.[16] Actors' faces become more visible; they mirror the plastered appearance of the playhouse walls. Elsewhere I have argued that many early modern writers who satirised the use of facial cosmetics compared the thickly painted face to plastered walls.[17] In the 2005 revival of *Measure for Measure*, directed by John Dove, designer Tiramani chose again to use white makeup. This time, after having conducted experiments using egg glaze and crushed pearl, she decided to paint the male actor playing Mariana with the same chalk and oil concoction, but brushed with a light dusting of crushed pearl. There is evidence in Thomas Tuke's 1616 anti-cosmetic tract that pearl may have been an ingredient used by the wealthy classes in Renaissance England. The pearl creates a shimmering effect, the lustre that Renaissance love poets demanded of their mistresses' complexions. Crucially, the shimmering effect would increase visibility in the playhouse and would have had specific value in a candlelit indoor space, where paint does not show up as well, leaving actors to rely upon egg glazes and pearl so that their faces would be enhanced by the light of the candles.[18]

These experiments proved to be valuable in that they raised further questions. For example, who applied the makeup in the tiring house? Actors, hired men, tiring men or women? Also, how was makeup removed quickly during quick changes? And finally, what was the effect of using face-paint on younger male actors?[19] So far, these are questions to which archival research has yielded no answers. Having seen and analysed the makeup experiments at the Globe thus far, it is arguable that experiments in reconstructed venues using 'original practices' could begin to identify early modern conventions of stage makeup. A question to ask now that the current artistic policy is to discontinue 'original practices' is how far should such experiments go, and who should conduct them? Mark Rylance addressed this question in discussing plans for his own production company, Phoebus Cart:

We cannot, for politically correct reasons, cast a white actor as Othello, and we were struggling with what that meant in terms of 'original practices' . . . Does that mean that the play is not really a play you can do in period anymore?[20]

Rylance is right to point out the danger of the Globe using black face-paint, and it is unlikely, regardless of the radicalising potential of the space, that a modern audience would be open to such a fictive theatricalisation of race. However, what my research demonstrated to me was that face-paint on the stage, regardless of its colour, was controversial, radical and bold because of its much deeper associations with gender and female sexuality than with race. Richard Burbage's painted black complexion in the very first performance of *Othello*, while obviously serving as a marker of an exotic race and religion, was more radical because of its connotations of sexual licentiousness. Painted faces on the Renaissance stage were meant to evoke sexuality and femininity; and blackness was a colour associated with sexuality and corrupted femininity.

However, the question of who should conduct such experiments is a burning one for scholars and practitioners to take up. Does the Globe have a responsibility to the academic community to continue experimenting with 'original practices'? Or is it indeed, as Dominic Dromgoole has suggested, that 'original practices' was a product of a unique collaboration within a specific space over a specific period of time? Alan Dessen wrote in 1990 that 'for both the academic and theatrical community, one of the attractive possibilities inherent in this project is that the new Globe may serve as a laboratory or testing ground where actors and scholars working together can investigate how Elizabethan plays could or would have been staged'.[21] The Globe has proven itself to be a dynamic, modern, experimental and revolutionary performance space and it must continue to test the boundaries of theatrical performance and the skills of the modern actor. The theatre should not be held to ransom by the academic investment in historical staging practices. Yet, having come up against the restrictions imposed by a fragmented recovery of history through archival searches, and having witnessed the revelatory power of Globe experiments in early modern stagecraft, just as the scholars saw the potential in the experiment before it was a theatre, I also see the 'attractive possibilities' yet to be discovered.

NOTES

1 Alan Sinfield, 'Poetaster, the Author, and the Perils of Cultural Production', in Material London ca. 1600, ed. Lena Cowen Orlin (Philadelphia: University of Pennsylvania Press, 2000), p. 75.

2 Jonathan Gil Harris and Natasha Korda, Introduction to Staged Properties in Early Modern English Drama (Cambridge University Press, 2002), p. 17.

3 Ibid., pp. 4 and 2.

4 Catherine Silverstone, 'Shakespeare Live: Reproducing Shakespeare at the "New" Globe Theatre', Textual Practice 19 (2005), 32.

5 See Jenny Tiramani, chapter 4, 'Exploring Early Modern Stage and Costume, Design'.

6 Mark Rylance, Claire van Kampen and Jenny Tiramani saw the difficulties posed by the word 'authentic' and subsequently referred to their work as 'original practices'. In the early days of the Globe Theatre, it was acknowledged that the 'practical problems of collaboration between different categories of people working at the Globe' would need to be solved. For example, 'designers would need constant help from academics but are sometimes frustrated by the lack of practical answers' (Globe Research Bulletin, Issue 1 (November 1997)), 7. This notion of needing 'constant help' is interesting, but never came to fruition since academics eventually were excluded from artistic decisions at the Globe. The academic community, however, has never ceased its intellectual investment in the space.

7 Andrew Gurr, 'Staging at the Globe', in Shakespeare's Globe Rebuilt, ed. J. R. Mulryne and Margaret Shewring (Cambridge University Press, 1997), p. 159.

8 W. B. Worthen, Shakespeare and the Force of Modern Performance (Cambridge University Press, 2003), p. 28.

9 Cynthia Marshall, 'Sight and Sound: Two Models of Shakespearean Subjectivity on the British Stage', Shakespeare Quarterly 51, 3 (Autumn 2000), 354.

10 Mark Rylance, interview with the editors, 17 April 2007.

11 Jessica Ryan, The 2002 Globe Season, The White Company: Twelfth Night, Globe Research Bulletin 26 (July 2002), 4.

12 Christopher Rawson, 'Stage Review: Globe's Twelfth Night Shows Comedy, Heart', Pittsburgh Post-Gazette, Thursday 13 November 2003 (Post-Gazette.com).

13 William Shakespeare, Twelfth Night, The Norton Shakespeare, ed. Stephen Greenblatt et al. (New York and London: W. W. Norton, 1997). All subsequent references are to this edition.

14 David Nicol, 'Twelfth Night, Performed by the Company of Shakespeare's Globe at the Middle Temple Hall, London, February 2002', Early Modern Literary Studies 8, 1 (May 2002), 10, 20.

15 Worthen, Shakespeare and the Force of Modern Performance, p. 63.

16 Interview with Mark Rylance (April 2007).

17 See chapter 6 of *Cosmetics in Shakespearean and Renaissance Drama* (Edinburgh University Press, 2006).

18 Martin White's AHRC-funded candlelight experiment at Bristol University, using costumes and designers from the Globe, revealed that bright colours and painted faces did not register visually as they did at the Globe. See p. 64.

19 Even more interestingly, what physical effect over time would the ingredients have had on boy actors' faces? (This is not a question that could ever be answered through experimentation obviously.)

20 Interview with Mark Rylance (April 2007).

21 Alan C. Dessen, '"Taint not thy mind . . . ": Problems and Pitfalls in Staging Plays at the New Globe', in *New Issues in the Reconstruction of Shakespeare's Theatre: Proceedings of the Conference Held at the University of Georgia February 16–18, 1990*, ed. Franklin J. Hildy (New York: Peter Lang, 1990), p. 135.

MUSIC AND SOUND

6 Musicians, *Measure for Measure* (2004), Shakespeare's Globe

CHAPTER SIX

MUSIC AND AURAL TEXTURE AT SHAKESPEARE'S GLOBE

Claire van Kampen

I was sceptical when in 1996 I arrived at a building finished enough to launch a 'Prologue Season' – for which I wrote the music for *The Two Gentlemen of Verona*. In the professional theatre world, creating productions of Shakespeare had had very little connection with, or interest in, any sense of an 'authentic' way to perform Shakespeare. In fact, when it came to playing Shakespeare, debates about 'authenticity' had divided the worlds of scholars and theatre practitioners into polarised camps that seemed, by 1996, to be resolutely separated by turbulent seas of mistrust. Though we did not attempt to recreate any sense of Shakespeare's own period until 1997, the Prologue Season was perhaps our own road to Damascus; audiences, far from shying away from standing through a performance in a typical inclement English summer had demonstrated, by record attendance, that not only were they hungry for the experience that being in the Globe's architecture afforded, but that somehow they felt that there was something here that was all their own. The energy of five hundred people standing was an enormous shock to all of us in the cast of *The Two Gentlemen of Verona*, and there was an eerie but ecstatic feeling that the play could not be controlled from the stage alone.

Given that most members of the audience in 1996 would never have opened a scholarly book about the first Globe theatre building before coming to the reconstruction, it was stunning that they seemed unperturbed by the brave new world that they found themselves in, as if they already knew it, that the 'Globe experience' resonated deeply with a theatre practice which, though long forgotten, was tantalisingly being remembered. Our first audiences' easiness and familiarity with the space encouraged us to dip our toes into the hornet's nest of 'authenticity', to see if we could answer Sam [Wanamaker's] initial mission for the Globe, which was to discover and recreate Shakespeare's company's working practices in the original Globe theatre. My challenge, therefore, was to look at the practice of Renaissance music, and, working with early music practitioners, to marry modern reconstructions of Elizabethan and Jacobean music to Shakespeare's texts for performance in the Globe using only reconstructed period instruments without amplification or electronic aids.

ENCOUNTERING AUDIENCE EXPECTATIONS

In 1996 we felt that modern audiences going to Shakespeare plays 'set in Elizabethan period' had up to that point witnessed productions that settled for a 'period generality' that demonstrated no accurate historical period at all, but just looked and sounded a bit 'long ago and far away'. Rather than hunting for authenticity, what we decided was indeed possible – and interesting – was accurate period reconstruction using carefully sourced evidence and referenced material. As we were chiefly interested in exploring what we knew Shakespeare's company would have been familiar with, and was capable of, we termed this experiment 'original practices'. One could say that the aim of 'original practices' productions was to observe what effect this carefully recreated period might have on the relationship between actor and audience within the architecture of the 'Wooden O'. Would a modern audience be alienated or embraced by productions that sought to 'recover' period clothing and music? Would a mutual vocabulary develop as a result of the experience of 'hearing' the plays in the Globe Theatre? There were doubts and fears: in particular, would an all-male acting company lack 'truth'? Would period instruments sound 'untuneful' and thus negate the purpose of having music at all within the plays? Come to think of it what *was* the purpose of music within Shakespeare plays, when its twenty-first-century soul-mate, theatrical lighting, had been banished?

Because in the modern Globe our expectations of production sophistication are informed by the kind of Shakespeare we have seen elsewhere and, perhaps more importantly, by the level of aural and visual information we are used to receiving via film, music in the present Globe has, in a sense, to be part of a consensus of 'creating an Elizabethan world' for its audience. In that sense, the wide and varied textural palette of instrumentation that takes the audience on a journey is necessary to inform and envelop a modern audience that has briefly stepped inside a theatre space for which there is no common currency, no familiar references. It is a new world that we are asking them to accept very quickly, within five minutes at an 'original practices' production. We are asking them to suspend their disbelief, to accept men playing women – dressed in exotic clothing, whitened faces and hemp wigs – instruments that sound weirdly, slightly out of tune, a language that is complex and archaic, and all this within a theatre architecture that may be as exciting as it is undeniably exclusive of comfort: hard seats, overheard aircraft, movement among the groundlings and no theatre lighting to help focus on the story or the actors on the stage.

ARCHITECTURAL DISCOVERIES

By looking at where the musicians were placed within the theatre architecture, it is clear that the presence of music within the plays had an iconographic and classical significance, besides its other functions of narrative support and the strengthening of character and status. The music gallery, or 'room', being placed directly above the stage, in the centre of the *frons scenae*, is at the most powerful visual point in the stage picture. What is more, in an 'original practices' production, musicians are dressed in Elizabethan clothing, which is colourful, far from the standard black uniform of the modern performer. They also wear hats, which they remove and replace if asked to bow, either as musicians receiving audience applause, or in character to an actor on stage. In the present Globe reconstruction, the music gallery completes the middle circle, which, unlike the upper and lower gallery, runs all the way around the stage. For 'original practices' productions, audiences were therefore seated on either side of the music gallery, in the lords' rooms, thus being behind the stage itself, on the line of the *frons scenae*. (Interestingly, from this position, audibility of the text is increased, though visibility of the action is reduced.)

The position of music performance in the theatre architecture supported the archetype of the Muses, known to an Elizabethan audience. Music therefore in this heightened scenario became even more sensitive, more significant; the instruments to which the text refers contain a meaning beyond the sound they make. The instruments that Elizabethans and Jacobeans considered signifiers of the music of the spheres – recorders, viols, lutes – invoke quite a different response in a modern audience, for whom these instruments are not part of their current popular musical vocabulary. Shakespeare's audience also identified specific musical instruments with hierarchy, function and/or qualities: *hautboys* (forerunners of the oboe) were considered 'marginal' instruments that could 'dance with the devil'; trumpet and drum calls were a known and current language of infantry and cavalry signals; use of trumpet and cornet flourishes, the lute and the viol signified a royal or noble character of wealth and power. Both in the first Globe, and in the present 'third Globe', music was placed between the world of the gods above, and the earthly stage of mankind, below. Music is, thus, not only heard but **seen** as the expression of the Muses as it transmits heavenly impulses to Man below on the earthly stage.

Contrast this powerful and present musical statement of the Elizabethan playhouse with music performed in a contemporary (twenty-first-century) theatre,

where musicians are generally placed unseen in a music studio entirely discon-
nected from the stage action other than through a visual monitor and headphones,
and their playing is 'piped in' to the auditorium via a sound system. For theatre
practitioners, this very prominent visual statement of musicians entering to play
is often felt to be a distraction to the stage picture. Curiously, though, the many
audiences who have given their feedback, both negatively and positively, to both
modern and 'original practices' performances of plays in the Globe, have never
once reported that they have been distracted by musicians being so prominently
displayed throughout the performance.

Two key questions had to be asked from the outset: did Elizabethan companies
use professional musicians, and how sophisticated was theatrical music of the
period? While working on *Julius Caesar* (1999), *Richard II* (2003) and *Richard III*
(2003) it was clear that it had been pragmatic for Shakespeare's company to use
the excess trumpeters and drummers that were on the court lists, waiting for
the Royal Command to be sent to war, as these early 'Drum and trumpet plays'
are crammed with tuckets, flourishes and alarums. These battle calls would have
been recognisable to many in an Elizabethan audience. There are both aural and
visual advantages to the narrative afforded by each stage 'army' possessing its own
trumpeter, drummer and standard bearer; these musicians would have appeared
both in the music gallery and also on stage.

ACOUSTIC REALITIES

Acoustically, in the Globe, sound is specific, not general. Individual instruments
retain their own character and personality while contributing to the ensemble of
which they are a part. Add to that the effects of the greatly differing air temper-
atures and moisture content, ambient noise from 1,500 people in the auditorium
(700 standing) and overhead aeroplanes, and the composer quickly finds that the
instrumental combination heard in the comfortable and resonant ambience of the
rehearsal room – a familiar acoustic that lends itself to the artificially enhanced
modern theatre auditorium – seems to have aurally disintegrated.

A discovery emerged from working with trumpet and drum calls and other
musical experimentation even within the rigorous parameters we had set ourselves
with the 'original practices' work: our modern desire to show off our Elizabethan
soundworld of 'natural' trumpet calls (signifying cavalry) and drum calls (infantry),
and later on with off-stage 'loud music', demanded that, at times, these instruments
had to be placed outside the fabric of the tiring house; in fact they were placed on the
public stairwell used by office staff. This was mainly due to the fact that for the most
part, early modern wind instruments do not have a volume control, but are designed
to be either 'loud' or 'soft'. I felt we were justified in exploring a rich palette of sound

when textual stage directions made reference to music being played while on-stage characters were continuing to speak, as in, for example, *Much Ado About Nothing* and *Love's Labour's Lost*. By creating a context for '*music within*' to help confirm an outdoor scene, where there is no lighting change to define movement from indoors to outdoors, we were providing an invaluable vocabulary in both Elizabethan music and stage practice.

However, unless positive evidence emerges that the tiring house had extensive upper rooms extending backwards, with doors that could be closed between them, we have to assume that Shakespeare only used, as underscore, the kind of music that, even under speech, could be played backstage *within* the confines of the tiring house. We found that the lute and the bass viol (used in a production of *Measure for Measure*, 2004/5) were the only instruments not to pull the audience's ears away from the text, when played on stage or off, remaining within hearing distance of the stage from the performer's position. Also we had to bear in mind the cueing system that we, even now, follow in the Globe. Actors generally take their own cues by listening through the 'grates' in the stage doors and musicians do likewise from above. This is in stark contrast to the modern theatre where music and lighting cues and actors' entrances are all controlled centrally by one person from an electronic board. Given that over-audibility from the audience's point of view would have been an issue for all combinations of '*loud music*', we noted that Shakespeare is very careful not to specify 'loud' music while text is being spoken (only the drum, a volume-adjustable instrument, is used under speech in the military plays). However, I think it would be a mistake to apply this logic to indoor theatres. What has emerged is that the Globe may have had a very specific musical culture unique to the amphitheatre playhouse.

DRAMATURGICAL DISCOVERIES

By performing the plays in an open-air amphitheatre, and not a 'normal' theatre auditorium, where the seated audience's attention is quiet within the darkness, we noticed that Shakespeare's dramaturgical placement of songs seemed to be pragmatic and deliberate. Shakespeare's skilful dramaturgy moves the audience through many changes of focus and energy, until, by Act 4, the atmosphere, even among the groundlings, is unfailingly focused and still. Space has thus been created for the audience to accept the indulgence of a hiatus in the action while a song is performed. Like the jig at the end of the play, this structural device may have been familiar to the audience; songs, usually performed by talented boy singer/actors clearly accompanying themselves introduced a note of purity as a 'message' from the heavenly worlds (Brutus' page Lucius, *Julius Caesar* 4.2)[1] or fates that expressed melancholy in love/emotion (Mariana's song, *Measure for Measure* 4.1), the opening of the door into the supernatural world (Caesar's ghost, *Julius Caesar* 4.2) or the demonstration of the distortion of pure love into 'madness' (Ophelia, in *Hamlet* 4.5).

What makes me think this dramatic device might have been a usual custom is that the idea is wonderfully parodied in *Love's Labour's Lost* 3.1 (note, Act 3 where audiences are yet to be drawn into the stillness of Act 4). Armado, the Spaniard, asks his boy page to 'warble' because he wishes to 'make passionate my sense of hearing' (3.1.1). Moth/Mote sings not a delicate love song but 'Concolinel'[2] which would seem to have been a naughty French chanson full of French words that had a parallel in sound to the words for female genitalia in English, all of this entirely incomprehensible to Armado. A post-Armada Elizabethan audience would have relished the joke. These boy performers seemed to have been in contrast to the male actors playing female roles. It is notable that Mariana does not sing herself in *Measure for Measure* but brings on the page specifically to do so. This could tell us either that Mariana was being played not by a boy, but by a young man whose voice had broken, or that such songs always required the special talents of boy singers who could accompany themselves on the lute or harp.

It seems possible that the lack of a song being given by Shakespeare to Mariana directly (or Cleopatra, or Gertrude) indicates that these roles were being played by male actors who specialised in playing female roles (as in the Japanese 'onnegata'[3] tradition) but, due to their broken voices, maintained suspension of disbelief as long as they did not sing, thus breaking the illusion of cross-gender. With this in mind, we felt that, for the most part, female roles in our 'original practices' productions were convincing when they were played by men whose natural speaking voices were in a high lyric tenor range and who were of smaller than average height and build. Due to the restrictions in modern theatre practices it was not possible for us to experiment by casting boy players, even in the singing roles.

'TWELFTH NIGHT'

Our experiment with *Twelfth Night* in 2002 was useful in confirming that indoor and outdoor playing, in two socially very different environments, demands specific musical instrumentation. For our three weeks of performances over 'Candlemass' in the Elizabethan Hall, prior to moving the production over the river to the Globe, we decided to try the 'broken' consort, playing arrangements of Morley's music, amongst others. In the Hall's indoor 'wet' acoustic – which is very challenging for speech – the music was resonant and loud enough to be heard over applause. The bandora provided a wonderful rhythmic basis for dancing the galliards[4] in the end 'jig'. It is entirely possible that Burbage's company employed the use of such a consort for such a wealthy and privileged audience.

What was interesting to contemplate as a result of this experiment was the seemingly unlikely influence of court masques on Jacobean performances in the Globe. When we transferred the production to the Globe two weeks later, the same music was rearranged for 'loud music' shawms, sackbuts, curtals and rauschpfeifes, plus field drum. Their sound was just about perceived over the applause, even though in the rehearsal room they were deafening. It is interesting to note here that for the jig at the end of the play we used the Fool/Feste's final song, which he sang accompanied by a theorbo from the gallery in both spaces. This piece of music transformed into a jig for the entire company by the addition of the instruments of the rest of the band, for both indoor and outdoor performances. For both 'incarnations' the tune of Morley's 'Lavolta'[5] was used instead of the traditional tune commonly known in partnership with the words 'When that I was', for when we checked our references, this traditional tune belonged to a considerably later period.

COMPLEX MUSICAL ARRANGEMENTS

Bearing in mind that the first Globe, like the third, was a commercial theatre disinclined to waste money, it seems unlikely that a consort of recorders or viols would have been hired only for rare and important moments, particularly given that these musicians would not have doubled on drum and trumpet. It is possible that, like our wind bands over the last decade, the versatility among six wind players does allow for a huge variety of both 'soft' and 'loud' music to be played; however, we have established that the first Globe, at least until around 1610 or so, was a simpler affair than ours, musically speaking, due to the lack of facilities to create off-stage music cues effectively.

It is therefore tempting to speculate on the wide variety of music employed in plays such as The Tempest and The Winter's Tale. Both of these plays, when performed in the Globe, would have had to answer complex musical questions, even if the masque in The Tempest was cut, or drastically reduced. Both call for 'heavenly music' in Act 5. How was this achieved? When we created a three-man production of The Tempest in 2005 we decided to use both the Jacobean and modern worlds; the music was 'sounded' by six early music/opera singers dressed in the attire of the Muses as depicted in the auditorium. I arranged music from the 1611 Atalanta Fugiens by Michael Maier. For the Masque I rearranged masque music by Robert Johnson (from Ben Jonson's The Masque of Oberon, 1611). The advantage of having singers as the only instrumentalists was that I could employ underscore of the quietest kind. In this regard, I was not seeking to recreate a Jacobean score for an 'original practices' production of The Tempest, but was rather introducing the audience to both the exotic and esoteric world of Michael Maier, a Bohemian emissary at court, and the main court composer for masques, Robert Johnson. The choice to use underscore of this nature in the production was because I felt a contemporary audience had to be able to 'feel' a sense of magic, of intrusion by an unearthly world. Where a Jacobean court audience may have achieved this feeling simply by listening to a hundred lutes and recorders, I felt today's listeners demanded a greater range of 'oddness' to achieve the same effect.

MUSICAL PERFORMANCES BY THE ACTING COMPANY

Therefore, through a range of experiments, we explored the role of the musician on stage; however, we were also curious to discover if the actors themselves contributed to the music of performance. It is unlikely that the acting company played the famous 'hautboys' that are remarkable in Shakespeare's stage directions[6] as this instrument had a disturbing spiritual significance to an audience of the 1600s, and was probably best played by specialists such as the City Waits.[7] However, it would seem that in the 'Drum and Trumpet' days the company fool, Will Kemp (then later on Robert Armin), would have presented a major star turn, and thus provided songs, capers and comic entertainment. The roles of Feste and Autolycus seem specially created to please the crowd before, during and after the show, these characters perhaps coming into their own with the jig at the end of the play. There are some puzzles here, however. One is the jig referred to by a member of Shakespeare's audience, Thomas Platter, which he witnessed at the end of a performance of *Julius Caesar*. He remarks that 'at the end of the comedy, according to their custom, they danced very marvelously and gracefully together as is their wont, two dressed as men and two as women';[8] Platter does not mention the clown's famous extemporising abilities, though this is not to say that there definitely was no clown or jig and caper at the end of the production that Platter witnessed. Having earlier described *Julius Caesar* as a 'tragedy' Platter's passage states that there was some satisfying resolution, which took place after the play itself was finished. The 'marvelous' and 'graceful' nature of the dance could refer either to the nature/complexity of the musical accompaniment (i.e., more than just a drum) or it may of course refer to the dancing style which seems to have been refined, or 'graceful'. If the music was instrumentally complex, and the dance therefore perhaps more than a jig and caper (would Platter have referred to a jig and caper as 'exceeding fine'?) then this would not seem to be having to battle against audience applause, as our current jigs have to. The notion of a 'curtain call' is too ingrained in modern audiences to cope with the idea of appreciatively but silently watching four actors dance a pavane at the end of a long play. What is possible to draw from this reference is that there could have been a coda, or final 'turn' at the end of the play, which perhaps may have included a song (like 'Singing Simpkin',[9] although strictly, Platter does not mention it), ended by an 'exceeding fine' dance performed 'marvelously together' to bring the audience out of the 'magical' nature of the drama, and put them firmly on the earth before setting them free on Bankside.

During the Prologue Season in 1996 we tried such a 'Singing Jig' at the end of *The Two Gentlemen of Verona*. It was 'rap-like' in its structure and form; the music was very simple (mouth-organ and percussion played from the stage), and was rather successful with the audience, many of whom requested copies of the text.[10] The *Julius Caesar* jig in 1999 was more aggressive, and consisted of three actors performing magnificent leaping galliards against a background of the rest of the company (fifteen in total) clapping and stamping to the music above, two of whom in the all-male company were dressed as women. The *Twelfth Night* jig told complex stories of each character through the choreography (Olivia and Orsino were 'confused' as to which twin was which). Perhaps increasingly in this area we have been pulled towards the audience's honest desire to show their appreciation for the actors in a Dionysian outburst of unbridled passion that denies musical subtlety. We must conclude that rather than having failed to reproduce an 'authentic jig' we have in fact arrived at a consensus: a 'modern' Globe audience absolutely expects there to be a 'jig' at the end of a Shakespeare play, and would consider the play 'unfinished' if it were not there.

THE NEW GLOBE AUDIENCE

However ignorant, or innocent of Elizabethan musical terms and 'codes' the audience may initially have been in Shakespeare's Globe in 1996, it has been a fascinating study to observe how quickly over a ten-year period the audience has become an informing entity in its own right. The Globe audience in 2007 has absorbed a unique vocabulary of musical signals that are played by instruments generally only seen by that audience in the context of Shakespeare's Globe. This audience, without always knowing why, responds to those signals with recognition. Our exploration of some of the aspects of the original playing practices of Shakespeare's company was in the main inspired by the similar work explored forty years earlier by the Early Music Movement, and notably pioneered in England in the 1960s. In particular the work of the charismatic David Munrow has been influential. Munrow brought scholarly textual analysis and reconstructed instruments together with musical interpretation based on primary and positive evidence. Healthy diversity and debate abound within the Early Music Movement particularly with regard to the interpretation of Renaissance instrumentation and musical realisation. Adding the original architecture of the performance space into these debates makes it appropriate to imagine that there are now many more roads open for the exploration of Shakespeare's company's working practices in theatrical performance.

By 2005, it was clear that the audience at Shakespeare's Globe was comprised of many who were returning annually, and to more than one production, exploring forms of historically informed experimentation, and that this type of audience, a 'Globe' audience, is not only eager and willing to take on board a good deal of extra-ordinary visual and aural information, but is able to store and build upon its experiences in the space. In Shakespeare's Globe the audience, if you like, has become a theatre practitioner, and thus truly able to 'play' with the company, responding to the many different aspects of new evidence from the play-texts, and from the Elizabethan stage, to contribute to the discoveries coming out of this exciting space.

NOTES

1 'If thou dost nod thou breakst thy instrument; I'll take it from thee, and good boy, good night' – Brutus to his page Lucius: *Julius Caesar* 4.2.323–4, *The Norton Shakespeare*, Stephen Greenblatt *et al.* (London and New York: W. W. Norton, 1997). All subsequent references are to this edition.

2 There is no extant song for 'Concolinel', mentioned in *Love's Labour's Lost*. Following Shakespeare's lead in *Henry V*, where the French Princess and Alys engage innocently in misquoting the English words 'foot and gown' to sound as *foutre* (to fuck in French) and 'coun/con' (cunt) thereby highly amusing the Globe audience at the expense of the French, I reconstructed 'Concolinel' as 'con-cul-inel' (*cul* means arse or bum in French) after the style of the French chanson, which liberally uses words that we now would consider extremely bawdy, if not offensive. Moth sings 'Con-cul-nel' to Armado, a proud Spaniard who is clearly the butt of English humour in the play. The French chanson reconstruction was based on Claude Sermisy (1490–1562). The French chanson itself derived from the Italian *popolaresca lirica*; many Italians were employed as musicians at the French Court.

3 From 'onna + kata' means 'woman's manner' in Japanese. Onnegata are male Kabuki actors who perform the roles of women as a speciality.

4 From *galliarde* in French, this dance and musical form was popular all over Europe in the sixteenth century. The dance is improvised, with the dancers combining patterns of steps which occupy one or more measures of music. In one measure, a galliard typically has five steps. In French, this is called a *cinq pas*, written in English sources as 'sinkapace'. It is an athletic dance, characterised by leaps, jumps, hops and similar figures. The physical needs of the galliard inform the tempo of the music, which on modern recordings is generally played too fast to accommodate the leaps of the dance.

5 The piece 'Lavolta' is ascribed to Thomas Morley. However, it appears in the *First Book of Consort Lessons*, 1599, which is a collection, by Thomas Morley, of consort music 'made by divers exquisite authors for six instruments to play together; the treble lute, the Pandora, the Cittern, the Base-violl, the flute and the treble-violl'.

6 '*Music of the hautboys is under the stage*', *Antony and Cleopatra* (4.3.9).

7 Originally watchmen of the town 'piped' the hours. The City or Town Waits were musicians whose business it was to play before the Mayor and Aldermen on festive occasions. Their number in the fifteenth century (see Calendar of Letter-books of the City of London: King

Henry VI) appears to have represented the Muses (nine), which in later years was reduced. The Waits, in the sixteenth and seventeenth centuries, were hired for many occasions which ranged from following condemned prisoners to the Tower to playing entr'acte music in the intervals for the indoor theatres.

8 Thomas Platter was a young Swiss traveller from Basel, who visited London from 18 September to 18 October 1599. Thomas Platter, 'Travels in England', trans. Clare Williams, cited in Andrew Gurr, *Playgoing in Shakespeare's London* (Cambridge University Press, 1987).

9 Entered in the Stationers' Register on 21 October 1595 was 'Kempe's newe jigg betwixt a soldier and a miser and Sym the clown'; this jig was preserved in translation among the five published in the German collection of 1600. It proves to be identical with 'Singing Simpkin', one of Cox's drolls published by Kirkman in 1663 in a collection called 'the Wits, or Sport upon Sport'. The vogue of the jig (it travelled around the country at fairs and wakes) survived the silencing of the public theatres by the Puritans. 'Singing Simpkin' (180 lines of lively doggerel) is a 'salacious operetta of intrigue' written to be sung to a variety of well-worn tunes by five characters.

10 The text for this jig was written by Cindy Oswin. Oswin is a writer, actress and director who has worked with many theatre companies, both classical and innovative, including the English National Opera and Shakespeare's Globe.

CHAPTER SEVEN

MUSIC, AUTHENTICITY AND AUDIENCE

David Lindley

There is a curious way in which music in the theatre – and indeed in television and film – often seems to stand outside any kind of historical location that a production might otherwise seek to invoke. For though on occasion the use of twenties jazz or fifties rock-and-roll can work to establish and confirm a particular period setting, in far more cases there is little connection between music and action in terms of its historical definition. The costumes of Gregory Doran's 1996 Stratford production of *Henry VIII*, for example, appeared to the audience to be meticulously accurate to the time of the play's action; Henry himself and Queen Catherine might have stepped out of their Holbein picture-frames, yet the setting of the song 'Orpheus with his lute' by Jason Carr was in a style that might best be described as 'universal stage-musical'. Television audiences who would write angrily to condemn the slightest departure from historical accuracy in the detail of the setting or costuming of a Jane Austen adaptation will cheerfully overlook scores of unashamed modernity. One might think that this is testament to a modern audience's ignorance of the history of musical styles – but exactly the same was true of the Victorian and Edwardian productions which on the one hand made a virtue of the historical exactitude of their recreation of period detail, but on the other accompanied their performances with a mish-mash of music often drawn from a variety of chronologically different sources from the later seventeenth century onwards. This suggests that music in the theatre is felt to be a system of signification that may operate independently of the other signifying systems of language, costume and scenery in the creation of a coherent, historically located world. Historical specificity generally (and perfectly reasonably) comes low down in the order of priorities, but even where some kind of gesture is made towards a coherent musical characterisation of a period, this will tend to be part of an effort to relocate the early modern text somewhere else than in the sixteenth/seventeenth centuries. Very few 'mainstream' productions have made any attempt to use early modern music.

There are, and have been, however, exceptions to this general practice. William Poel, one of the earliest enthusiasts for historical performance of Renaissance drama, was, from the very beginning of his experiments with his Elizabethan Stage Society, closely associated with the contemporaneously emergent early music movement. Arnold Dolmetsch, who provided music for Poel's first production and all those which followed until 1905, was one of the most significant advocates of the rediscovery of music and of instruments from the pre-Baroque period and of the attempt to find a performing style which might be considered an accurate recreation of that of the sixteenth or seventeenth centuries.[1] The faith which propelled both these pioneers was essentially the same – that to try to recapture the physical conditions of the first performance of music or play would guarantee something more 'authentic', be truer to the author's original intention, and therefore more vital to their contemporary audience. It must certainly have been the case that to theatregoers used to a full symphony orchestra providing the incidental music for Shakespeare, as for all other theatre, the small ensemble of various combinations of viols, recorders, virginals, pipe and tabor which Dolmetsch provided must have sounded surprising – even if, as with the acting, the musical performance might sometimes be rather amateurish.

While a few productions in succeeding years followed Poel's musical lead, in the event the pursuit of early musical performing practices was more widespread and continued at a very much faster pace than attempts to reproduce the Elizabethan theatrical space. It grew throughout the twentieth century, and, aided by the wide dissemination made possible by recordings, turned concerts by musicians such as David Munrow in the 1960s into major events with large, enthusiastic audiences.[2] There have always been 'mainstream' musicians resistant to the claims of early music specialists – Thomas Beecham, for example, memorably described the sound of the harpsichord as that of 'two skeletons copulating on a tin roof', and Vaughan Williams trenchantly dismissed the 'latest orders from Germany' that Bach was 'to be performed as "period music" in the precise periwig style', stating:

We cannot perform Bach exactly as he was played in his time even if we wanted to, and the question is, do we want to? I say emphatically, No! Some music dies with its period, but what is really immortal endures from generation to generation. The interpretation and with it the means of interpretation differ with each generation.[3]

Vaughan Williams's belief in the transcendent universality of great music speaks very much from its moment in 1950, at the beginning of the massive growth in interest in early music performance practices. As the movement continued to gather strength, Will Crutchfield observed that 'it is startling to note how far the "authentic performance" movement, once so insular and gentle of cast, has come to resemble a juggernaut, a steamroller or a conquering army'.[4] It was precisely the increasing prominence of the early music movement and the confidence – even hubris – that went with it about the authenticity of performances on historically accurate instruments which inevitably led in the 1980s and 1990s to vigorous questioning of the aims and achievements of the movement, and to a searching exploration of the theoretical basis for the claims being made on its behalf. Among many who seriously challenged the authenticist assumptions, Richard Taruskin (himself both a musicologist and a performer of medieval and Renaissance music) was one of the most determined and persistent critics. In a sequence of prominent and influential articles[5] he argued that merely to deploy original instruments guaranteed nothing, since there was simply not enough surviving evidence of the ways in which music was actually performed to enable practitioners to claim that they were replicating historical styles. Indeed, he argued that the style which passed for historically 'authentic' was in fact determined by modernism, so that performances, far from being historically accurate, were 'authentic' only to the modern moment of their creation. He observes:

So is Early Music just a hoax? Are the Brüggens and Bilsons deceiving us, or themselves? Is 'authentic' performance as inauthentic as all that?

Not at all. It is authentic indeed, far more authentic than its practitioners contend, perhaps more authentic than they know. Nothing said above about Messrs. Brüggen, Norrington, and Bilson or the rest should be taken in itself as criticism of the results they have obtained. They have been rightly acclaimed. Their commercial success is well deserved. Conventional performers are properly in awe and in fear of them. Why? Because, as we are all secretly aware, what we call historical performance is the sound of now, not then. It derives its authenticity not from its historical verisimilitude, but from its being for better or worse a true mirror of late-twentieth-century taste.[6]

Taruskin, then, conducts a complex negotiation with the early music movement. He does not deny that research into original instruments, or into what can be adduced of historical performing practice, or careful and scrupulous editions, are valuable and important; but he argues that their value resides in the degree to which they release performers into the expression of their present moment.

Taruskin's work, and indeed the early music movement itself which he interrogates, is predominantly concerned with performance and performers, and with the (im)possibility of replicating historical practice. Yet this questioning of underlying assumptions bears a strong resemblance to the slightly more recent literary critical movement which labels itself 'presentism'.[7] It sets itself in opposition to the dominance of the critical scene by 'new historicism', and deconstructs its claims and ambitions in terms that are very similar to those deployed against the 'authenticists' in music. So, for example, Terence Hawkes writes:

. . . none of us can step beyond time. It can't be drained out of our experience. As a result, the critic's own 'situatedness' does not – cannot – contaminate the past. In effect, it constitutes the only means by which it's possible to see the past and perhaps comprehend it. And since we can only see the past through the eyes of the present, few serious historians would deny that the one has a major influence on their account of the other. Of course we should read Shakespeare historically. But given that history results from a never-ending dialogue between past and present, how can we decide whose historical circumstances will have priority in that process, Shakespeare's, or our own?[8]

Like Taruskin, Hawkes does not deny the importance of historical research, but like him he considers the recreation of the past to be conducted from our present, and wishes to focus critical attention precisely on the act of reading from the present into the past. Not surprisingly, perhaps, Hawkes has little time for the work of Shakespeare's Globe, judging that 'its commitment to nuts-and-bolts authenticity ensures that *déjà vu* will always hold centre-stage'.[9] Ewan Fernie goes farther. In his argument for the 'crucial importance of Shakespeare *now*' he argues that 'presentism relinquishes the fantasy of recovering the text's previous historical reality in favour of embracing its true historicity as a changing being in time', and dismisses 'contemporary Shakespeare and Renaissance criticism's turn toward context, which in practice means anything but the text . . . This contextual framing and focus tames the text's challenging otherness.'[10]

The notions underlying the search for 'authenticity' and historicity in both performance practice and in critical writing have come under attack. The assault on the possibility of historically informed performance of music is answered in Claire van Kampen's chapter, pp. 79–89. I would only observe that the use of original instruments cannot but raise significant and interesting questions about the nature of the musical experience in the theatres of Shakespeare's time, and that exploration of performing practices may well have the effect, not of 'taming' but, as Laurence Dreyfus observed, of defamiliarisation.[11] I do wish, however, to take up issues that are raised by Fernie's comment quoted above, and which are complicated by Hawkes's observation that: 'The new Globe can never inherit the cultural role of the old one because that culture has irretrievably gone. Specifically, the new theatre can never under any circumstances recreate the single most crucial element of the Elizabethan playhouse: the audience.'[12]

To take Fernie's comment on contexts first: no doubt everyone has encountered readings of texts on which his observation might be just – the essay which avoids and dissolves the complexity of a text by deploying 'background' to recast it as merely a conventional articulation of a simplified commonplace, or, in the context of this chapter, explications of musical events in Shakespeare plays which insist on seeing them only and always as exemplifying notions of cosmic harmony. But in truth it is a huge overstatement. For, as Gary Tomlinson observes:

Meaning . . . does not inhere in individual signs but instead is determined by their interaction with other signs. Together congeries of such signs, groups of signifying acts, make up contexts in which individual signs or acts gain significance. Without context there is no meaning.[13]

This, he argues, is as true of musical events as any other. Music's meanings are elusive and indeterminate (one reason why moralists have always been made uneasy by the art), but they do not inhere only in the internal structures of the music itself. They are created out of the multiple and complex associations of particular musical styles and modes of performance with wider cultural contexts.[14] In Fernie's vision – and to greater or lesser extent that of Taruskin and Hawkes, the primary context can only be the present; that is the lens through which the past is seen and comes into focus.

This, however, is to resist the possibility that certain kinds of knowledge of historical context enable the observer to escape from the confines and contexts of the present, and thereby to approach and understand the text in ways which, precisely, challenge the present(ist) prison to which, taken to extreme, these arguments would confine us. Nonetheless, Tomlinson's further comment, that 'the boundaries of the meaning of a work cannot be drawn at the edges of the score, but must be located anew by each perceiver according to the work's participation in his or her own context of meaning' might seem to accord with a 'presentist' position. But he continues: 'This leads to another corollary: since the meaning of a musical work does not wholly reside in the work, it cannot be conveyed fully by means of performance.' Then, in what amounts to a reversal of Fernie's position, he writes:

A performance can present little more of a work's original context than the portion of it that exists within the work itself . . . This is only a part of the conceptual worlds in which the work took on its first meanings: and any performance, therefore, amounts at best to a relatively thin context for authentic meaning. A thick context must result from an elaborate work of cultural interpretation.[15]

Tomlinson's vocabulary indicates clearly that he is writing at the time of the begin-nings of what came to be known as 'new historicism', and so he might simply be taken as a representative of the outmoded manner that presentism seeks to dislodge. But his words both chime with and challenge Hawkes's point about the modern Globe audience. The central and essential issue is how far, where and in what circumstances it is possible to disturb the simple (or the sophisticated) 'pre-sentist' response of an audience. To which the answer may be – not easily in the theatre, but more readily in the study.

This is obviously the case with the language of early modern plays. In the theatre the local detail of meaning may escape the audience (as it not infrequently seems to escape actors); but while reading a good edition the footnotes should at least help to recover lost meanings and untangle unfamiliar syntax. With sufficient experience, though the associations of words and phrases can never be as ready, or as full as one might assume they were for an original audience, a student may come to a familiarity with language that was once simply alien. The same might, to some extent, be true of early music and of musical events also, especially since, despite the efforts of practitioners for the last century, to most modern members of a theatre audience the language of sixteenth-century music is as unfamiliar as classical Greek. But equally important is the understanding of the multiple contexts within which the music of the theatre might be placed.

A simple case is that of the various military signals that punctuate so many of the histories and tragedies. Stage directions call for 'alarum', 'retreat', 'march', 'dead march' and so on. In the modern theatre these will probably be translated into various fanfares for trumpets and drums – but while such excited noise will generate the energy that no doubt was part of the intended function in the original performances, it cannot, for a modern audience, convey the precision of meaning that might have been available to an audience for whom the language of military drums and trumpets was familiar. So, for example, the dramatic action which precedes *King John* 3.3, is summed up in the stage direction '*Alarums, excursions, retreat*'. The stage is first crossed by soldiers, whose fighting is incited by the 'alarum' – not any old noise, but, as Gervase Markham indicates, one of the six main signals which a soldier needed to know, a call 'which sounded, every man (like Lightning) flyes upon his enemie, and gives proofe of his valour'.[16] The sounding of the retreat then clearly marks the ending of the fight, so that the shape of the battle is economically depicted in and through the instrumental cues. In many plays Shakespeare, for example, uses these musical signals with very precise significance.[17] But these effects can only now be recognised by a reader; they cannot be recreated in the theatre, even if valveless trumpets and authentic kettle drums are used, nor can they be comprehended by a modern audience for whom there is no musical language of war. To be aware of the precision of musical signals such as these is not to construct the past from the perspective of the present, but to recognise accurately the way meanings may be dependent upon a language and a context that is gone, but whose implications can be reconstructed.

This may be to build too much on a relatively simple example, but a much more complex case is the singing of Ophelia. According to the first quarto she enters the stage '*playing on a Lute, and her haire downe singing*'. It is an episode which has attracted critical attention from a contemporary feminist perspective,[18] and thereby participates in discussions of the representation of the relationship of women and music which achieved prominence in the latter part of the twentieth century.[19] This is, one might say, a very obvious example of the way in which the nature of our focus on the past is determined by current preoccupations. That, however, is not, I think, the whole story.

If one attempts to consider the historical contexts which may have contributed to the meaning of this episode, then first among them might be the consideration that while dishevelled hair was a conventional sign of distraction, it would seem that the addition of singing to the depiction of the madwoman is an invention of the early modern theatre, and perhaps of Shakespeare in this play.[20] If this is so, then the shock of novelty for the original audience is one we can imaginatively understand as contributing to its effect. More important, however, are the contexts within which this theatrical presentation of a singing woman was located. Upper-class women were supposed to learn musical instruments, but to restrict their playing to domestic and private environments. For Ophelia to enter on to a public stage singing is to transgress gender norms and social expectations (in a way that Desdemona, singing privately to her maid in *Othello*, does not). The lute that she (may) have carried adds further to the picture. It was the instrument that young women of the upper classes learned – but on the Renaissance stage it is also the instrument played by Franceschina in Marston's *The Dutch Courtesan* and by Bellafront in Dekker's *The Honest Whore*. Ophelia's infringement of the rules of conduct for her social class, then, carries associations with the whore, associations which are then further encouraged by the sexual content of the ballads that she sings. It does not seem to me that awareness of these contexts in any way 'tames' the scene – rather they intensify and complicate our response to it. But, once again, this intensification is available only in the study as one brings historical scholarship to bear on the scene. A modern production might choose to intensify the sexual transgressiveness of Ophelia, but the specific associations of lute and singing simply do not resonate in the present.

The question then arises of what and how Ophelia sings to the accompaniment of her lute. There are no surviving musical scores for her songs, though it is generally accepted that 'How should I your true love know' would have been sung to the ballad tune 'Walsingham', and it is probably safe to assume that her other songs were similarly accommodated to already existing and well-known tunes. This marks one of the most obvious divergences of practice between Shakespearean and modern theatre. Where the modern production will commission a new score, specially designed for the particular production, this was not the case in the adult theatre – at least before 1608 and the King's Men takeover of Blackfriars, with its larger musical resources. Until then the hectic repertory system and the absence of a separate cohort of musicians meant that most of the music would have consisted of instrumental items from repertory, and songs with words accommodated to well-known ballads or lifted from already published music.[21] This, of course, was the common practice of the broadside ballad itself, rarely published with any music, but advertised to be sung 'to the tune of . . . '[22] Its implication for the nature of the communication between actor and audience, however, is something that a modern performance would find difficult, if not impossible, to recreate. A familiar tune associated with unfamiliar words sets up multiple possibilities – of identification and simultaneously of defamiliarisation – that no modern Ophelia could reproduce. As Bruce Smith says:

with respect to the present [ballads] serve as reference points to the past, as gestures towards experiences that the audience, like the protagonists, is presumed already to have had. Ballads establish a commonality of memory that unifies the audience and imbricates its members in the fictional world of the play . . . .Ballads in Shakespeare's plays help to establish a sense of common culture. The ground for that common culture is not chronological knowledge but *feeling*.[23]

Even if a modern Ophelia sings the 'original' plangent tune of Walsingham, though it might have an effect of strangeness and intensify pathos, it cannot engender the same complex of feelings as was available to a seventeenth-century audience. But this does not mean that, with historical imagination, one cannot speculate intelligently about the situation of that original audience and its possible range of responses to the scene. Such scholarship and imagination does not mask the way in which modern critics will inevitably approach Ophelia's scene with a particular agenda and awareness deriving from their own situatedness. But it is to suggest that seeking contexts of various kinds can enrich and extend the modern reader's sense of the possibilities that the scene can sustain.

Bruce Smith notes that we live in a time which has 'altered for ever the condition under which human beings all over the world now hear. Two inventions – electricity and the internal combustion engine – make it difficult for us even to imagine what life in early modern England would have sounded like.'[24] This is one among many obvious reasons why a modern audience at the reconstructed Globe clearly does not get unmediated acoustic access to Shakespeare's world, no matter how historically informed the musical performance may be. Another fundamental difference, one which profoundly affects the nature of an audience's relationship to musical events on stage, is that while we are now accustomed, in film and television as well as theatre, to truly 'incidental' music – or, to use film terminology, 'non-diegetic' music which is heard by the audience, but not by the participants in the action, the evidence suggests strongly that at least until the later part of the seventeenth century all music performed in the theatre was assumed to be heard by both. This is a matter of contention,[25] but if it is true, then it requires us now to unlearn some of the 'natural' assumptions we make about theatrical music. So, for example, it is easy for a modern audience to take the music which accompanies the raising to life of Hermione's statue in *The Winter's Tale*, or the inanimate body of Thaisa in *Pericles*, simply as emotional intensifiers, or as in some way illustrating and underlining the strangeness of the events they accompany. But for an Elizabethan audience this music might be believed to cause the action to happen, to bring about the resurrection or the cure. In the early modern theatre, music is always active, and causative, reacted to by characters on stage, and often familiar to its audience. In the modern theatre, and before a modern audience, whether in the Globe or the Royal Shakespeare Theatre, it will always tend to slip back into the decorative and illustrative. As such it may often work powerfully, and performance of contemporaneous music on accurately reproduced instruments may contribute in varied ways to that power, but I would contend that the attempt to recover and to comprehend some of the circumstances and contexts within which the music of the original production functioned can valuably expand, contradict or estrange me from the present(ist) perspectives that are, still, however, inevitably going to play a significant part in prompting the questions I want to ask of a text. Just as we are likely now to speak of 'historically informed', rather than 'authentic' performance practice, I would want to draw back from some of the more extreme historicist formulations – but not to renounce the belief that without contextual awareness the study of dramatic literature is debilitated.

NOTES

1 See Harry Haskell, *The Early Music Revival: A History* (London: Thames and Hudson, 1988). On Arnold Dolmetsch, see Margaret Campbell, *Dolmetsch: The Man and his Work* (London: Hamilton, 1975); on Poel see Robert Speaight, *William Poel and the Elizabethan Revival* (London: Heinemann, 1954), and Marion O'Connor, *William Poel and the Elizabethan Stage Society* (Cambridge: Chadwyck-Healey, 1987).

2 Howard Mayer Brown states that 'the decisive event in the popularization of early music in Britain was the emergence in the late 1960s of David Munrow and his Early Music Consort of London. Munrow combined personal vitality with a desire to communicate with a large audience'. 'Pedantry of Liberation', in *Authenticity and Early Music*, ed. Nicholas Kenyon (Oxford University Press, 1988), p. 48.

3 Ralph Vaughan Williams, *National Music and Other Essays* (Oxford University Press, 1963), p. 171.

4 Will Crutchfield, 'Fashion, Conviction, and Performance Style in an Age of Revivals', in Kenyon, *Authenticity*, p. 19.

5 Conveniently collected in Richard Taruskin, *Text and Act: Essays on Music and Performance* (Oxford University Press, 1995).

6 *Ibid.*, p. 166.

7 The label is not without its problems, having rather different uses in different disciplines. How far this will turn out to be a genuine and widespread shift in literary criticism remains to be seen. For a critique, see Robin Headlam Wells, 'Historicism and "Presentism" in Early Modern Studies', *Cambridge Quarterly* 29 (2000), 37–60.

8 Terence Hawkes, *Shakespeare in the Present* (London and New York: Routledge, 2002), p. 3.
9 *Ibid.*, p. 139.
10 Ewan Fernie, 'Shakespeare and the Prospect of Presentism', *Shakespeare Survey* 58 (2005), 169, 179, 176–7.
11 Laurence Dreyfus, 'Early Music Defended against its Devotees: a Theory of Historical Performance in the Twentieth Century', *Musical Quarterly* 69 (1983), 306–8.
12 Hawkes, *Shakespeare in the Present*, p. 140.
13 Gary Tomlinson, 'The Historian, the Performer, and Authentic Meaning in Music', in Kenyon, *Authenticity*, p. 118.
14 This truism is one which has not always been easily accepted by musicologists. See, for example, Martin Clayton, Trevor Herbert and Richard Middleton, eds., *The Cultural Study of Music: A Critical Introduction* (London: Routledge, 2003).
15 Tomlinson, 'Authentic Meaning', pp. 122–3.
16 Gervase Markham, *The Souldier's Accidence* (London: 1635), p. 64. See also Paul A. Jorgensen, *Shakespeare's Military World* (Berkeley and Los Angeles: University of California Press, 1956), chapter 1.
17 See David Lindley, *Shakespeare and Music* (London: Thomson Learning, 2006), pp. 112–22, for more detailed discussion of the semiotics of martial music in the plays.
18 See, for example, Leslie C. Dunn, 'Ophelia's Songs in *Hamlet*: Music, Madness, and the Feminine', in *Embodied Voices: Representing Female Vocality in Western Culture*, ed. Lesley C. Dunn and Nancy A. Jones (Cambridge University Press, 1994), and Jacquelyn Fox-Good, 'Ophelia's Mad Songs: Music, Gender, Power', in *Subjects on the World's Stage: Essays on British Literature of the Middle Ages and the Renaissance*, ed. David C. Allen and Robert White (Newark: University of Delaware Press, 1995).
19 A book which initiated widespread discussion of this topic is Susan McClary, *Feminine Endings: Music, Gender, and Sexuality* (Minneapolis: University of Minnesota Press, 1991). On the Renaissance, see Linda Austern's seminal articles, '"Sing Againe Syren": the Female Musician and Sexual Enchantment in Elizabethan Life and Literature', *Renaissance Quarterly* 42 (1989), 420–48, and '"Alluring the Auditorie to Effeminacie": Music and the Idea of the Feminine in Early Modern England', *Music and Letters* 74 (1993), 343–54.
20 It was to become a widespread convention in the later seventeenth century. See Dolly MacKinnon, '"Poor Senseless Bess, Clothed in her Rags and Folly": Early Modern Women, Madness and Song in Seventeenth-Century England', *Parergon* 18 (2001), 119–51.
21 This is the suggestion of Ross Duffin, in his *Shakespeare's Songbook* (New York: Norton, 2004), which prints all known surviving music, together with suggestions of popular tunes to which the remainder might be fitted. This is an area where I think much more research needs to be done, since I suspect the picture is rather more complicated than this model implies.
22 See Tessa Watt, *Cheap Print and Popular Piety, 1550–1640* (Cambridge University Press, 1991), and Claude M. Simpson, *The British Broadside Ballad and its Music* (New Brunswick, NJ: Rutgers University Press, 1966).
23 Bruce R. Smith, 'Shakespeare's Residuals: the Circulation of Ballads in Cultural Memory', in *Shakespeare and Elizabethan Popular Culture*, ed. Stuart Gillespie and Neil Rhodes (London: Thomson Learning, 2006), pp. 196, 200.

24 Bruce R. Smith, *The Acoustic World of Early Modern England: Attending to the O-Factor* (University of Chicago Press, 1999), p. 39.

25 Martin White, for instance, in *Renaissance Drama in Action* (London: Routledge, 1998), p. 154, argues: 'After experimenting extensively with music, language and action in a range of plays . . . I am certain that music would have been used . . . in a manner not dissimilar to the way it was used to accompany action in early cinema and in film scores today.'

ACTOR/AUDIENCE INTERACTION

7 Mark Rylance as *Richard II* (2003), Shakespeare's Globe

CHAPTER EIGHT

RESEARCH, MATERIALS, CRAFT: PRINCIPLES OF PERFORMANCE AT SHAKESPEARE'S GLOBE

Mark Rylance

CC: Was the Globe Theatre an experimental space in your mind? And if so did you have a hypothesis that you were setting out to prove to begin with, or was it just an empty space that you wanted to play in?[1]

MR: It has always appeared to me as the most experimental theatre space in England. The space itself is an experiment. I do not think I had a hypothesis that I was setting out to prove. I think my arrival here was in response to an invitation to take up what Sam [Wanamaker] and the people around him had proposed, which was a challenge that they would build, as faithfully as they possibly could, a theatrical tool from four hundred years ago, that had specific plays written for it that we knew, and that we would try and mount those plays in that tool. In my mind, it is a bit like someone discovering the original cello, or the original violin and saying, 'Mozart wrote for this instrument, not for the modern one we're using, so who will take up the challenge to try and play his music on this instrument?', and that seemed a very exciting challenge. I have always had a particular purpose with Shakespeare, which is to reach audiences in as full a way as possible, so that it is a physical, soulful and spiritual experience. I did not come with a particular objective, although I was encouraged to be radical by the people who selected me. I remember that they were aware, even in the earliest stages, that there was a reputation problem, that the Globe's reputation and outer appearance did not match its inner character.

But then things developed. What developed first of all was the observation of three principles that Sam was employing in the reconstruction of the Globe. The first of which was that there was to be the most accurate **Research** possible and that all theories would be brought together, battled out and weighed for credibility and then decisions would be made after consideration of this extensive research. So the first thing Sam's closest advisors, Professors Andrew Gurr and John Orrell, demanded was very faithful research. The second thing was that **Materials** for the building would be sourced as accurately as possible to the original. Great difficulties were encountered by Sam and his friends, like trying to get a licence to have the thatch, or taking down all the balusters that had been made by computer and making them again by hand, finding 1,000 oak trees, exploring and finding out how to use lime plaster for the first time in hundreds of years.

In discussing materials, I have slipped into the third thing which was *Craft*; human craft. Wherever possible, wherever affordable, Sam's architect, Theo Crosby, insisted that original craft would be rediscovered and exercised in the project. Research, materials, craft – these were three things that Sam handed on like a father to a son – these are the principles of the work here and it became apparent right away as we considered the question of costuming, particularly with Janet Arnold's extensive work on the clothing of Shakespeare's day, that there was not any costume anywhere that had followed any of these principles with any faith.

The whole idea of being faithful to a period, while very familiar in music, thanks to the early music movement, is pretty unfamiliar in the theatre. Theatre directors and designers feel they have a free hand really just to imagine whatever they want and there are very few people who are working in the theatre with a sense of detailed realism about a period. So those three things became our guiding principles. They were tempered at first because, although it is hard to believe now, we were not even sure that anyone would come and stand for a show in this 'old' building. No former reconstruction had dared to have standing room even in warmer, drier climates. What would people do when it rained? We had no Arts Council funding to support our work and the experiment would be fruitless if audiences did not fill the yard and galleries. There were all kinds of things that we did not know about how a modern audience would react to the reconstruction, and those things affected, not only the rigour with which I approached 'original practices', but they affected the very construction of the building.

The lower gallery is, in my view, totally wrong, and it is so because of natural nervousness about the yard when we opened. There are all those ingresses into the yard and actually the evidence is against them. It should be a high wall with iron spikes to stop people moving between the yard and seats! We put ingresses there to encourage people to walk down from the seats into the yard and stand. We were not at all certain anyone would stand, so a very large lower gallery was created that you could only enter from the front in order that people would use the yard. I am not saying this was consciously done, but our unfamiliarity with adopting the customs of a former theatrical period in history affected the degree of rigour we applied. To our delight audiences have wanted more and more rigour. They love the fact that it is an unusual theatrical experience. They led the way by favouring 'original practices' [OP].

The Globe experiment is particularly groundbreaking when artists accept the challenge to really assume the rather unfamiliar, uncomfortable theatrical disciplines of that period. But unfortunately the established theatre community felt completely the opposite of the initial audiences. With 'original practices' productions, we were taking on disciplines that were difficult and many directors would turn me down; they could not accept that as a way they wanted to work. Even 'freehand' productions were still scary for directors because of the lack of lighting and the strong given character of the stage and theatre.

I should explain that I considered two streams of work to be valid experiments, 'original practices' and also 'free-hand' work. 'Free-hand' meant that theatre artists of our own day should apply their unchained modern instincts to the building. It seemed like both responses were appropriate for the Globe. Something like Katherine Hunter's *Pericles* (2005), with circus skills, and all kinds of things fashionable in theatre today, was a good experiment and might lead us through an instinctive approach to make discoveries about the play and building just as much as the disciplined OP relationship with scholarship. Surely the point of building a working model of the Globe was to discover things scholars had not imagined or grasped from the written records. 'Free-hand' play revealed many aspects of how the space might have worked originally.

Clearly, it was always going to be a place which would have to have a relationship with theatre scholars and artists, and make some kind of friendship between those generally antagonistic groups; at least they were quite antagonistic and fearful of each other when I began. The scholars who had owned the project, much more than we artists, were very fearful that we were not going to see it through as the scholarly experiment, which people like Andy [Gurr] and John [Orrell] had sold to their fellows all around the world.

C C: Did you find those principles a restriction or did you feel liberation within them, like the structure of a sonnet, for example?

M R: Eventually, great liberation within them but at first they were very difficult. They were unusual, playing *Henry V* (1997), for example, without his costume getting worn down at all during the course of the play. I had played it a few years before in New York. When he was a young man Henry was shot with an arrow through the eye piece of his helmet and it came through his cheek and out. Because I felt my face was a bit gentle for Henry V, I had a scar painted on my face when I played it. I had always done naturalistic things like that to bring myself to the character. That naturalistic makeup was deemed to be not really right for this space, so I had to change my normal way of playing the part, of approaching and believing in myself as the part. I had to become a storyteller as well as a part inside the story. That is just a little example of the challenge to acting practices.

The practical hurdles, like strewn rushes all over the floor, were a much larger challenge. Of course, for me, I understood why we were imposing these disciplines. I had thought them through and agreed to them in principle long before we got to rehearsal. I think it was quite quick sometimes for my fellow actors to take on board why they were going to have to cope with all these extra historical experiments as well as the space itself. The space was so demanding for us, the lack of lighting to focus the audience, the rain, aeroplanes, the magnetic pull of the groundlings, the wild spirit the building seemed to inspire in the audience, whether you were in 'original practices' or in 'free-hand' productions, you had to deal with these things, and there was no book of instructions.

CC: This raises an interesting point; it is the notion of shifting from psychological realism to storytelling. You and the audience are together in a creative process rather than you presenting an artefact to them for appreciation.

MR: Yes, exactly. I think, very quickly, with the first *Winter's Tale* (1997), it became very apparent how vitally important the story was in this space. It was a very beautiful production, but in a few places, it lost the movement of the story, and you could see the audience shifting and wandering. In my five years at the RSC, I had never focused on the story so much. We had focused on finding a certain interpretation of a scene and the director would put together these interpretations into a complete interpretation of the play. In my mind it was a bit like going to see a football match where the two teams had practised an interpretation of the beautiful game. If we went about it that way, rather than actually playing the game, it became apparent very quickly that we were approaching the Globe in the wrong way. We needed to make interpretive choices, but the choices were only how best to serve the story, so it could be played with the audience in one time, one space. They were hungry for the story itself, not a story about the story.

CC: The RSC approach you were describing presupposes that you know the story already whereas this does not. It assumes that you may be coming to it fresh, for the very first time.

MR: Yes. The magic of it is that if your players 'play' like they have never experienced it before, they will convince the audience that the story is actually happening for the first time. To be fair, there are many RSC approaches, and the story approach I am describing was something I learned at the RSC when playing Hamlet two hundred times for them. I found if I came out speaking 'to be or not to be' as if it had not been cooked before, but I was cooking it that very moment, ingredient by ingredient, as if the proscenium just happened to find me thinking, 'I've got to a place where I don't know what the hell to do. To be or not to be, that is the question', it provoked a different response from the audience. Shakespeare comes to life when we speak and move with the audience in the present, particularly with the famous speeches like that one. It is one of the only ways to counter the terrible nerves and feeling that there is no point even trying to say this speech when people know it so well and it has been done so well before! But if you actually take it step by step, you know, 'to be or not to be, that is the question'; then imagine the audience saying, 'What do you mean, that is the question?' And go on, 'Whether 'tis nobler in the mind to suffer the slings and arrows of outrageous fortune', there is a sense of dialogue with the audience who are playing the role of Hamlet's conscience at that moment.

This approach really helps the actor to avoid the dreadful pre-cooked explaining of Shakespeare which I can never understand. Of course all this is so much easier when you can see the audience you are speaking to, when actor and audience are not blinded by the light, which was the condition Shakespeare wrote for (even indoors there was candlelight). I now like to imagine moving through soliloquies with an audience like you move through a landscape; over hills, round corners, to dead ends, backing up again, realising you have to go through that river, there, then being wet for a few lines because you have gone through a river and you are in a different place. It is the sense of taking an audience in the present through this text that became paramount.

It also became paramount to say to the actors, 'Don't speak *to* them, don't speak *for* them, speak *with* them, play *with* them.' Eventually, in my last years, I really came to feel that it was not just about speaking, it was about thinking of the audience as other actors, and not only when you were projecting on to them the role of the helpful crowd, like Henry's army or the citizens of Venice at the trial in *The Merchant of Venice*. It was more about the fact that anything they did was like another player on the stage doing something, so they were always there and when you were alone they were your conscience or your soul. A soliloquy suggests that the character speaking has divided into two so the audience becomes that part of you that is so silent and very rarely speaks back, that you long for some guidance from, be it the idea of an ancestor like a grandparent, or a lover who is not present, or at times, enemies.

As I say, many of these things I learned before at the RSC, but the Globe sorted the chaff from the wheat, so to speak. The space told me what was essential and what was just vanity and fashion. There is an enormous pressure on institutions like the RSC, and I was saddened that there was so much antagonism from many of their artists when we opened and were stumbling to find our way. Funnily enough, I believe the Company's Mission Statement of the 1960s, which has dominated its approach since, has the word 'style' in it. The RSC is constantly hunting for its style of Shakespeare. I think the hunt for a style is way off the point. It is so hard to play Shakespeare really well, eight times a week, even if you have a great production, it will not always be great on the night; any more than a great football team will always play well and win. So to be bothering about style rather than the play and the audience, for me, as an actor, does not seem so helpful.

'Original practices' was an enormous release because the world we were concerned with was the Globe Theatre and we did not need to worry about style, the style was the relationship between audience and actor in that building. Our building was demanding our style of play whether we liked it or not because our style was to hold an audience's heart and mind for a few hours in that space. The principles of that world were very clear and could be followed, and therefore we could really focus on playing the story. Now this, of course, drew attacks from people, that we were anti-intellectual and anti-director, that I specifically was. I was demanding something different of directors. I have gone through that intellectual obsession with Shakespeare. I love it and indulge in it often elsewhere than on the stage but it is not helpful for actors, particularly in this playing space. Playing the story spontaneously, speaking it truly, moving it between its hidden and open passages, letting it run, reining it in, this is the work of the actors. Let the audience interpret what is happening because the best interpreted production will die after ten, twenty performances if the actors do not have a way of keeping it alive, by changing it and making it spontaneous. Actors have to learn how to give and take focus, and find new ways of playing the essential situation of the story in this building.

CC: Do you think then that the Globe is an actor's theatre that upsets the hierarchies that are present in theatres?

MR: The Globe is an audience's theatre. Audiences come to a play long after the director and critics have gone. Who is still there? Actors. In mainstream British theatre, I think the Globe does upset some hierarchical concepts. Mostly I think it challenges how we treat audiences in modern theatre architecture and practice. I think the major changes taking place at the RSC, the new predominance of the actor/audience relationship, the stress on ensemble, a thrust stage, international companies, £5 tickets, £10 tickets down at the National – I think the Globe building has affected theatre practices more than people want to admit. This architecture does demand much more from an actor. It demands we get over our fear of the audience; that we convince them eye to eye of our reality, that we light our stage with our voices. It gives the audience a different power. Directors who work at the Globe have to dismount their trained circus ponies and learn to ride wild horses. Audiences want to have something more happen than they did twenty years ago. I do not think they are happy to sit quietly in the dark and admire us with their minds.

CC: That is one of the things I am interested in pointing out, that by placing the Globe and the RSC in opposition, you actually miss the fact that there has been a general movement towards a more participatory kind of theatre.

MR: Yes, companies like Kneehigh and PunchDrunk really break the assumed boundaries between actor and audience. In the Globe the audience is being played upon by each other as well, and one often had the feeling as a player that the consciousness of the audience as a whole was larger than the consciousness of any individual audience member or actor. This is where the Globe's spirit as a building comes into play. The sacred geometry of the architecture generates a particular collective spirit in the people gathered. The group consciousness was very surprising; it would teach you things that were funny, and things that were moving in the play that you never imagined to be so. Then you had the choice as an actor and director whether to suppress a response or employ the response (such as laughter at an unexpected moment). It was much easier to get a sense of where the imaginative energy was from the Globe audience and adjust yourself to make the most of that energy. In fact, the setting of the play was the imaginative energy of the audience. It must be said that there is a lot more humour in a Globe audience than elsewhere. Is that something truly revealed in Shakespeare's writing by the reconstruction? I came to feel it was. I feel the writer wanted to us laugh much more than we do at his plays. We are still a bit Victorian in our reverence.

Of course, for placing the story so unabashedly between us and the audience, giving it to them completely at times, we were accused of being pantomime-like or selling-out to the audience. There was a big debate among us as well, right from the start, about what was right or wrong when responding directly to the audience. To find our measure we had to make mistakes and explore. I have to really resist the desire to get the audience to do what I want them to do as a storyteller. In *Measure for Measure* (2004/5), for example, I was very keen that they could feel that they were allowed to laugh at me early on, that I had not figured everything out as a character, so I would stumble very early on in my speech and search for my words. John Dove (the director) and I were also very keen to make the Duke very present. If he was someone who planned everything out, it was not such a good story, but if he was someone who woke up one day and thought, 'This hasn't worked. Strictness hasn't worked, liberality hasn't worked, I don't know what to do, I'm going to just leave and then secretly come back and watch and see what happens.' Rather than having the whole thing planned out, he is making it up. We felt that presenting someone who is slightly withdrawn and private, uncertain, was key to the dynamic of the story. I think the text supports this as well.

I do not know how it works, but I find I can be in the story and in the audience making fun of myself in the story at the same time, in certain places in Shakespeare. Now this may sound like a contradiction of what I was saying earlier about not commenting on the story, but if we are all in the story, audiences and actors alike, then I found I could flip between these two seemingly contrary realities as if they were one. The actor and the audience are one group of imaginers somehow. I know we would have arguments about it as actors sometimes. In *Henry V* one heavily armed actor playing a French Duke wanted to jump into the yard and kill a small group of groundlings for throwing things and laughing.

CC: So the actors learned from one another how to use the space? Was there a difference between those actors and those directors who worked on 'original practices' and those who worked on the 'free-hand' productions? Or were they entirely intermixed?

MR: They intermixed. But gradually Tim Carroll became the serious OP director and a core of experienced actors grew around him.

CC: Did one group learn from the other or influence the other?

MR: I think so. Certainly *Twelfth Night* (2002) was directed by Tim [Carroll] right after directing a very radical 'free-hand' *Macbeth* (2001) for the Globe. I feel that many things Tim was praised for in the OP *Twelfth Night*, the movement, wit and singing of the company, he learned or discovered in the 'free-hand' *Macbeth*. He certainly learned that reading theatre critics was a waste of time and he encouraged me to be more radical with 'original practices', which Jenny Tiramani and Claire van Kampen had been urging for a while. I think his experience with *Macbeth* gave him enormous courage to approach 'original practices' much more vigorously. I did *Julius Caesar* (1999) quite vigorously and Richard Olivier was very brave with *Henry V* (1997). Giles Block researched his decisions on use of the yard in *Antony and Cleopatra*. I suppose all the 'original practices' directors were very selfless, since they were never going to get any brownie points in their career for doing OP work.

For the first time with *Twelfth Night* Tim [Carroll] stopped staging things, so we played with free movement. We would settle on certain moves but he never asked us to stay in one place. He gave enormous responsibility to the players. Mike Alfreds's 'free-hand' revival of *Cymbeline* (2001) reminded us all of the benefits of free movement, but Tim brought that spontaneity to 'original practices'. By the time of John Dove's *Measure for Measure*, Colin Hurley and I, who had done a lot of things together with Tim, we just knew that we could move and react to whatever the other did. We were really playing with the ball of the story in many different spontaneous ways. Even Bill Stewart and the older actors did this and it became wonderfully playful and it was a wonderful thing to go out and play with the other actors who had been in these plays for a while. We were creating with an audience, not recreating.

CC: This discussion leads me to ask has your approach to and your opinion of 'original practices' changed over the ten years and, if so, how have you developed in your thoughts?

M R: I think each time we tried something and the audience liked it and it worked in a production, then we thought, 'Well, what can we do next?' and frontiers that were ahead of us included more work with makeup. I can remember when we did *Antony and Cleopatra* (1999) I had a very expensive £800 Asian-hair wig for Cleopatra as I tried to naturalistically convince that I was a woman. For Olivia, in *Twelfth Night*, I had a silk wig that I sat on my head. The twins, I remember when I first saw their silk wigs, I raised questions about them as Artistic Director. I was worried that they were so stylised that it might just remove the audience. But the wigs did not remove them, quite the opposite. I think what happened was as we developed our voice work we developed the ability to vary our voices in order to be more convincing and let the story be carried by the words. There would always be someone who could not see our faces, so the only storytelling tool we could rely on in that space was our voices. The voice can hide and reveal the soul of the play more than the face.

My training at the RSC was very much about understanding the text. Clarity, clarity, clarity was the thing that was being worked on all the time and, as I was saying, you run the risk as an actor of explaining your lines to an audience rather than playing your lines, so I had always been very keen on trying to find the emotional reality behind my line, my need to say the line. Because I have read a lot of Sir Francis Bacon's thoughts on the purpose of theatre in Shakespeare's day, I believe the emotions are of primary value in Shakespeare. They are more primary in Shakespeare, I believe, than the thoughts and actions which follow to reveal their emotional source. But the Globe made me realise that what I had not encountered was the physical beauty of the line; the actual sound of the consonant and the vowel. This is a much more visceral space. Most theatres have the three balconies and the people seated, but this place brings in this yard which has people standing literally up to their necks in the physical reality of the stage. It is the introduction of the physical into the theatre, dropping it down into a physical, visceral level, which is very offensive to some critics and theatre people, and very new. It is so crude, and that crude chaotic cheap energy is in there empowering the space. I feel with Shakespeare that he has a particular story to tell about hierarchical structures of consciousness. From *Love's Labour's Lost* through to *The Tempest*, the senses are not to be denied but often provide the essential key to enlightenment. He will time and again give to the most chaotic character, the Dogberry or the Bottom, a key resolution of the plot, a discovery through their chaos of some major thing that releases the plot. In this way, the sensual, the Caliban, is credited with as much importance as Friar Francis or any of the very enlightened characters that give advice from a subtler consciousness.

This always seemed to me a wonderful thing which this architecture had to say about the playing of Shakespeare, that we should rediscover and 're-love' the sensual, visceral nature of the whole experience, particularly in our age of information, in particular, the language, the sound of Shakespeare. When I entered the profession as an actor, Gielgud and Olivier were rejected by my generation as beautiful speakers who were hiding the truth behind a flamboyant decoration, it was only the stuttering MarlonBrandos that were carrying the truth. Now, of course, this idea carries through to presidents, you know, a president is to be trusted because he cannot put together two words, therefore how could he pull the wool over your eyes? And it carries through in the inarticulateness of so much movie acting. But if you are speaking beautifully, like Martin Luther King did, for example, it does not mean he was speaking falsely. He was trying to move you in a particular direction, but it was not from a false intention or to cover a truth. I was really aware in my ten years here how much, as an actor, I myself had to encounter that prejudice about the sound of speech.

What happened, of course, is that as soon as you drop Shakespeare into the earth and awaken the senses, the collective spirit of Shakespeare has a grounded vessel to enter once again. Many people comment on the unusual spirit of performances in the Globe architecture. I think that welcoming the visceral will also awaken some kind of spirit. That spirit, in my awareness of it at the Globe, is a force of nature; nothing to do with religion or sentiment. The spirit of nature is not sentimental. It manifests itself in visceral aspects; it is ruthless; it is not sentimental at all. The great river falling over Niagara Falls is a very powerful thing, but it has got no sentiment as to who it throws over the falls. I have a feeling that Shakespeare and others in his culture knew much more about harnessing the nature of theatre than we do. I firmly believe that Shakespeare artists in two hundred years will think our work on Shakespeare is as crude as we now feel Tate's Restoration rewrites were. I suspect they will wonder why we did not turn the engine on and employ the ritual energy of the plays. If I knew how to do this I would do it. I have witnessed it on a handful of occasions and wondered why it happened.

CC: There is certainly a powerful sense of a collective audience at the Globe. Do you think that is one of the reasons the 'original practices' productions have been so popular with audiences?

MR: I always felt if this was just an experiment in recreating the past, then it would fail. Part of why the plays occurred originally was that they were connecting with the themes of the day; they were topical. The great benefit of this experiment, as opposed to the many models and drawings of the Globe which preceded it, was that someone had taken the trouble to build it in its actual size, and to get the fire department to allow us to open it so that people could come. If the audiences had come just to watch an experiment it would not have worked; the place had to have some meaning for them, and my job really was to build a community. We had a community of scholars and artists but we did not have a community of audiences, we did not have a community of actors, so we needed to build, with the audiences and actors, a community to work the building, to inhabit it. At first, the seasons were to do with discovering where the community we had was. What had happened to people in the four hundred years since they inhabited a Globe theatre? Well, they wanted to throw things at Shakespeare for one. They wanted to bring him down, which I think was quite healthy.

The very special, unique thing, I may never again experience, was that the audience was learning how to be in the Globe just as we actors were learning. They were changing and growing and finding their feet with us and over time some of their cruder responses went away and they got more interested in other responses to the productions. The building itself was more popular than anything we did in it, which was in one way humbling, and in another way, it was kind of nice, because unlike other theatres, we had a clear thing that we were serving, which was this building, and in that way we were with the audience; they were just like us. Eventually, we had no one coming along pretending to be a member of an Elizabethan audience or throwing things. Quite the opposite, they were still, witty, lively, imaginative, everything you would want from an audience; and a great many of them were taking a chance on their first Shakespeare play, because of the building. What a privilege. Once there was an audience and there was a community I knew they were hungry for the performances to be good. The audience was ahead of us most of the time. They were ahead of my modern theatre community in their hunger for new ideas about the plays.

F K C: I was going to ask what 'original practices' would you have pursued farther here?

M R: Well, I am particularly interested in the space being changed now architecturally. It was built as a laboratory and it was built on the scholarship of the time which lacked any practical experience. Now we have ten years' experience, so for the last six to seven years we have been arguing in the architectural advisory group for changes to the building. We are gradually moving through a painstaking process to publish our findings, get responses back and hopefully get a Board and Trust who will put that at the centre of this project, and rebuild and adjust the space. The interior spaces are not decorated, which is absolutely wrong. There are all kinds of things we know are wrong now, and are very problematic for the artists and the audiences in my opinion. Well, even if they are not problematic, the credentials of the place rest with its faithfulness to research. It must not just kow-tow to modern tastes but keep reintroducing modern tastes to this period; to me there is no point to it if it is not doing that, no point at all.

FKC: What is fascinating about that too is the notion of a body of practice as a body of research.

MR: Yes, that is right, that is the unique idea of the place. But I think that in terms of playing, yes, there are certainly things to be discovered. There is an enormous amount to be discovered about speaking and sound, which has very much fallen away in our modern sensibilities and society. I think we should stick to our guns and explore this period as rigorously as possible and the audiences will follow. They like that and the theatre community will eventually come round to see that too.

NOTE

1 This chapter recounts a conversation between the editors and Mark Rylance which took place at Shakespeare's Globe Theatre on 17 April 2007.

CHAPTER NINE

DEMOCRATISING THE AUDIENCE?

Christie Carson

Is the Globe Theatre a democratic and therefore accessible theatre space? Rather than addressing the 'historical romanticism'[1] of recapturing both Shakespeare's meaning and the experience of his audiences I would like to approach the contemporary romanticism which tends to pervade the Globe Theatre project. In many ways the starting point for this theatre has been to create a sense of drama around itself which reaches out to the local, the national and the international communities. Shakespeare's Globe has a reputation for 'accessibility', which draws together the related but very different ideas of physical, cultural and intellectual accessibility. While I suggest that the merging of these three concepts into one is not entirely helpful it does serve to highlight the expectations of audiences as well as the cultural debates that surround this theatre project.

Critical reception has moved beyond the initial reaction which was to deride the enterprise as a cultural theme park, a cross between Disneyland and a National Trust property.[2] Many critics now see it as a profoundly democratic theatre space that has caused actors and audiences alike to reconsider their ideas about the plays and about the nature of the theatrical event. The Royal Shakespeare Company has been seen to be elitist and monolithic by comparison. Pitting the Globe against the RSC in a David and Goliath struggle presents an attractive image and there is certainly something to be gained from a comparison of the contrasting working methods and actor/audience relationships developed by these theatre companies. However, the placement of these two theatre companies in opposition oversimplifies the nature of the discoveries made at Shakespeare's Globe, which are as much to do with current audience tastes as they are to do with the theatrical practices of the Elizabethan period. The RSC's development since the 1960s has been determined, to a large extent, by conventional actor training and by the tastes of its audiences which have, in turn, had an impact on theatre architecture. The Globe Theatre by contrast began as an architectural and scholarly project where actors and audience members have

8 Colin Hurley as Autolycus in *The Winter's Tale* (2005), Shakespeare's Globe

been confronted by the passivity of their respective roles. To understand the success of the Globe Theatre it is necessary to place this theatre in a wider social, political and theatrical context, acknowledging the profound shift that has taken place in the perceptions and expectations of our current theatre audiences in response to a digital communications world.

The shift towards a more participatory audience began in the 1960s. As Susan Bennett highlights in *Theatre Audiences*: 'In the explosion of new venues, companies, and performance methods, there is a non-traditional theatre which has recreated a flexible actor-audience relationship.'[3] Therefore to see the establishment of Shakespeare's Globe Theatre as being outside this general movement towards readdressing the audience as active participants in the meaning-making process of the theatre is misleading. However, the particular practical hurdles presented by the new building have raised quite fundamental questions that might well not have been asked had the architecture of the space not been a primary concern in the project. The Globe can be seen as an experiment in first principles of the theatre. It should not be seen, however, to represent a huge departure from the general direction of contemporary theatre practice.

Looking at the cultural placement of this theatre it is useful to begin by addressing the position of its seeming rival the Royal Shakespeare Company. For much of the twentieth century the RSC remained largely unchallenged in its position as the preserver and the presenter of legitimate Shakespearean performance. From this position of safety the RSC developed to reflect the changing cultural climate at its own pace and in its own way. It is interesting to note how architecture has taken a central role in that process. In honour of the closure of the Royal Shakespeare Theatre in Stratford for its substantial renovation, Michael Billington charts the shifting perspective of this long established company:

The Stratford stage, in short, offers a mirror of the times: postwar romantic pictorialism gives way to 1950s heroic individualism which, in turn, is replaced by a 1960s Brechtian collectivism. And, in the 1970s, there is an attempt to reflect a more communal culture in which theatre becomes not just a 'show', but some form of shared experience.[4]

There are many ways in which the RSC can be seen to be monolithic; however, to position this company as immovable and unchanging in the face of audience opinion and cultural change is unjustifiable. If we look again to the architectural changes as an indication of shifting ideas about Shakespearean performance, then the addition of two new theatre spaces in Stratford, not to mention the shift to a variety of London venues, must be seen as evidence of adaptation and change. As Billington points out, these new spaces offered new opportunities to actors and audiences alike: 'The opening of the Other Place in 1974 and the Swan in 1986 also changed the ecology of Stratford. Every actor, director and designer wanted to work in these spaces rather than rise to the challenge of the daunting main theatre.'[5] The fact that the Royal Shakespeare Theatre is now undergoing a thorough restructuring indicates a renewed desire to move with the cultural times. The architectural changes at the RSC have been motivated throughout its history by the desires of the theatre profession and the expectations of audiences. The Festival theatre has continued to house the large and popular productions throughout this time; however, a second strain of more radical and participatory activity began to take place in the smaller experimental spaces. Therefore, the passivity of the mainstage was contrasted by the alternative theatrical practices of the studio theatres starting in 1974.

The interactivity achieved in these smaller spaces in the Globe Theatre is expanded into its main house space. The additional unpredictability that is the result of outdoor performances intensifies that audience interaction, creating a new kind of performative specificity. The architecture of the Globe Theatre inverts the accepted relationship between ticket price and proximity to the stage, reinventing the pre-Restoration norms. Suddenly the passivity of the darkened space is contrasted by a space where actors and audience members are exposed to natural light as well as to wind and rain. The audience is vertical and surrounds the acting space, but it is a divided group, not a uniform mass, and is addressed as such. Tim Carroll points out in the chapter that begins this section of the book that an actor performing on the Globe stage can address all of these audiences at once, or can choose to address a particular group of audience members. The playful relationship between actor and audience and the consciously variable nature of the performance, which acknowledges the conditions of that performance, creates an atmosphere that is enjoyably different for every show.

This variability of performance contrasts dramatically with the established, branded and reliable product model that the RSC developed in the 1980s, as typified by its international franchise of the musical Les Misérables (a model that incidentally was directly emulated by Disney). Where the RSC in the 1980s and early 1990s aimed to present the standard delivery of the industrial model, the Globe audience in 1996 was presented with a shifting performative event that revelled in the unique differences that result from the work of a group of artisans. The formality of the RSC's audience interaction was suddenly contrasted by actors who, in Bridget Escolme's words, were not just 'familiar to us' but were 'familiar with us' as audience members.[6] A visit to Shakespeare's Globe is affected by the time of day, the temperature, the weather, the political moment and the personal circumstances of the individual audience member. While in other theatres these external factors are to a large extent excluded from the performance, at the Globe Theatre they become a part of the theatre-making process.

Two examples taken from the 2005 season illustrate the uniqueness of individual performances at the Globe, but also the means by which a drama that is larger than an individual performance is created. In May of that year I attended the first performance of *Pericles*, when John McEnery played the title role after Corin Redgrave had been forced to leave the production following a heart attack. The audience were alerted to this state of affairs at the beginning of the performance and told by the narrator that 'this one is for Corin'. As a result the performance, which was not well attended, became the theatrical equivalent of St Crispin's Day. 'We few, we happy few' (*Henry V* 4.3.60)[7] that attended helped to relaunch this production after the personal tragedy of the central character/actor. Similarly, the final performance of *Measure for Measure* in October of the same year, Mark Rylance's last on the Globe stage, was charged in a way that was largely dependent on the audience members' knowledge of the importance of the moment for the Artistic Director. This atmosphere was enhanced by the recognition of the many actors, directors and supporters who attended that performance, including a very frail-looking Corin Redgrave, all of whom were in full view of the audience. If there was any doubt about the significance of the day, the final 'curtain call', followed by the parade of gifts that appeared at the front of the stage, and the impromptu speech by Mark Rylance, made the audience very aware of the fact that it was a special performance.

This popular and inclusive approach to the audience is not limited to the activity that takes place inside the theatre building. The Exhibition and Education Departments' remits extend the activities of Shakespeare's Globe to a very wide audience indeed. The annual birthday party held in Shakespeare's honour throws open the doors of the building in a very public way. The exhibition tours that carry on throughout the year mean that there is rarely a moment when the theatre is empty. More often than not several activities are going on simultaneously. This plethora of activity and of audiences in the building stands in stark contrast to the private and formal environment created at the publicly funded theatres. It seems ironic that this very public open-door policy is created in a building that is almost entirely commercially funded.

It would be unfair, however, not to point out that even in the subsidised theatres some changes have taken place to accommodate audience demands for access. The National Theatre has increasingly been moving towards public engagement, presenting itself as a venue not only for the long-established foyer concerts but also, under Nicholas Hytner's leadership, as a venue for public debate. The Travelex £10 tickets and the summer series of free outdoor performances now draw a very large and largely young audience, who might not otherwise attend the theatre. The RSC has been rather more formal in its presentation of public events and has instead moved to develop debates based around the themes of the plays, although the public birthday celebrations and the £5 tickets now available for RSC productions for audience members under twenty-six must be acknowledged.

It is difficult to unpick the relationship between these developing programmes given that the press now reflects the romanticism of the David and Goliath narrative. Charlotte Higgins, in an interview with Mark Rylance in the *Guardian*, enquires:

Does he [Rylance] think the theatre world has adjusted itself in the direction of the Globe? It was doing £5 tickets long before the National Theatre's Travelex season; and now the RSC is revamping its main house in Stratford along Renaissance lines, with a thrust stage that will revolutionise the way the audience and the players interact.[8]

This shift towards critical sympathy for the influence of the Globe Theatre must be seen to be somewhat ironic given early assessments of the Theatre and its achievements. This sense of irony can be seen in Rylance's response: 'I think it's really good that the RSC is changing . . . It would be nice if they acknowledged that we had had a massive effect on them . . . They need a change . . . They have been stuck in a certain way for a long time.'[9] Both the question and this response link very much into the vision of the Globe Theatre as the great theatrical innovator and the embattled underdog of Shakespearean performance. Rylance in this interview goes on to compare the financial situations of the two theatre companies, bemoaning the RSC's complacence given the huge public subsidy it receives. Actor Paul Chahidi similarly supports the notion that the RSC has been influenced by the Globe's work when he says: 'I also think that the new theatre, the Courtyard, is a result of the realisation of the vitality, freshness and engaging nature of the Globe. I am convinced of that.'[10] But the question remains: how do these impressions stand up to evaluation?

In order to understand the shift in audience expectations in the theatre more widely it is useful to draw on Philip Auslander's ideas about 'liveness' as well as his vision of a 'cultural economy . . . in which different media enjoy different degrees of cultural presence, power and prestige at different points in time'.[11] In his book entitled *Liveness*[12] Auslander articulates his ideas about cultural dominance:

I propose that audience perception was likely to be most influenced by the dominant media of the time and that spectators would bring expectations based on that influence to bear on their experiences of non-dominant media. In my narrative, television (in its extended form as 'the televisual') assumed the role of dominant medium, while all forms of live performance were relegated to the position of dominated media.[13]

In Auslander's terms the theatre is one of the dominated media, but this does not mean that it is a cultural endeavour without influence:

Even though the theatre has, in my terms, much lower cultural presence and power than, say, cinema or the Internet, it may enjoy greater prestige because it continues to be perceived as a high art form requiring specific educational and cultural capital to appreciate.[14]

So to Auslander the theatre is a dominated but prestigious form.

While in 1999 Auslander believed that a televisual aesthetic determined audience expectations, writing in 2006 his opinion shifts:

It once seemed that television could absorb any cultural discourse and turn it into itself; now, that capability characterises the digital, which has absorbed the televisual among other discourses.[15]

I quote Auslander at length in order to support my supposition that at least part of the Globe Theatre's success has been due to the cultural moment of its creation. The Globe Theatre successfully defied the expectations of critics rooted in televisual traditions by appealing quickly and directly to the new digital aesthetic which demands at least a sense of democracy and fuller individual participation.

While the intimacy of the live theatrical experience at Shakespeare's Globe, stripped of technological intervention, seems to be the antidote to mediated forms of liveness, these performances present an interesting and complex example of the way the new digitally dominant world has influenced audience expectations. The rarefied and unusual nature of the physical and visual experience, and the specific location of the theatre at Bankside, position this type of performance as culturally remote for many. However, the theatre generally has for some time been trying to address, on the one hand, an aging audience that want to hold on to the cultural prestige of a situated private theatre event and, on the other hand, a young audience with no training or experience in the behaviour expected in this kind of communal environment. One significant reason for the Globe Theatre's success, I suggest, is the fact that it has something to offer both of these audiences. While the Globe Theatre was initially set up as a scholarly project, it is run as a commercial venture and has succeeded largely because of the broad appeal it has for a range of new and old theatre audiences.

Returning then to the initial question about the three kinds of accessibility the Globe Theatre purports to offer, how do these claims hold up under scrutiny? To look at the issue of physical accessibility, the central London location of the Globe makes it a relatively easy place to get to. The RSC in Stratford or until recently at the Barbican has, by comparison, appeared more physically remote. But physical accessibility can be extended to include the comfort audiences feel entering and leaving the theatre as well as their comfort during the performance. Interestingly, Shakespeare's Globe does not provide a physically comfortable environment at all. Standing for three hours is physically taxing. Sitting on hard wooden benches is only marginally more comfortable for that length of time and the audience is exposed to the elements as well as the uncomfortable seats. Yet it is easy to leave the theatre during the performance and re-enter at will. For many of the younger members of the audience the ability to move around is prized over the ability to sit still in a comfortable seat. The audience relationship that exists in the Theatre is based partly on the fact that everyone, both on stage and off, must endure the cold or the heat, although some are more protected from the rain. It is interesting that physical discomfort in this environment seems to add to, rather than take away from, the enjoyment of the performance and the vision of the Theatre's accessibility. The physical effort of standing or even sitting in a place of discomfort actually helps to engage the audience in the participatory nature of the event. There seems to be something egalitarian and Shakespearean about a theatre that is open to the elements, forcing actor and audience member alike 'to answer . . . the extremity of the skies' (*King Lear* 3.4.91–2).

The intellectual accessibility that the Globe Theatre appears to offer seems to stem from the combination of a heightened awareness of the comedy in the plays and the increased actor/audience engagement. While David Starkey's ungenerous suggestion during the BBC broadcast of *Measure for Measure* that the audience laughed in the wrong places[16] illustrates an early impression of audience responses at the Globe, increasingly this audience has been seen to be particularly challenging and discerning. In Paul Chahidi's words the audiences 'really want to enjoy themselves'.[17] The idea of going to the theatre prepared to become involved in the meaning-making process stands in contrast to a view of the audience as standing outside the performance trying desperately to understand. What is often seen as a lack of reverence for the texts can also be recognised as an approach to the text which assumes the development of mutual understanding. This is a practical illustration of the critical shift away from a sense that the plays hold meaning that is irreducible. In this view, as W. B. Worthen points out: 'the modern stage becomes a site of interpretation rather than a place of production, a place where "meanings" are found rather than made'.[18] At the Globe Theatre the meaning of the plays is remade each day as a result of the coming together of the actors, the audience, the architecture and the elements both physical and cultural. Addressing the principles that sit at the centre of the Globe project it is important to note the kind of audience that is encouraged to attend this theatre and how that audience is positioned in relation to the action on stage. Shakespeare at the Globe is seen as a popular playwright and the work is approached in a way that retells the stories for a new audience. While this was initially seen as a criticism of the work at the Globe, increasingly this aspect of performance is being seen as one of the Theatre's greatest successes.

This leads to the final kind of accessibility that the Globe Theatre both credits itself with but also is credited more widely with possessing, cultural accessibility. On a basic level this claim can be supported by the fact that the ticket prices are achievable for the majority of the population at just five pounds to stand in the yard. It can also be supported by the audience figures that indicate that 43 per cent of those attending the Theatre are first-time visitors.[19] The already mentioned open-door policy produces an atmosphere which generates an astonishing 97 per cent positive response rate to the question: Did you find the Theatre 'welcoming and accessible'? These statistics are drawn from the Globe's first audience survey conducted in 2006. The survey positions the Theatre not within other cultural events so much as it places it in the environment of 'other London attractions'. The Theatre building is seen as a 'must see' London venue. Interestingly, this places the architecture above the events that go on inside that structure. Of all of the forms of accessibility that circulate around the Globe Theatre the notion of cultural accessibility seems the most interesting and complex.

In many ways I see this debate as inspired by a cultural divide. The Globe Theatre is in many ways an organisation which puts forward its American founder's view of a commercial venture that celebrates Shakespeare as a playwright of the people. Rylance indicates the popularity of the work of the Globe with an American audience: 'The Globe was very popular in America, much more popular than it was ever here in the press or in my theatre community. Mostly actors in my theatre community apologise to me because they haven't been to the Globe.'[20] Of those attending the Globe Theatre from overseas 47 per cent are from the United States. The Globe Theatre project could not exist without the substantial support it receives from American audiences and donors but I suggest that it is the rather un-British attitude towards Shakespeare that this theatre owes most to its American founder. The work of the Globe Theatre goes to the heart of the question of the role of Shakespeare in forming British identity. Bryan Appleyard, writing in the *Independent* in 1995, identified the challenge that was being laid down by this theatre even before it was completed, stating:

From its inception this project seems to have been specifically designed as a provocation or rebuke to English cultural attitudes. Shakespeare is, after all, more than just the greatest creative artist we, or perhaps humanity, has produced. He is also an embodiment of England. What you do to him, you do to us.[21]

There are many members of the theatrical and intellectual communities who would prefer to maintain the exclusive and illusive status of this writer and it is these people who have had the greatest difficulty coming to terms with the presence and popularity of the Globe Theatre. Actors and directors, as Rylance points out, often condemn the Theatre without visiting it. Increasingly, critical opinion in the press has swung towards favouring the work at the Globe because of its popularity with audiences. Meanwhile academic discourse has begun to take the Theatre more seriously as an influential London theatre as the study of performance has worked its way into the mainstream of Shakespeare studies.

Shakespeare's Globe Theatre undoubtedly presents a challenge to established ways of thinking because the space itself is so unfamiliar at first. Given that almost half the audience are visiting the building for the first time the performing conventions and rules of social engagement must be established at the beginning of each performance. As a result this theatre provides an international, intercultural collective space that allows for a negotiated audience/actor relationship rather than a space that reaffirms traditional behaviours and hierarchies. The Globe Theatre confounds many people's expectations because it is intellectually accessible yet challenging; it is both revolutionary and reactionary; it is new and old at one and the same time. The audience and the performers have had to relearn their roles and their relationships in this new space. While some elements of the experience are recognisable, this theatre forces the stark exposition of audience expectations and theatrical traditions.

In thinking about the increasing cultural influence of the Globe Theatre over the ten-year period under discussion, I suggest it is interesting to look at the work and position of the BBC in this cultural debate. While for many years the authoritative television adaptations of Shakespeare used in education were produced by the BBC, relying heavily on RSC actors and directors, increasingly there has been a shift away from this focus. The BBC has broadcast two live productions from the Globe Theatre on the newly established culturally rich channel BBC4. The BBC has also produced its own modern adaptations of the plays in the *Shakespeare Retold* season. Most recently, when the World Service produced a broadcast performance of *King Lear* to go out on the four-hundredth anniversary of the royal performance of the play, Boxing Day 2006, to the largest single audience of a Shakespeare performance in history, the producers chose to record that performance at the Globe Theatre. Rather than an undiscerning audience this production recognised that at the Globe Theatre those in attendance would produce a more engaged and sensitive response than in a conventional indoor theatre. Watching the audience on that occasion I can attest to the fact there was a sense of collective responsibility in the audience for maintaining a level of engagement that is unparalleled in my theatre-going experience. The audience had clearly come to be part of the performance not just to listen to it.

The intervention of the BBC in the debate around the cultural placement of the work of the Globe Theatre I think is important. The Globe Theatre has presented work over the years that has appalled as many people as it has enthralled; however, the essential work of this theatre must be its ability to force a reassessment of the fundamental definition of what theatre is and what the theatrical experience should entail. How Shakespeare should be approached by an actor has been largely redefined by the experiments on the Globe stage. The role of the audience has moved in new directions and audiences have had the opportunity to readdress what they want from the theatrical experience. The remit of the BBC to inform, to educate and to entertain which has fuelled public-service broadcasting for half a century has been adopted, to a large extent, by this unconventional commercial theatre. The publicly funded theatres, on the other hand, seem in some ways to be holding on to earlier (and ironically later) forms of theatrical production and an industrial sense of a commercial product rather than a genuine engagement with the current cultural debate. What the Globe Theatre has done to a large extent is to open up a range of theatrical performance styles to choose from, introducing competition in Shakespearean performance. The Royal Shakespeare Company and the National Theatre are no longer the only venues for classical theatre, and the style of acting that these theatres have nurtured and developed over many years has been presented with a radical alternative. This new approach fundamentally challenges the hierarchical and formal nature of theatre-making in the English tradition. It also sets up a potentially interesting debate about the role of theatre in society as an influential, even if not dominant, force.

The work of the Globe Theatre has destabilised what had been seen as accepted truths about Shakespearean performance. In this way it must be seen to be a success insofar as it has opened up new possibilities for the future of British theatre. This Theatre has altered not only the audience response to the theatrical event but has also pointed out the limitations of current critical approaches which do not address the specificity that is required to interpret a single Globe performance (rather than a production) within a wider cultural and theatrical context. Shakespeare's Globe has therefore succeeded through a combination of factors. Partly it has been supported by a general shift away from cultural and intellectual hierarchies, and this has been combined with a desire in audiences for increasing physical closeness and a sense of community. The push for a sense of democratic participation, as well as a truly live and unpredictable experience, comes from both embracing and rebelling against the dominance of a digital world. The changes taking place in terms of the position of Shakespeare in cultural and educational policy, as well as the need for a public debate about the nature of British identity, have all also helped to further the development of this uniquely placed theatrical enterprise.

Howard Brenton, whose play In Extremis was performed at the Globe Theatre in 2006 and again in 2007, expresses his opinion about the importance of the Globe's role in the face of these social changes:

By understanding how the Globe works, a new theatre can be imagined . . . It may encourage playwrights to turn from the solipsism of individual alienation that has dominated the best new writing of the past decade. If we follow the Globe rules in play-making, we can rediscover public optimism. Out of the old wooden theatre, something new.[22]

It seems ironic that the free-market model which the Globe Theatre puts forward has somehow managed to develop a collective spirit of engaged public debate that has largely disappeared from the publicly funded theatres. The important social role this theatre has played is something that critical writing has failed to fully address. By presenting an alternative to the established model of Shakespearean production, the Globe Theatre has destabilised the centrally funded, controlled and authorised model established by the publicly funded theatres. Shakespeare has to some extent been freed of his institutional position by this theatrical 'upstart crow'.

NOTES

1 W. B. Worthen, quoted in Bridget Escolme, *Talking to the Audience: Shakespeare, Performance, Self* (London: Routledge, 2005), p. 16.

2 For a further discussion of this line of criticism through the work of Dennis Kennedy and W. B. Worthen see the Introduction to Part III.

3 Susan Bennett, *Theatre Audiences: A Theory of Production and Reception* (London: Routledge, 1997), p. 19.

4 Michael Billington, 'The Final Curtain', *Guardian* 28 February 2007, p. 23.

5 *Ibid.*

6 Bridget Escolme, *Talking to the Audience*, p. 19.

7 *The Norton Shakespeare*, Stephen Greenblatt et al. ed. (New York and London: W. W. Norton, 1997). All subsequent references are to this edition.

8 Charlotte Higgins, 'Praised and Confused', *Guardian*, 24 February 2007, p. 29.

9 Rylance, quoted in *ibid.*

10 Paul Chahidi, interview with the editors, 16 February 2007.

11 Philip Auslander, 'Is there Life after Liveness?' in *Performance and Technology: Practices of Virtual Embodiment and Interactivity*, ed. Susan Broadhurst and Josephine Machon (Houndmills: Palgrave Macmillan: 2006), p. 194.

12 Philip Auslander, *Liveness: Performance in a Mediatized Culture* (New York: Routledge, 1999).

13 Auslander, 'Is there Life', p. 194.

14 *Ibid.*, p. 195.

15 *Ibid.*, p. 196.

16 David Starkey's commentary in *Measure for Measure*, Globe Theatre live broadcast BBC 4, 2004.

17 Interview with Paul Chahidi, 16 February 2007.

18 Worthen, 'Staging "Shakespeare": Acting, Authority and the Rhetoric of Performance', in *Shakespeare, Theory and Performance*, ed. James C. Bulman (London: Routledge, 1996), p. 16.

19 Globe Theatre audience survey, 2006 (all subsequent statistics about the audience in attendance are drawn from this report).

20 Rylance, quoted in 'Praised and Confused'.

21 Bryan Appleyard, 'History Rebuilds Itself, this Time as Farce', *Independent*, 9 August 1995, p. 13.

22 Howard Brenton, 'Playing to the Crowd', *Guardian*, Saturday 12 May 2007.

GLOBE EDUCATION AND RESEARCH

INTRODUCTION

Farah Karim-Cooper

Shakespeare's Globe is a centre that accommodates three primary areas of work: Theatre, Education and Exhibition. The work of Globe Education, often neglected by scholarly discourse on the Globe, is inclusive, comprehensive and continuous year round; the focus of Part II of this book is Education's particular relationship to learning and scholarship, as well as its engagement with the work of the Theatre department. The following chapters will demonstrate the particular ethos of Globe Education as an autonomous department, and will demonstrate how its methodology can be viewed in experimental terms.

Before describing what the following chapters set out to do, it might be useful here to discuss the critical enquiry into the role of scholarly research at Shakespeare's Globe. In the Afterword to *Inside Shakespeare: Essays on the Blackfriars Stage*, Paul Menzer asks how 'meaningful research' can be 'pursued' at the reconstructed Globe and at the Blackfriars Theatre. What follows is, loosely, a critique of the methodology that was established when Andrew Gurr was Director of Globe Research. In particular he finds fault with research into the early performances at the Globe undertaken by Pauline Kiernan (former post-doctoral scholar at Shakespeare's Globe). Menzer argues that the approach reflected in Kiernan's work does little to take into account key questions: 'What counts as evidence? What qualifies as discovery? What constitutes documentation? Against what kind of control are "tests" and "trials" conducted?'[1] As already discussed in the introduction to this volume, the language used to discuss research into performance at the Globe has been unfamiliar to many literary scholars. 'Experiments', 'tests', 'discoveries' and 'documentation' are terms not commonly seen in literary approaches to Shakespearean studies, and Menzer usefully interrogates, as this book aims to, the meaning of 'experiment'. Menzer deconstructs Kiernan's methodology of determining 'conclusions' based on the testimony of modern actors and directors using the space. He says, 'the casual deployment of terms derived from scientific experimentation – or anthropological fieldwork – promises empirically demonstrative "finds". Yet in the main, the "experiments" often result in vague invocations of "what works".'[2] Menzer most clearly articulates the more generally held sense of disappointment in the outcomes of practice-based research felt by many literary and theatre-history scholars.

In a similar fashion, Rob Conkie's study of the Globe published in 2005 appears discouraged by the seeming demotion of scholarly input represented by the evolution of Globe Research from Gurr's pursuit of authenticity to the simple documentation of what happened in the space:

Jaq Bessell, the person Gurr secured to succeed him as head of Globe research, fulfilled a very different role to that originally intended as a tester of ideas and hypotheses about original staging. She expertly records the rehearsal processes of the productions between 1999 and 2001 and she provides scholarly input on a range of matters...This work represents a hybrid perhaps of dramaturg, assistant director and researcher, and is obviously a significant distance away from Gurr's original intentions for research at the new Globe.[3]

Conkie's conclusion is that after Bessell left and Education absorbed research, effectively, there was no research mandate at the Globe, 'a fact registered by the loss of the extremely informative *Research Bulletins* for the seasons of 2003 and 2004. With the appointment in 2004, after a two-year hiatus, of Farah Karim-Cooper as Globe researcher, perhaps this type of work will be restarted.'[4] What both Menzer and Conkie are suggesting is that the potential for research at the Globe has never been fully realised, a sentiment I do not contest. However, what these scholars also suggest is an attachment to theoretical ideas about the role of scholarship in experiment-led work investigating the original staging practices of Shakespeare's company, theoretical ideas that have been challenged and found wanting in the first years of the Theatre's operation.

Since my appointment in 2004 Globe Education has restructured the Research department and as a result the methodology, the strategy and the desired outcomes of scholarly engagement. Rather than simply restarting the original approach to research, as Conkie hoped, new approaches to scholars and scholarship are now being devised. Building on and expanding the original purpose of research is crucial, but so is its repositioning within Globe Education. As part of this restructuring process fundamental questions are being asked. Beyond the Architecture Research Group, which stands guard over the reconstructed theatre building, what purpose is there in creating a research programme within a theatre? Why does the Globe need scholars that are not focused on architectural history? If the Globe is, as Dennis Kennedy suggested in 1998, a form of 'edutainment' and a 'heavily mediated touristic site', why would early modern scholars want to work there?[5] Fundamentally, scholarship is central to the Globe and to Globe Education's interest in discovery and its commitment to quality teaching. By developing a broader-based research profile in the academic community, creating a postgraduate community on site and working with the Theatre department to provide dramaturgical support, Globe Research is becoming increasingly integrated into the work of the organisation as a whole, thus enabling critical exchanges between Globe Education Practitioners, academics and theatre artists. The large-scale research tool promised to scholars by Sam Wanamaker has been built; the scholarly community therefore has a responsibility to make itself a permanent home there with its own practitioners researching, lecturing, observing, constructing, teaching, reading and interpreting without denying the ideological and epistemological significance of the entirety of the Globe experiment, which includes the experiments in learning that Globe Education have been conducting.

The first chapter in this section, written by Patrick Spottiswoode, Director of Globe Education, provides the basis for the experiments in learning and research that currently characterise the work of this department and its unique relationship to the work in the Globe space. He traces the history of the individual programmes and establishes a context for Globe Education's fascinating autonomy, while acknowledging the social and cultural factors that have contributed to the development of the department's work, as well as the complexities and challenges faced by the early proponents of a Shakespeare's Globe 'centre'.

In the next chapter, James Wallace discusses his experiences as co-ordinator of the *Read Not Dead* staged readings that were established by Patrick Spottiswoode as a way of decentralising Shakespeare's work through bringing the plays of his contemporaries to a modern audience. Wallace outlines the projected aims of the experiment and the hitherto undocumented outcomes. Wallace is by no means the only co-ordinator of staged readings, but has co-ordinated over thirty of them, and thus is able to comment on the rigour of the process and the actors' responses to working under such extraordinary conditions (one rehearsal in the morning with a performance later that afternoon). Before drawing his conclusions, Wallace spends time usefully discussing the problems faced by producers in the commercial theatre keen to familiarise audiences with non-Shakespearean early modern drama. The volunteer nature of the *Read Not Dead* readings, according to Wallace, provides a significant step towards resurrecting non-Shakespearean drama in a theatrical way, giving greater context to Shakespeare's work.

Fiona Banks, Head of Learning for Globe Education, focuses her chapter more narrowly upon the practice of learning that she has spent the last ten years developing. Reinforcing Spottiswoode's idea that the department's methodology is to place the learner at its centre Banks indicates the way that Shakespeare and the Globe's history, architecture and space have become vehicles through which to develop a student's or teacher's understanding of the plays and period. A former schoolteacher herself, she makes useful parallels between an actor on the Globe stage and a teacher in the classroom: 'both know the challenge of engaging an audience in an environment that is unpredictable and potentially distracting'.[6] Banks traces the developing history of education in Britain over the last ten years and maps on to that the objectives of Globe Education within this shifting environment. She asserts that a key objective of Globe Education is to raise the profile of the theatre artist as an educator. The centrality of practical experimentation in the work of Globe Education consolidates the ongoing engagement between the Theatre and Education departments.

The final chapter in this section returns to the relationship between the Globe Theatre and the academic community. The question left hanging by Menzer's essay and Conkie's book is what should be the fate of Globe Research? This is a question that Martin White's chapter engages with directly, as he sets out the stages of development of Globe Research and looks forward to its importance to the construction of an indoor playhouse at the Globe. He focuses first on the mission of the Architecture Research Group (ARG), which is to oversee and propose any necessary changes to the building in the light of new research. Shifting his focus to historical stage practices, White aligns 'original practices' with the early investigations into historical staging techniques conducted at universities worldwide, highlighting the pitfalls in conducting such experiments in buildings that are not entirely historically accurate.

Following on from the ideas raised in this section Ralph Alan Cohen of the American Shakespeare Center, Virginia, provides a 'rule book' for directors working in reconstructed playhouses in the final section of this volume. What influences his conclusions is his own experience as a theatre director, theatre builder and academic, as well as the Artistic Director of the Blackfriars Theatre. Cohen sits on the Globe's Architectural Research Group where he contributes his knowledge of the reconstruction process but also gleans from the group what the Globe has learned, with a view to reconstructing his own Globe in Virginia. Cohen's ambition mirrors Sam Wanamaker's vision to build, in addition to the Globe amphitheatre, an indoor playhouse. As Spottiswoode's and White's chapters demonstrate, the formerly named 'Inigo Jones' theatre is an exciting prospect. Historically aligning themselves with James Burbage and his 'two playhouse-plan' (to borrow Andrew Gurr's phrase)[7] for the Lord Chamberlain's Men, the Shakespeare Globe Trust and the American Shakespeare Center will be able to conduct theatrical experiments of a more focused nature, as theatre artists and academics will be able to observe the changes to a play and a production as it is transferred from outdoors to indoors. Being able to determine what happens to the play, its running time, the alterations to the design, costume, makeup and actor/audience relationship, as well as the changes to music that will need to take place as a production moves between indoor and outdoor venues, will redirect the aims of research at the Globe and at Cohen's Blackfriars. However, the development of a sophisticated, comparative-research approach to practical experimentation will require an equally sophisticated approach to the analysis of this work.

NOTES

1 Paul Menzer, 'Afterword: Discovery Spaces? Research at the Globe and Blackfriars', in *Inside Shakespeare: Essays on the Blackfriars Stage*, ed. Paul Menzer (Selinsgrove: Susquehanna University Press, 2006), p. 224.
2 *Ibid.*, p. 227.
3 Rob Conkie, *The Globe Theatre Project: Shakespeare and Authenticity* (Lewiston: The Edwin Mellen Press, 2006), p. 196.
4 *Ibid.*, p. 197.
5 Dennis Kennedy, 'Shakespeare and Cultural Tourism', *Theatre Journal* 50, 2 (1998), 175–88.
6 See Fiona Banks, 'Learning with the Globe', p. 159.
7 Andrew Gurr, *The Shakespeare Company 1594–1642* (Cambridge University Press, 2005), p. 10.

CHAPTER TEN

CONTEXTUALISING GLOBE EDUCATION

Patrick Spottiswoode

The Globe is unique among theatres, in my experience, in its commitment to education. From October to April, Globe Education has exclusive use of the stage so that all workshops and courses can include practical work in the theatre. Further stage access is provided during the summer. I do not know of another theatre in the world where stage crews regularly strike a show so that students or teachers can work in the theatre at midnight or at seven in the morning. The Education department is not answerable to the Marketing or Theatre departments. We do not educate for the box office. The Artistic Director and the Director of Globe Education are colleagues. We work in support of each other but also on independent projects for our own particular audiences. The dynamic and creative exchanges between our two worlds enable us to pursue Sam Wanamaker's idea of a maverick theatrical experiment with education at its heart.

EDUCATION FROM THE BEGINNINGS

Globe Education was founded in 1989, eight years before the theatre opened, but Sam Wanamaker had experimented with theatre, education and exhibitions on Bankside since 1972. That year he opened a Museum in a warehouse in Bear Gardens that presented changing exhibitions on topics as varied as blood sports, the Thames watermen and the Clink prison. Few people seemed interested. Bankside was then a deserted stretch of the Thames and most of the buildings were derelict warehouses. Streets were poorly lit and dangerous after dark.

Sam entered into a partnership with the Curtain in Shoreditch in the late 1970s to establish a schools programme in the Museum. The Curtain was an Inner London Education Authority (ILEA) drama centre providing workshops for primary and secondary schools. He extended the Museum into the larger warehouse next door and created an exhibition on Elizabethan and Jacobean Theatres with a focus on

Bankside. Children were greeted by an 8-foot-tall bear, a prop from the National Theatre. Models of the Rose, Swan, Globe and Blackfriars were borrowed or commissioned and put on display.

The Cockpit Arts Workshop, another drama centre north of the river, decided to throw out its ply-board working reconstruction of the seventeenth-century Cockpit Theatre stage. Sam hired a team to pull down the Cockpit, transport its 'timbers' across the river and build it into the upstairs room of the larger warehouse. An intimate Jacobean theatre that could hold up to a hundred people now sat above the exhibition in Bear Gardens. In years to come Al Pacino would use the theatre as the setting for the opening of *Looking For Richard*.

Relations with the Curtain soured in the early 1980s. ILEA staff left in 1983 taking their exhibits with them. I was employed in April 1984 to re-establish a presence for the project on Bankside. As well as a new exhibition, Sam wanted to develop an education programme that would attract university students and the general public in addition to school groups. This was at the time when Southwark Council had reneged on its agreement to provide the land for the new Globe. Sam wanted to maintain a presence in Southwark during the campaign to fight the Council's decision.

I was also tasked with restoring relations with Southwark Cathedral. Sam had established an annual Shakespeare Birthday event in the Cathedral which included a sermon – an idea copied from the annual Shakespeare birthday sermon given at Holy Trinity in Stratford-upon-Avon. In 1974 he asked Warren Mitchell, who had acted for him in *The Threepenny Opera* in 1956 (the UK's first Brecht production), to give the sermon in the persona of his infamous comic TV character, Alf Garnett.[1] The Bishop and clergy walked out in high dudgeon and refused to speak to Sam or celebrate the birthday with him again. It was therefore particularly poignant when Warren Mitchell returned to the Cathedral pulpit in 1994 to speak at Sam's memorial, one Jewish actor recognising the feat of another who would be given his own plaque next to the Shakespeare monument in the Gentile Cathedral.

The awkwardly named Bear Gardens Museum of the Shakespearean Stage opened in autumn 1984. Poster information and models traced the development of theatres in London from the Red Lion Playhouse of 1567 to the closing of the theatres in 1642. The last image was a woodcut depicting the beheading of Charles I in 1649 on an outdoor scaffold stage surrounded by a groundling crowd.

Placing the Globe in a wider theatrical context had always been of importance to Sam and to Theo Crosby (the architect who joined Sam in 1971 and who helped him shape his vision for the new Globe Centre). If the Globe were to become the 'custodian' of early-modern-theatre history in London it would be important for visitors to understand that not all playing spaces were outdoor thatched wooden Os and that from 1608 the King's Men had secured the indoor Blackfriars Playhouse for winter performances. Scholars advising Sam and Theo were keen advocates of building an indoor theatre. As no plans for the Blackfriars survive, plans for an indoor theatre discovered at Worcester College, Oxford, by Don Rowan, who believed them to be by Inigo Jones, were chosen for the second theatre.

Sam's campaign led to the discovery of the Rose foundations in 1989. The Museum of London's archaeologists would not have spent so much time examining the Elizabethan 'layer' at the expense of finding remains of Roman Southwark had Sam not consistently drawn people's attention to Bankside's theatrical past. It must have been galling for him to see the great and the good suddenly take interest in Bankside once the Rose foundations were discovered, and even more galling to be excluded from discussions regarding the Rose's future by the first rather ramshackle troupe of Rose Trustees.

The Bear Gardens Museum had a modest bookshop and a counter that doubled as a theatre bar. The amateur Bankside Theatre Company was presenting short seasons in the Cockpit Theatre when I arrived, but professional companies began to stage plays by Shakespeare and his contemporaries too. In 1985 a company called Phoebus Cart produced *Othello* in the Cockpit. Iago was played by its Artistic Director, Mark Rylance.

A second upstairs room was used for workshops, rehearsals and as a studio theatre with an audience capacity of thirty-five. On some evenings there were performances in both 'theatres'. With two theatre spaces, an exhibition, a shop, coffee bar and an education programme, the Bear Gardens Museum was a dilapidated doll's-house version of the Centre that Sam and Theo were planning for the future.

GLOBE EDUCATION

Globe Education has been developing programmes since 1989 for three different but not mutually exclusive audiences: school students and teachers; undergraduates, graduates and scholars; and the general public. The department has grown steadily, as its skills have developed, from three full-time staff and a few freelancers in 1989 to twenty-three full-time staff, fifty freelance Globe Education Practitioners and two researchers on PhD studentships.

It is fitting that a theatre that has shed so much light on the importance of the audience should place such emphasis on education and should engage with a diverse range of audiences. The new Globe celebrates an audience at play in a way that the Globe which Sam saw in Chicago in 1934 did not. The Chicago Globe, and the Shakespeare Festivals that followed, were more concerned with creating an Elizabethan stage façade for the actor to play against than with exploring the audience's place in the theatre. The stage was seen as the only place the play 'happened'. The very titles of my student text books emphasised the stage: *Early English Stages*, *The Elizabethan Stage*, *The Shakespearean Stage*, *The Jacobean and Caroline Stage*. Theatre education departments similarly focused their efforts on introducing audiences to the play on the stage rather than using the play to explore the worlds of their audiences. The spotlight was on the actor. Audiences remained in the dark, unseen.

A PROGRAMME FOR THE PUBLIC

As the Globe took shape and as the Friends of Shakespeare's Globe grew in number, regular seasons of events for the general public were organised around themes chosen for the *Read Not Dead* series of staged readings. We succumbed, I confess, to using Shakespeare's name as a marketing tool for seasons of lectures, seminars, readings and events: for example *Shakespeare and Spain*, *Shakespeare, Gresham and the City* or *Shakespeare Framed*.

We seek themes that can involve a variety of audiences. *Shakespeare and Shoes*, chosen for 1998–9 to prepare for the (ill-fated) opening of the Millennium Footbridge, celebrated the shoemaking industry in Southwark and the pedestrian groundlings whose importance had been one of the most startling discoveries of the Globe's opening seasons. Readings were staged of *The Cobbler's Prophecy*, *The Shoemaker's Holiday* and *A Shoemaker, A Gentleman*. A shoe-design project and workshop exercises on the pentameter's five feet were developed for schools. The presence of the cobbler acquired particular resonance in Mark Rylance's 1999 production of *Julius Caesar* as the 'Commoners' of the play mingled in the yard with the groundlings before climbing up on to the stage during the opening scene.

Themes have complemented theatre seasons, commemorated anniversaries and have explored political and cultural issues. While *Othello* was not staged at the Globe until 2007, increasing animosity towards Muslim communities in the UK post 9/11 prompted Globe Education in 2004 to mark the four-hundredth anniversary of the first recorded performance of *Othello* with an exploration of Anglo-Islamic relations in the sixteenth, seventeenth and twenty-first centuries.

Shakespeare and Islam ran for eighteen months with cross-cultural, interdisciplinary, inter-faith and cross-generational projects. *There's Magic in the Web*, a devised piece based on *Othello*, toured schools in cities around the UK. *Othello* workshops in English, Arabic and British Sign Language were led for children with special educational needs. Students around the world created designs, inspired by Islamic designs, for the handkerchief from Egypt 'spotted with strawberries' which Othello gives to Desdemona. Ninety were hand-embroidered and sewn together to create the lining of a Tent for Peace – now used for storytelling. Over four hundred Southwark primary and secondary students presented *Othello* on the Globe stage

9 Southwark schoolchildren perform a scene from *Othello* as part of the annual *Our Theatre* production (2004)

as the annual *Our Theatre* production (see figure 9). To demonstrate the power and presence of the handkerchief as a character unto itself, this production deliberately had a hand-embroidered love-token clearly visible at Desdemona's first entrance in 1.5, unlike many productions in which a small modern hankie is not seen until 3.3, thus marginalising its role in the play.

Finally, lectures on European relations with Islamic lands in the Renaissance period were complemented by staged readings of plays featuring Moors and Turks. Photographs of Islamic lands by Peter Sanders were projected on to the walls of the Globe, enfolding the theatre, for the launch of Islam Awareness Week.

As Shakespeare's Globe does not receive Arts Council funding, it requires sponsorship to fund these initiatives and other commissions that enrich particular seasons such as new sonnets, translations of plays by Ariosto, Lope de Vega and Lessing or a new score by Claire van Kampen for the Asta Nielsen silent film of *Hamlet*.

In 1996, Thomas Middleton's poem *The Ghost of Lucrece* was staged in the Cockpit for a season that explored writers' responses to *Lucrece*. It was directed by Claire van Kampen (who also composed the music) and designed by Jenny Tiramani. Joy Richardson played Lucrece, in a modern white hospital gown and asylum straitjacket. Mark Rylance played the narrator as Middleton, dressed in Jenny's first experiment with handmade period clothing. The conversation between past and present looked forward to several of Claire, Jenny and Mark's experiments with 'original practices'.

'READ NOT DEAD'

Organised from the outset by Deborah Callan, now Head of Globe Education and Head of Events, *Read Not Dead* was initiated in 1995 to shed light on plays written between 1567 and 1642 that were *not* by Shakespeare. A few of us were unhappy with the name 'Shakespeare's Globe' on the grounds that it was misleading and might encourage the project to become too Shakespeare-centric. I had insisted on Globe Education as a department name and not Shakespeare's Globe Education for the same reason. 'Shakespeare's Globe' had helped to differentiate the Bankside Globe from the one in Shaftesbury Avenue but the latter was renamed the Gielgud Theatre in 1994 – a change that honoured Sam, who had died the year before, as well as Sir John.

Colleagues agreed to experiment with a pilot season of four readings. One of them was *Westward Ho!* and, shamelessly, we approached members of the West family – Prunella Scales, Timothy West and Sam West – who were supporters of the project, to take part. The season's success convinced us to embark upon a thirty-year project to stage readings of all the non-Shakespeare plays of the period with professional casts and to record them for the archive. The collaborative importance of the audience has been evident from the outset. Actors who curse themselves during the read-through for wasting a Sunday over a dead script leave the theatre after the performance wondering why the play has suffered such neglect. Twelve years on we have heard over one-third of the extant plays from the period.[2] We hope the readings will encourage other theatres to experiment with productions, or at least readings, of the lesser-known plays from the early modern period. All plays in the recent RSC 'Jacobethan' season had already been staged as readings at the Globe.

Theatres tend to fall back on the same non-Shakespeare plays via the theatrical 'hubs' of Marlowe, Jonson and Webster and then rarely experiment much beyond *Dr Faustus*, *Volpone* and *The Duchess of Malfi*. We have, sadly, grown accustomed to the two very different plays that are the two parts of *Tamburlaine* being conflated into one production on grounds of box-office economy. I long to see a production of Webster's *Appius and Virginia* rather than yet another production of *The Duchess of Malfi*. In 2000, I eagerly attended a seminar on 'the non-Shakespeare repertoire' at the Shakespeare Theatre Association of America conference only to discover 'non-Shakespeare' meant shows like *A Christmas Carol*.

Read Not Dead has brought us into contact with scholars who are working on plays in our series but who may have never seen a production of the play before.[3] The readings also brought many actors into the fold at a time when there was considerable suspicion about the project within the profession. Deborah Callan sees *Read Not Dead* as offering a valuable training for young actors who learn from working alongside more experienced colleagues. The series was the first step in a developing initiative to support the training of young actors and directors. The series also prompted the Globe Quartos editions that provide audiences, directors and academics with accessible and affordable copies of some of the plays. First-time editors were encouraged to step forward and were mentored by a prestigious editorial board.[4]

'LIVELY ACTION' FOR SCHOOLS

John Marston, and not William Shakespeare, provided the name for Globe Education's schools programme. In his letter 'To the Reader', Marston apologises for publishing *The Malcontent* as it had been written 'merely to be spoken'. All he hopes is that his readers will remember 'the pleasure it once afforded' them when it was presented with 'the soul of lively action'.[5]

It is difficult for students, who may feel that Shakespeare wrote his plays 'merely to be examined' and who probably have never been to a theatre, to explore the 'soul of lively action' as they confront rows of words on rectangular pages on rectangular desks in rectangular classrooms. It is also difficult for teachers who do not have experience of teaching drama to encourage students to approach the plays as words spoken in action.

Shakespeare's place in the school curriculum was gaining prominence as the Globe was taking shape in the 1990s. Standard attainment tests that developed into the current 'Key Stages' in 2002 meant that Shakespeare and the Globe were of particular interest to primary-school teachers who were teaching 'The Tudors' and to secondary-school teachers who had to prepare all fourteen-year-olds for a compulsory Shakespeare test. Crowds who gather around the Globe stage are asked to consider, literally 'from many sides', the personal and/or political implications of words in action. It is difficult for students to consider a play's resonance for themselves or their community if they are only being questioned about the language, characters or themes within a particular scene.

Theatres have an opportunity to introduce students to the 'soul of lively action'. Shakespeare's place in the curriculum, nationally and internationally, means that Globe Education is inundated with requests for one-day or half-day workshops to enhance the students' visit to see the Globe. Globe Education Practitioners rouse words into action and help students to see the theatre 'feelingly' and not just digitally. However, our most ground-breaking work takes place in cross-curricular and longer-term projects. Fiona Banks writes eloquently in this book about the role of Globe Education Practitioners (GEP) and about our experimental and experiential approaches to teaching and learning that support different areas of the curriculum. In 1997 we rather meekly asked actors in the Theatre Company and elsewhere if they might like to consider training to become GEPs. There is still a stigma among actors in some theatres about working for education departments. The tables here have now turned. Actors from Globe Theatre companies rather meekly enquire if they might become a GEP. Having shared the same light with audiences in the Globe, they are considerably less nervous of sharing the same light with students in a workshop room.

GLOBE EDUCATION IN SOUTHWARK

Long-term relationships involving outreach and performance work on site are possible with London and, particularly, Southwark schools. Our teaching practice would be a lot poorer without the experience of creating sustainable projects with local nursery, primary, secondary and special educational needs (SEN) schools. Bankside attracts people from across London, the UK and the world but Sam was always insistent that the Globe should remember its Southwark community. Southwark stretches southwards to Dulwich and eastwards to Bermondsey. It is now home to hundreds of diverse communities and so our challenge is to engage with all sectors of our constantly evolving multicultural community. With up to sixty young people arriving monthly from overseas requiring a secondary-school place, and more than a hundred languages spoken, Southwark is a borough that is constantly in transition. We have been working to build a solid relationship with the community over the last twelve years. The Globe's opening Festival included the first annual production funded by PricewaterhouseCoopers and given to a packed house by over four hundred students from Southwark primary, secondary and SEN schools. It is called, symbolically, Our Theatre.[6] The Southwark Community Projects team has four members of staff who seek to involve every nursery, primary, secondary and SEN school in a project over a three-year period, creating community ownership and pride in a theatre that inevitably has a national and international profile.

GLOBE TO GLOBE

'The child in Stornoway' was invoked in committee meetings in the 1980s as representing all students around the world who would not be able to visit the Globe. The word 'Internet' did not appear in the OED of 1993, the year Sam died. The

World-Wide Web, however, has enabled us to share our practice internationally and create distance-learning projects with schools and universities across the globe.

William Caxton defended print from those who preferred hand-copied texts because movable type allowed more people to have the book 'at once'. The Web is an almost perfect vehicle for enabling people around the world to follow the ephemeral act that is theatre even more immediately than Caxton's 'at once'. GlobeLink – born out of a campaign involving schools around the world to raise money for the 'heavens' over the stage – houses Globe Education's interactive Web resources for students, practitioners and scholars, sharing insights and discoveries through distance-learning projects, podcasts and blogs.

The Web came just at the right time. I was loath to produce the ubiquitous education pack for each play. Most packs reduce the 'soul of lively action' into poorly written synopses, turgid notes on 'characters' and 'themes' and an array of photographs of very past productions. The pack promotes a sponsor's logo on the cover to prove that funding has been put to educational use. Typically, the lion's share of the sponsorship is siphoned off to fund the production. The web has allowed us to abandon teaching packs and explore more interactive schemes that celebrate process and performance. *Adopt an Actor* takes advantage of new technology to enable students to follow an actor's evolving journey from first rehearsal to last performance. Students ask questions of their adopted actor and receive weekly bulletins. GlobeLink now houses an archive of interviews with actors from every production since 1998.

HIGHER EDUCATION

American universities were the first to commission courses from Globe Education in the late 1980s.[7] Semester courses for liberal arts majors included lectures, seminars, production visits and, crucially, involved the students working in small groups with professional directors before presenting scenes on the Cockpit stage. The combination of theory and practice provided students with a more experiential approach to the plays than they could get on campus.

Since 1997 undergraduates have been able to present scenes on the Globe stage (see figure 10). Playhouse practice is incorporated into courses provided for two hundred undergraduates every year with growing interest from German and UK universities. Students attend Globe productions and work with resident faculty including 'Masters' of text, voice, movement, clothing and music. Having theatre staff on site has allowed us to develop specialist courses for theatre majors such as a one-year intensive course for conservatory actors from Rutgers University or summer schools for groups like the Young Shakespeare Company from the Shakespeare Globe Centre, New Zealand. The Conference of Drama Schools brings students

10 A Rutgers movement session on the Globe stage

from the leading drama schools in the UK to the Globe in an annual Sam Wanamaker Festival and several students have gone on to be cast in Globe productions.

The growth of undergraduate courses and the creation in 1999 of our first MA in *Shakespeare Studies: Text and Playhouse*, with King's College London, enabled Globe Education to employ a full-time Lecturer. While *Text and Playhouse* is an English Department MA, students also benefit from working with theatre practitioners at the Globe. They are never able to forget that plays were written for the stage, especially as their study carrels are the dressing-tables the actors use during the theatre season. MA modules and a collaborative MA with King's College London's Education Department are helping to develop a significant graduate presence on site.

There are potential scheduling conflicts between the schools and higher education programmes. The Shakespeare Globe Trust continues to invest in new workshop studios for Globe Education but there is only one Globe stage. The current approach to time-tabling was born out of a mix of ideology and need, arising from the Bear Gardens days when all workshops included work on the Cockpit stage. Priority is given to primary and secondary schools in the mornings and early afternoons. Undergraduate and graduate students arrive late afternoon and often work on site and stage until eleven in the evening. It is a logistical Rubik's Cube for the operations team.

RESEARCH AND GLOBE EDUCATION

In 1996, Andrew Gurr (former Director of Globe Research) secured a Leverhulme
three-year grant for Reading University to support research into Globe productions. The grant funded two Post-doctoral Research Fellows to be 'rapporteurs' for
each production, sitting in on rehearsals and producing *Research Bulletins* at the end
of each season. The funding also secured video equipment and the recording of
multiple performances of productions from three fixed-point cameras. Most theatres film one performance for archive and for understudy use. Globe productions
are recorded specifically for research purposes. Gurr knew that performances at
the Globe would evolve and change from day to day depending on the audience,
weather, time of day. Multiple recordings thus help trace the development of productions and provide valuable research material for scholars visiting the Globe's
archive and library.

When the Leverhulme grant ended and when Gurr retired as Director of Globe
Research, a Head of Research continued to provide dramaturgical support, write
bulletins and supervise the library and archive. However, it was impossible for one
person to cover all rehearsals and, without funding, the Globe could not afford
further 'rapporteurs'. In these early years, research at the Globe focused on Globe
productions, recording use of the space by different actors and directors. When the
Head of Research left for a new post, Globe Education began to oversee research
at the Globe. Farah Karim-Cooper was appointed Lecturer in 2004, and was given
the task of re-establishing a research culture. Two researchers on PhD studentships
are now based at the Globe. Since 2004, we have sought to extend research beyond
particular Globe productions and the architecture of the building as the introduction
to Part II of this book details.

Sam always hoped that the Globe would become a meeting place for scholars,
students and theatre artists. The current trend within Higher Education to promote
'knowledge transfer' is working both ways, with practice-based research undertaken by theatre practitioners at the Globe feeding as well as being fed by the
Academy. Globe-inspired approaches to the teaching of Shakespeare and the creation of cross-curricular projects in primary and secondary schools are enlivening
students' encounters with Shakespeare's plays and are liberating the 'soul of lively
action' that Marston feared would lie imprisoned on the page.

Sam was a maverick and the Globe was a maverick idea. However, the changing
place of Shakespeare within the curriculum, interest in site-specific theatre, shifts
in scholarly discourses, the Internet and the heritage industry not to mention the
regeneration of Bankside, with the Tate Modern showcasing contemporary art,
have all contributed to the Globe's popularity. I doubt if the Globe would still
be here today if it had opened, as Sam hoped it would, in the 1970s or 1980s.

The time would not have been right. It would have suffered the same fate as the St George's Elizabethan Theatre in Tufnell Park that competed for attention with Sam's Globe in the 1980s. St George's opened in 1976 and was closed by 1989.

As Bankside is slowly swallowed up by corporate London and as some of the old 'liberties' are being colonised into an area called 'More London', it is imperative that the Globe retains a maverick spirit, continues to sit happily in the margins of the cultural establishment, challenges rather than comforts ideas about heritage and offers much more than more Shakespeare.

NOTES

1 Alf Garnett was a racist bigot in *Till Death Us Do Part*, which inspired the US series *All in the Family*.
2 Maggy Williams has provided programme notes for all the readings. John Wolfson, a collector specialising in early modern plays, has recommended titles and lent quartos and folios of plays for exhibition. His collection of Shakespeare sources, of pre-Restoration quartos and folios and of Restoration adaptations of Shakespeare's plays will form the nucleus of the new Globe Library.
3 Globe Education also stages readings especially to support editions of plays, for example *Mahomet and his Heaven* for Matthew Dimmock's Ashgate edition (2005).
4 Nick De Somogyi's transcripts for actors and audiences developed into the Globe Quartos series published by Nick Hern Books. See Appendix 6.
5 *The Malcontent*, ed. Bernard Harris, New Mermaids (London: A. and C. Black, 1967, 1993).
6 In *Our Theatre*, each school works on a 'chapter' of a play before coming together to present the whole play at a festival. It has provided the model for festivals in Manchester and St Louis, Shakespeare Lives! programmes in Buffalo and North Carolina and for Globe Education Academies in Davis and Baton Rouge.
7 Ralph Alan Cohen and Thomas Berger commissioned these for James Madison and St Lawrence Universities in the late 1980s.

11 *Read Not Dead* staged reading of *Philotas*

CHAPTER ELEVEN

'THAT SCULL HAD A TONGUE IN IT, AND COULD SING ONCE': STAGING SHAKESPEARE'S CONTEMPORARIES

James Wallace

Of the thousands of plays that were written for professional theatre companies between 1576 and 1642 some 470 survive to add to those by Shakespeare.[1] 'The majority of these plays are rarely published or read, let alone dug out from the graveyard of the bookshelf to have life breathed into them again by performance. The *Read Not Dead* project aims to stage readings of them all. In doing so it investigates in practical ways the largest body of primary evidence of early English theatre that there is. After describing the project's development, and the nature of the event, I will explore whether the staging of these readings suggests anything about staging processes and audiences then, and if there are new ways to approach this kind of work now. I have co-ordinated, acted in or seen half of the 160 readings staged so far, so this essay is a partial as well as a personal survey of a project that is now twelve years old.

THE PROJECT

The first aim of the project was to give staged readings to all the surviving plays by Shakespeare's contemporaries, by whom I mean all those who wrote plays for professional theatres, both adult and juvenile, from the time of the opening in 1576 of the first public playhouses until the closure of all theatres in 1642. My figure of 470 extant plays excludes masques, pageants, entertainments, literary translations, academic and Latin plays, and closet plays. *Read Not Dead* has also allowed the staging of 'bad' Shakespeare quartos, adaptations of Shakespeare (from Restoration versions to a staging of Edward Bond's *Lear*), of narrative poems, and a couple of new plays (by Rowan Joffe and John Wolfson). Patrick Spottiswoode had two other motives when he initiated the project. One was to get more actors involved in the whole Globe project, especially after the death of Sam Wanamaker (himself an actor). Patrick wanted to bring in more 'mad blood', and so far over a thousand actors have taken part. His second motive was to keep attention on the whole of the early modern drama. His department is, as he puts it, Globe Education, not Shakespeare Education. It was always part of Sam's vision to explore all aspects of the dramatic arts from that time, both for their own sake (it would still have been a golden age without Shakespeare), as well as to contextualise the plays of Shakespeare within their original conditions. The building of an indoor theatre specifically for Shakespeare's contemporaries is one part of Sam's dream that has yet to be fulfilled. I believe that *Read Not Dead* shows that it remains a worthwhile dream.

There are anywhere from twelve to fifteen readings a year, in three seasons. The summer readings are chosen to complement the Globe Theatre season. The autumn and spring readings are part of seasons of events including lectures, seminars and symposia themed around particular professions, people or places. One drawback of this approach is that the plays in a season have sometimes had little relation to each other. Groups of plays can be chosen that are more tightly bound, that can illuminate each other in a more focused way. This has happened where a particular writer or theatre has provided the theme (James Shirley or the Fortune). These days seasons are being chosen along similar lines (Thomas Middleton, the Blackfriars, boy-company plays). Each reading is accompanied earlier in the day by seminar introductions. Deborah Callan has been the person who has run the project in practical terms (scripts, props, programmes and so on), and she has been the effective casting director to them all.

THE EVENT

At ten on a Sunday morning the actors and co-ordinator meet at Bear Gardens, rehearse the play once through, then perform it at three that afternoon. At the start of the day the co-ordinator can outline briefly the plot, context and style of the play, and alert the actors to its particular demands and opportunities. Props can be assigned and costume or clothing sorted out. As the project has developed, and due to time-pressure, it has become usual practice to give out entrances and exits at this point rather than during the rehearsal. As a result, the rough logic of places (indoors, outdoors, where doors lead to and from) can then be established, and the rehearsal allowed to run more freely. Then rehearsal begins.

In the early days of *Read Not Dead*, there were readings that involved a semi-circle of chairs on stage, with actors simply standing up to act when needed. Though simple, this was never satisfying. Such readings never aspired to the level of a performance. They denied the playwright control of both stage numbers (many of these plays rely on the energy of a crowd scene at their end, for example), and the capacity to create effects by the introduction or removal of characters. By keeping them all on stage this method left the actors without space for preparation before an entrance. It also limited the potential for the actors to rehearse by themselves. This was the greatest shame, because an amazing amount of work can be done simultaneously during rehearsal if the reading is staged with entrances and exits. Away from the main run-through of the play actors can run scenes by and between themselves. Songs and dances can be learned. Stage-fights or bits of business can be practised. Costumes can be sorted out, props prepared and sometimes even made. There is enough time for a co-ordinator to block the play, to sort out changing of furniture, to guide tempo, characterisation, situation and style, and to oversee the telling of the story as the main rehearsal runs; however, the best readings would also give the actors time and space to use their own initiative and creativity away from it.

Some things need to be done in advance: the composition of music, the gathering or making of props, the decision about the 'look' of the play. Sometimes the set is dressed (with drapes, or with garlands and flowers, for example) but that is rarely necessary. Clothing proves to be the most effective way of creating the visual world of one of these plays. Generally, actors are asked to exercise their own responsibility and creativity in fulfilling a dress code. The readings have been overwhelmingly in modern dress, or rather 'current dress' – in itself an original practice. Overall the rehearsal can be fairly manic, often finishing only minutes before the start of the reading. The readings themselves share this energy, one that is necessarily improvisatory and time-pressured, and amplified by the presence of an audience.

The theatre in Bear Gardens is in the style of an indoor Jacobean playhouse. It is small, seating an audience of up to ninety, twenty of those in the gallery. The stage itself is small. The façade of the back wall is two storeys high, with three entrances below. There are two single doors either side of the stage. There is a central double-doored entrance, above which a canopy supported by posts projects a few feet out on to the stage. This canopy is curtained, and so gives a thrusting balcony space above and a discovery or hiding place below. All the doors open inwards from the stage. Above the single doors are curtained balconies reached from behind the stage. It is also possible to climb up to or down from these spaces above from on stage. There are shallow stairs four steps high, leading from the auditorium on to the sides of the stage. The stage itself has a short rail running around its front. This simple, intimate stage, while not a 'best guess' reproduction, provides all the essential elements of the early modern indoor stage, bar a trap.

The co-ordinators, actors and musicians (and stewards) all give their time for free. This volunteer spirit combines with the improvisatory nature of the performances. The readings demand that the actor be extremely alert, listening intently to fellow actor and audience despite having one eye on a script. The audiences, comprising academics, students, actors, friends of the cast and of the Globe, share this attentiveness. They are smart and generous, quick-witted and appreciative. They encourage the actors, and, like the Globe audience, make their presence known, and in so doing help to create the event.

AN EXPANSION OF THE CANON

Each play throws up its own discoveries and questions, but it is also possible to draw some general conclusions from these readings, particularly about the current place of the plays of Shakespeare's contemporaries in the English repertoire. The canon needs constant re-evaluation, otherwise it remains trapped by the preferences and prejudices of the past. Very few of these plays are regularly given professional staging. The theatrical repertoire consists of most of Marlowe, two or three plays by Jonson, and two or three tragedies each from Webster, Ford and Middleton. And that is pretty much it. The RSC leads the field in producing a range of these early plays, but even they have been sporadic, averaging less than one a year through the sixties and seventies until a burst of activity in the eighties that coincided with the opening of the Swan. One actor from those seasons, Greg Doran, went on, as director, to encourage another burst in the middle of this decade. With one exception, no other British theatre has even produced an average of one of these plays per year since William Poel's one-off West End productions for his Elizabethan Stage Circle in the late 1920s. That exception is the Theatre Workshop Company led by Joan Littlewood, who directed all but one of the eight non-Shakespearean plays produced at the Theatre Royal, Stratford atte Bowe 1953–60, better than the Globe's record of eight in its first nine years.

Three of the Globe's eight non-Shakespearean productions were Marlowe's, yet Marlowe is a good example of the need to constantly challenge the repertoire. At present, if a slot for an early play in a theatre's programme is free at all and is not already filled by Shakespeare, it takes courage to take the further risk of choosing outside of the best known of early modern plays. And these have been made known by previous productions, and particularly by having been read. Commercial availability of texts becomes an issue, itself partly determined by school and university reading lists. These lists are subject to all the changing literary approaches and wider cultural influences that determine the curriculum at school and university levels. Shakespeare's contemporaries are often pushed into patterns to explain Shakespeare's development, so anything written after he stopped is largely ignored. The status of Marlowe is a good example of a reputation built largely on non-theatrical considerations, created by Victorian literary, moral and political tastes and passed on to us. He is given the status of John the Baptist to Shakespeare's Jesus and dominates, and is performed despite the mangled condition of plays such as *Faustus* or *Tamburlaine* (where the publisher decided to fillet out the comedy). Yet Marlowe went unpublished for over a hundred years until Robert Dodsley's twelve-volume collection of *Old Plays* in 1744 (when just *Edward II* was deemed worthy). The second edition of 1780 added one more, *The Jew of Malta*, though Marlowe remained unmentioned in the introductory survey by the new editor Isaac Reed. George Chapman, John Ford and even Richard Brome had more literary status into the nineteenth century. A complete works of Marlowe had to wait until 1826. Despite the success of Goethe's *Faust*, Marlowe's *Dr Faustus* only gained a reputation in the 1860s. He has had the benefit of being claimed as a precursor to the Romantics by literary critics in the 1870s, although he is practically ignored by the major Romantic poets themselves. He was claimed by radicals as a champion of free speech despite the unknowability of the reasons for his death.

Marlowe now is given primary status in discussions of Shakespeare's development. Arguably, however, John Lyly's influence was greater; certainly in writing comedy and in writing about love, but also in the use of characters from all strata of society (up to and including the pagan divine) and in the use of natural imagery. Lyly's influence can also be seen in Shakespeare's characters, who fashion themselves through choices made in the theatrical moment, rather than being presented as fixed emblems of vice or virtue. John Marston's preoccupation with the body disturbed Victorian critics, who dismissed his work as morbid and childish; consequently, acknowledgement of his extremely close links with Shakespeare's mid-career has suffered. It has now been recognised that Shakespeare collaborated with many of his contemporaries, including John Fletcher, Thomas Middleton, George Peele, George Wilkins and John Day, to name a few. With only a very few outlets for the medium of theatre, mutual scrutiny by theatre companies of each other's repertoires was necessary both artistically and economically. Shakespeare's plays are filled with echoes of plays that were repertorially in competition with his and are therefore just one side of a conversation that would happen on stage between companies and individual authors. To understand his work fully one has to place him among a wider range of authors beyond Marlowe. And, of course, a Shakespeare-centred valuation of plays ignores entirely those that follow him, despite the fact that playwriting keeps developing and in many ways improving.

Some playwrights wrote too few plays, or too few survive to establish a body of work that would demand attention, such as Henry Chettle. Some wrote too many plays, perhaps, and are therefore too time-consuming for busy practitioners to get to know, such as John Fletcher, Philip Massinger and Thomas Heywood. Some writers are simply unpublished, or only available in research libraries, or in century-old editions costing hundreds of pounds, even for relatively known playwrights. By the time this book is published the Globe will have launched Gary Taylor's long awaited *The Collected Works of Thomas Middleton* and a new online edition of the works of Richard Brome will also be available, but we still await the complete works of other prolific playwrights of the period.

The overemphasis on Shakespeare that forces him to dominate a literary story of development undervalues the historical conditions of playmaking as a collaborative and multifaceted activity. Current scholarship has begun to locate Shakespeare more firmly in the material circumstances of his time, both in terms of performance and publication, but we still lack proper histories of all the buildings and companies other than his. In re-evaluating the repertoire it also becomes clear how artificial the dividing line of 1642 is in terms of understanding post-Restoration theatre. Despite an eighteen-year gap, professional theatre-making resumed with many of the same actors, the same plays, the same playwrights, the same concerns and conventions, the same audience members and even the same theatres. Restoration comedy grows out of Jacobean and Caroline comedy. It is arguably Ben Jonson who is the playwright with the most lasting influence on British theatre. It is from him that we derive our comedies of character and manners, which were inherited by Brome and Shirley in the 1630s and then passed through Congreve and Sheridan to Wilde, and on to the present day.

INDOOR THEATRES

As much as we need the Globe to rediscover amphitheatre playing, we also need a theatre to rediscover these plays indoors. Not all of the readings sat entirely comfortably within the Bear Gardens theatre. The drum-and-trumpet war plays of the amphitheatres of the 1590s such as Robert Greene's *Selimus the Great* (1592), or *Locrine* (1594), or the later firework and spectacle plays of the Red Bull (such as Heywood's plays of classical myth) were designed to fill larger spaces. Some Paul's plays, particularly Marston's, seemed to ask for a greater degree of control over lighting than the other indoor theatres of the time. The court plays of John Lyly sometimes suggest discrete playing spaces within a room. Occasionally a play like Robert Wilson's *The Cobbler's Prophecy* (1594) would suggest promenade staging. It is right to consider all these plays as site-specific, and there is more variety to be found than is commonly supposed in Shakespeare-centred approaches. There were twenty-six other theatres besides the Globe in use during the period between 1576 and 1642. The vast majority of plays would have been written for a particular stage, and the attendant physical demands that it required. Of the surviving plays, the ratio of indoor to outdoor plays is roughly two to one. Given the dual use of indoor/outdoor sites by various companies, indoor requirements would have also influenced outdoor playing.

In the same way that music adapted to the intimacy of the indoor space, woodwind and string replacing brass and drum, so the acting style may have become quieter, more subtle. The proximity of audience allows and demands greater truth. The actor, needing to project less physically and vocally, can play more effortlessly, more naturally, more conversationally. The vocal range is extended to the whisper. A shout seems louder. Actors can just talk. This also allows a greater speed of delivery, which in turn makes it more like real speech. But the relationship between actor and audience remains declared in the move indoors. An indoor theatre such as the Blackfriars was used in the afternoon, had windows, and the angles through which daylight reached the stage is similar to those of the Globe (with its high galleries and stage roofing). Because the audience would have shared the light with the actors, in the readings it was usual to play with the auditorium lit. The audience is closer, more intimate with the actors than in the larger amphitheatres. As the actor becomes more visible to the audience, so the audience becomes more visible, more available to the actor. The reduction in the audience's size (while still filling the room) also contributes to greater intimacy and equality between audience members and actors. Audience awareness cannot be inimical to truthful playing.

SOME CONCLUSIONS

It would be easy to dismiss a process that only gives a day to prepare. We should remember, however, that companies in the early modern period would also stage a different play each day. Henslowe's records show this, while also showing a new play entering the repertoire of the Rose about every two weeks, from which it can be inferred that a fortnight would also be the average time to learn a new part. Of course, with more time together more could have been achieved in the readings, but it is still extraordinary to realise just how much can be achieved, if attempted, in just a day, certainly enough to allow a play to come to life, albeit with script in hand. Even with their lines learned, however, the actors of the Rose were still performing a new play for just a day or two as part of a continuing repertoire of near daily change. The experience of staging these plays reinforces the need to view these plays as material written for ensembles. Usual modern theatre practice has all creative decisions passing the director one at a time. These readings work without a single pole of authority, and instead ask for an ensemble responsibility from the cast, for performances as well as props and costumes. This responsibility liberates the actors, puts them more in control of rehearsal and performance. This ensemble responsibility must surely resemble early modern staging.

In performance the surprise to me is how many of these plays still appeal to an audience. There is a presumption that if an early modern play is relatively unknown then it cannot be any good. That simply is not true. If anything, it can be Shakespeare's plays that are obscure or difficult in comparison. The predominance of Shakespeare has blinded us both to the great variety and to the quality that exists in early modern drama. Conversely, there is a huge amount to be learned about Shakespeare by looking again at his contemporaries, discovering the changing world of theatre that he was part of and reacting to, and not just trying to fit that world around him. These plays are only dead if we let them lie dead.

With so huge a project, so many people working on so many different plays, much of the knowledge gained is too diffuse to mention here, or has already been lost. Disparate discoveries about particular plays live and die with each reading. There are, nonetheless, tangible results. Each of the readings has been recorded on audio, a record as much of audience reaction as of actors' delivery of lines.

A dozen or so of those plays which have already been staged have been edited and published in the Globe Quarto series, with the co-ordinator contributing to it. Both scholars and students have had the opportunity to see plays in live performance that they otherwise never would, and been reminded of their potential in the hands of actors. It is a usual reaction to be surprised at how entertaining these plays can still be, how exciting, funny and thought-provoking. Most of these plays were written with actors in mind, designed for the best performers of their day. Perhaps inevitably there is still an aspect of them best appreciated by actors who are trained to seek out those opportunities for performance that an academic can miss in a private reading. *Read Not Dead* allows these plays to become the things that they were originally meant to be – live events. In turn, many actors have had the chance to extend their knowledge of early modern drama, and to gain practical experience of its demands.

NOTE

1 Shakespeare, of course, supplies the chapter heading (*Hamlet* 5.1.70), cited from *The Norton Shakespeare*, ed. Stephen Greenblatt *et al.* (New York and London: W. W. Norton, 1997).

CHAPTER TWELVE

LEARNING WITH THE GLOBE

Fiona Banks

If the Globe were a school child it would, at ten years old, be in Year 6, the final year of primary education. This phase marks the end of the beginning as a learner. Students make the transition from the essential, formative primary stage of foundation learning and experimentation to secondary school with its broader, deeper curriculum. At this stage of education there is an expectation that learners will build on their existing knowledge and use it to help themselves develop, grow and mature. Among educators it is recognised as a simultaneously exciting and challenging period. In such a context this book could be viewed as a detailed end-of-primary-school review and this chapter a reflection upon what has been learned during that time about learning: the ways in which Globe Education has sought to develop learning at the Globe during its first ten years, and its endeavours to share discoveries made by theatre artists and educators with as diverse a constituency of learners as possible.

AN ETHOS FOR LEARNING

Learning has been at the centre of the Globe project since its inception. The act of reconstructing an Elizabethan playhouse not seen or played in for four hundred years came from a desire to rediscover forgotten knowledge and understanding. Put very simply, the Globe positioned all involved as learners, at the beginning of their education. Like a child moving through years of schooling, the process of creating work at the Globe has been a continuous stage-by-stage journey that is by necessity fluid and experimental. Learning at the Globe is real: a physical, active challenge, a daily necessity if the theatre is to function and its work move forward. It is not a cerebral 'add on' existing as a worthy sideshow or something that makes for good marketing and PR. Learning exists in the body of the organisation rather than just its head. Crucially, staff at the Globe have to learn by 'doing' and continue to learn each time they engage with the theatre. We learn from the building, the actors, directors, designers, stage managers, movement and voice experts and from the audience. This learning ethos informs all of Globe Education's work and provides a context and guiding principles for the type and quality of learning we seek to create.

Since it was founded Globe Education has championed learning by 'doing'. All programmes, whether ninety minutes or three years in duration are delivered using practical, active approaches to teaching and learning. Shakespeare wrote plays for actors to perform, not for them to read, and as Rex Gibson suggests in his seminal book *Teaching Shakespeare*: 'Active methods comprise a wide range of expressive, creative and physical activities. They recognise that Shakespeare wrote his plays for performance, and that his scripts are completed by enactment of some kind.'[1] The act of doing, however, is not just about encountering Shakespeare's plays – as plays – to be performed. It is also an act of experiential or kinaesthetic learning in which knowledge can become part of the learner's makeup and remain as a physical and/or emotional memory to draw on when he or she next encounters Shakespeare's words in a classroom or examination hall.

The notion that Shakespeare should be taught actively is not new. It is encountered as early as 1908 in an English Association pamphlet that warned: 'There is a serious danger in the class-room, with text books open before us, of forgetting what drama really means.'[2] The use of active approaches gained profile and momentum in Rex Gibson's 1986 *Shakespeare in Schools Project* and the following Cambridge University Press *School Shakespeare* series of plays. Yet twenty-one years since Gibson's project, and eighteen years since Globe Education began working with schools, this method of teaching and learning is still to be widely adopted. In a study of London secondary teachers carried out by Globe Education in July 2007, 100 per cent of teachers felt their students responded positively to active approaches to Shakespeare and these methods had a positive effect on students' learning, yet 53 per cent of them said that they do not use active approaches to teaching Shakespeare as frequently as they would wish.[3] It would be possible to offer multiple hypotheses as to why this might be so, but in the absence of any substantial evidence, Globe Education has begun a three-year research project into the effects of active approaches to teaching Shakespeare on teaching and learning at Key Stage 3.[4] At the time of writing, the outcomes, of course, remain to be seen; but we hope to be able to give teachers a mandate to use active approaches to learning in their classrooms without fear that they will be regarded as frivolous – with potential to jeopardise test results.

This process has already begun. The past ten years have seen a shift in attitude politically and culturally to the benefits of active learning. The notion that quality and depth of learning is directly related to the amount of time a student spends, head bent over books, at his or her desk is being challenged. In November 2006, the

National Strategy for school improvement, part of the then DfES, commissioned Globe Education to develop and deliver training to all of its English consultants across the UK as part of a national initiative to improve the quality of teaching and learning about Shakespeare.[5] As a result, approaches to Shakespeare pioneered in Globe rehearsal rooms and developed by Globe Education Practitioners are now being used by students in classrooms across the country, giving them a toolkit of approaches for exploring Shakespeare's plays that they share with the actors who play in them at the Globe.[6]

Globe Education does not confine the use of active learning to the exploration of Shakespeare's plays, but increasingly works to develop and share creative, arts-based approaches to active learning across the school curriculum. In 1998, the National Advisory Committee on Creative and Cultural Education published *All Our Futures*, a landmark report that explored the value of, and need for, creativity in education and highlighted the role that arts organisations could play in this process.[7] This move towards creative learning coincided with Globe Education's development of its range of programmes and projects for students and teachers. In 2005, as part of our work to interrogate notions of creativity and explore the relationship between education policy, arts organisation, artists and schools, we created an MA *Creative Arts in the Classroom* for teachers with King's College London.

Today the landscape of formal education looks very different from the way it did in 1997 when the Globe opened. The value of creative learning is now universally accepted. The arts are invariably cited as crucial to the development of creativity, which is being positioned as a third 'basic' skill alongside Literacy and Numeracy.[8] Creativity is featured heavily throughout the recent revisions of the National Curriculum and is already being incorporated to a greater degree into teachers' classroom practice. In response to this growing recognition and need, Globe Education has begun to offer training, initially for teachers in our local borough of Southwark, in the use of active approaches to learning across the curriculum. The practical and academic are less frequently seen as opposites and there is growing recognition that rigorous academic understanding can arise from, and be part of, practical exploration.

LEARNING THROUGH SHAKESPEARE

While there exists a universal expectation that Globe Education will teach about the work of Shakespeare and his contemporaries, it often comes as a surprise to discover that in all of our programmes we teach *through* Shakespeare as well as *about* Shakespeare. The universality of Shakespeare's stories and the dilemmas faced by his characters have great resonance with twenty-first-century students. On many occasions the best way into a play, scene or speech is to encourage students to make a personal connection with the situation or character. Workshops are often structured to engage students in the exploration of an issue or situation located in their own world before they move on to engage with the same situation as portrayed in Shakespeare's play. Learning about play, Globe and self sit together in all programmes, although, dependent on the length of the programme and the needs of the learners, the focus and weight given to each element may differ.

In some projects Shakespeare is used predominantly as a teacher, as a catalyst for learning. These are frequently projects developed for schools and colleges in our Southwark community where we have the opportunity to engage in partnerships with students and teachers over long periods of time. In 2001 Globe Education embarked on *Right to Reply*, a five-year project that used Shakespeare's plays to teach core communication skills to Southwark students at primary, secondary and post-sixteen stages of education. Most recently *King Lear* is providing a framework through which to deliver strands of the revised National Literacy Framework to students aged between five and eleven in Southwark primary schools. Teachers comment on the motivation, engagement and opportunities for empathy that using a play as a basis for such learning brings. Simultaneously, Shakespeare's plays cease to be 'high art', culturally unknowable and inaccessible and become inclusive; part of a student's everyday experience and a means by which they can develop 'core' skills and understand their own world.

CHILD-CENTRED LEARNING

At the heart of Globe Education's work with young people is the desire that it should be inclusive, accessible to all. Just as the audience in Shakespeare's original Globe would have come from a cross-section of society we seek to ensure that all students we work with regard the Globe today as 'theirs' and access to Shakespeare's plays as part of their cultural entitlement. Programmes range from early years (beginning at three years old) to postgraduate and cover all years and types of schooling. A five-year rolling training residency with Gosden House School, which specialises in creative learning for children with special educational needs, has enabled Globe Education to offer programmes for students with SEN.[9] Similarly, a sixteen-year relationship with Studienreisen England Tours in Germany has enabled Globe Education to create programmes to support German students from the age of eleven in their study of Shakespeare as part of the German school curriculum.

All programmes, of whatever duration, are bespoke and have the needs of the child at their centre. Schools participating in a 'one-off' ninety-minute session at the Globe can stipulate a play and play focus, while series of workshops and longer projects are devised with project partners to meet their needs and project aims. Project partners during the last ten years have been diverse, ranging from schools in Southwark, across London, nationally and internationally to the DfES and Metropolitan Police. The diversity of the work created by Globe Education, combined with its individuality, is central to its success. The best work is always that which is created in direct response to the needs of learners and their particular environment or situation. This ethos of collaboration is also central to our teaching. Just as a good actor on the Globe stage will be able to respond with subtlety to his or her audience and ensure that it becomes part of the performance, the best projects and workshops are those in which Globe Education Practitioner, teacher and student learn together and there is an exchange of knowledge, energy and understanding.

CREATING A COMPANY OF ARTS EDUCATORS

I arrived at the Globe, directly from teaching in a South London comprehensive school, in the opening week of Henry V in May 1997. In the green room, actors, playing at the Globe for the first time, could be heard voicing their response to the experience. The conversations usually progressed along the following lines:

Actor 1: It's really hard out there, different, you can see the audience and they can see you.

Actor 2: They move around, they can be noisy: even small noises can be disruptive if a lot of people make them.

Actor 1: They can see each other and they are sometimes more interested in what is going on over on the other side of the theatre than what you are doing. You have to work to get their attention and to hold on to it.

Actor 2: You don't know what will happen. They feel that they are part of the performance, sometimes they say things, it can be great but it can also be disruptive.

Actor 1: When you feel like you can work with the audience, and they become part of the play . . . and you're in it together . . . it's amazing.

I felt at home. It was all deeply familiar – a conversation that would not have been out of place if it had been held between two trainee teachers in a staffroom. The experience of actors playing the Globe stage is similar in many ways to the experience of a teacher in a classroom. Both know the challenge of engaging an audience in an environment that is unpredictable and potentially distracting. Equally, both can experience the joy of theatre and learning that is collaborative, that can potentially lead to what Tim Carroll refers to earlier in this book as 'a moment of beautiful revelation'.[10] This synergy between Globe actor and teacher provided a good starting point for the development of Globe Education's training of its own practitioners and for its teacher training programmes.

All of our projects and workshops are delivered by Globe Education Practitioners (GEPs), theatre artists (largely actors and directors), who train with Globe Education to become educators. Over the past ten years we have created a company of approximately sixty arts educators who bring their skill, knowledge and creativity as theatre artists into their work as teachers and seek to find innovative ways of sharing our discoveries about Shakespeare's work and the Globe with young people.

Artists of all kinds have been working successfully with and in schools for decades. At the time of the Globe's opening, however, surprisingly little formal consideration had been given to the value and role of such work. Equally, there were few expectations. Schools largely seemed to accept the value of working with an artist on face value, demanding very little from the encounter, other than it should take place. In a report to the Scottish Arts Council in 1993 E. Turner and I. Stronach observed:

A bridge is being built without a blueprint. On the one side, there is the education pier, solid but, perhaps, a little unimaginative. On the other side is the arts pier, a much more eclectic construction, exhibiting a range of styles. Both sides have set out to construct a linking span but it is not yet clear whether the connection will be made.[11]

While this comment is a little reductive in its view of the attributes of education and the arts, it does capture some of the core issues that artists and educators sought to address in the 1990s. In this climate it was also difficult for artists, often working alone, in schools for a long period of time, to find a voice and professional identity.

In 1997 Globe Education had a team of ten dedicated actor teachers (as they were called then) who were committed to developing active approaches to teaching Shakespeare. This team worked to introduce young people, to the Globe, and to the impact it could have on our understanding of Shakespeare's plays, long before the theatre itself became a physical reality. When the Globe opened the question most frequently asked among this group was: 'How shall we incorporate the Globe into our work now that we actually have it?' In many ways the work developed with Globe Education Practitioners over the past ten years has sought to address that question and to make meaningful, sustainable and innovative 'connections' between education and the arts.

Simon Rattle in All Our Futures (1998) states: 'To be a performing artist in Britain in the next century you have to be an educator too.' Part of Globe Education's mission is to raise the status and profile of artists as educators and to encourage the recognition of this profession as such. Our training programme is part of this mission. The development of this programme has coincided with growing recognition of the role artists can play in education and of the need for further training to enable artists to develop this part of their career. We recruit practitioners from across the acting and directing communities; some are experienced educators, while others are not.

All have a passion for Shakespeare, the Globe, learning and the genuine desire to share this with young people. All new practitioners undergo an initial training and induction process before becoming part of our company. An ongoing programme of observation and professional development is offered to all. Specific training needs are identified from this process and training days held each academic term.

The training we offer reflects and enables Globe Education's range of programmes and projects. These have grown dramatically since 1997, in size and diversity. Now on an average day approximately 800 young people (aged between five and eighteen) come to the Globe for a workshop, while we simultaneously work with approximately 120 students (from age three upwards) in schools. These figures do not take into account work with teachers, graduates and postgraduates. Practitioners begin working with us in one area, for example at Key Stage 2 (seven-to eleven-year-olds) and progress, as best suits their interests and skills, to teach across a range of programmes. An experienced practitioner might begin his or her day exploring *The Tempest* with three- and four-year-olds in a Southwark nursery; return to the Globe to lead a workshop with a group of fifteen-year-old GCSE students on *Macbeth*; then go on to deliver training for teachers on active approaches to Shakespeare's language. The number and range of programmes enable us to offer practitioners scope for development and a safe, supportive, space to hone their skills. It can be, in the words of one practitioner, a 'sweet shop' for a committed arts educator. For others it provides continuity. Some practitioners identify Globe Education as the longest relationship of their professional life – a home from which they can develop a parallel and complementary career.

The learning that takes place each theatre season, as new companies of actors play the Globe stage, is central to the development of our work. Increasingly each year actors and directors from the Globe Theatre have become GEPs. Ex-theatre company members now make up half of our practitioner team. They bring with them the physical and emotional knowledge gained from rediscovering Shakespeare's plays on the Globe stage and have learned ways of sharing these with their audience, albeit an audience they meet 'in character' rather than as themselves. The similarities between Globe actor and teacher, so apparent in the early days at the Globe, have enabled a holistic exchange between education and theatre and provided a framework through which ideas can be developed, explored and shared with learners of all ages.

LEARNING AND THE DEVELOPMENT OF NEW MEDIA

Globe Education's desire to facilitate the learning that can take place when artist, Globe and student meet drives our work. Sam Wanamaker charged us to work locally, nationally and internationally. His vision informs all of the programmes

12 Globe Education Practitioner Jack Murray leads a workshop as part of the *Excellence in Cities* programme

and projects we create. GEPs work in Southwark, across London and travel around the UK delivering specially designed outreach programmes to groups of teachers and students (see figure 12). International outreach work has ranged from conflict resolution workshops for students in the Lebanon (in conjunction with the English Speaking Union); to the creation of Globe Education Academies for teachers in California and Louisiana. A central concern, however, has always been the issue of access for students who may never come to the Globe, or work with a GEP.

The development of the Internet has increasingly enabled us to address this concern and begin to offer equality of access to the Globe for learners around the world. In 1997, Globe Education created the first Globe website. Its purpose was to provide a profile for, and information about, the Theatre and to provide a platform for GlobeLink: Globe Education's international association for students and teachers. GlobeLink was created with the aim of offering all students a means by which they could develop a relationship with the Globe and learn with us as our knowledge of the theatre developed. Since GlobeLink's inception we have worked to develop online projects and methods of sharing discoveries that reflect Globe Education's ethos of active, student-centred, collaborative learning.

Adopt an Actor was born out of this approach and out of the desire to offer material on the Web that did not replicate the static, expert-led, nature of the traditional-education teacher's pack. We wanted to demystify the process of making theatre at the Globe in order for students to be able to engage actively and organically with all aspects of production. In 1998, we asked ten actors in *As You like It* and *The Merchant of Venice* to voluntarily offer themselves for 'adoption' by schools around the world. They all agreed. Each week bulletins of their progress were posted on the GlobeLink website. Students were asked to respond to their actor's questions and help them to solve rehearsal room and performance challenges. Wherever they lived, students could have access to Globe actors. They could share, and in some cases help shape, their process as it developed. This project has continued since 1998. Its ongoing legacy is a comprehensive online resource that now covers twenty-nine productions.

GlobeLink has developed into the Globe's centre for learning online. Today learners can blog with Othello, travel with *Romeo and Juliet* on tour, or download Globe Research documents from a recent Stage Blood seminar. Soon students will be able to take part in video conferences with GEPs from the Globe Theatre. In spring 2008, Globe Education launched an online MEd module with Cambridge University, Faculty of Education, an online partnership which represents the first of its kind for the Faculty's MEd programme. The development of new media has given us the opportunity to extend access to the Globe in ways that would have been difficult to envisage in 1997 and to integrate a growing body of virtual learners into our daily work.

A THEATRE FOR YOUNG PEOPLE

Since there has been a Globe stage students have performed on it. Each year since 1997 approximately six hundred young people from sixteen Southwark schools have come together to perform in their production of a Shakespeare play, as part of the *Our Theatre* project. Each day from October to April students who visit the Globe for a workshop explore work on the stage as part of their visit. The process of 'playing' and performing offers opportunities for experiencing a play from the 'inside', and in longer projects for significant personal and social development. It is, however, only in recent years that Globe Education has begun to explore creating theatre productions for young people.

In 2004, we developed *Magic in the Web*, an interactive performance of *Othello*. Students worked 'in role' throughout a ninety-minute session in which they were cast as members of Othello's army; both audience and participants in the drama.

For many of the students involved this was their only experience of live theatre. It is widely accepted in schools that students should experience Shakespeare in performance. This notion has been given official endorsement in the 2007 revisions to the National Curriculum that state students should 'watch live performances in the theatre wherever possible to appreciate how action, character, atmosphere, tension and themes are conveyed'. Cost, time and availability of theatre productions can, however, sometimes become obstacles to making this vision a reality. There are also issues of suitability and quality: every teacher wants their students' experience of theatre to be positive, engaging, stimulating and challenging.

In response to this need, in 2007, Globe Education created the project *Playing Shakespeare with Deutsche Bank*. A full-scale production of *Much Ado about Nothing* provides the centrepiece of the project (see colour plate 7). This production was created specifically for young people and played for a week in the Globe to an audience of over 6,000 London fourteen-year-old students, all of whom received tickets for free. For some it was their first visit to a theatre, for all an opportunity to see in performance the play they were studying for their National Tests at the end of Key Stage 3 (eleven to fourteen years old).

The response of this audience was extraordinary. Unlike most members of the theatre-season audience, many of the students had no knowledge of 'black box' or 'fourth wall' theatre conventions, through which to channel their response to the Globe. Their reactions were spontaneous and intense. Costumes were cheered; kisses greeted with a wave of euphoria. Their reaction to the theatre itself was exuberant, the play sometimes difficult to start and the usual Globe pre-show announcements impossible to deliver. I was reminded of why our opening production of *Henry V* began with drumming; in anticipation of a raucous audience that never quite materialised. The experience was possibly the closest we will get to understanding how an Elizabethan audience, with no knowledge of twentieth-century theatre conventions, might have responded to a play. The feedback from students and teachers was overwhelmingly positive. The production was podcast on the DfES website and downloaded by students and schools around the UK and internationally. We have learned that the Globe can provide a unique space for young people to meet Shakespeare's plays as audience members: in which they are not distanced in the dark from the stage and actors who play down to them, but can become part of the theatre and 'share the same light' with actors who play with them.

CONCLUSION

Sometimes people talk to me about 'Globe Education Practice' and I am never quite sure what they mean. Of course, there are some ideas that are fundamental and some truths we hold to be 'self evident' – many of these I have explored in this chapter. But if our work is to be exciting, pioneering, rigorous, creative and worthy of the learners we serve, it must always be reflective, experimental, evolving. We must always be learning.

NOTES

1 Rex Gibson, *Teaching Shakespeare* (Cambridge University Press, 1998), p. xii.
2 Anon., *The Teaching of Shakespeare in Schools* (English Association, 1908), p. 7.
3 Globe Education, *Playing Shakespeare with Deutsche Bank: Research Survey into Active Methods of Teaching Shakespeare*, 2007.
4 This research is ongoing and part of the project *Playing Shakespeare with Deutsche Bank*. The research period will end in academic year 2009/10. Key Stage 3 or KS3 is the first phase of secondary education and covers ages eleven to fourteen.
5 DfES is the Department for Education and Skills. When Gordon Brown became Prime Minister in June 2007 the structure of this department was changed. It has been renamed the Department for Children, Families and Schools – DCFS.
6 Globe Education Practitioner is the term used to describe theatre artists who deliver Globe Education's projects and programmes. See the section 'Creating a company of arts educators' in this chapter.
7 This report was commissioned by the DfES and the DCMS – Department for Culture, Media and Sport.
8 This idea is discussed by Eric Booth in *Impressions from the UNESCO Conference in Lisbon: What I Observed at the First-ever Worldwide Arts Education Conference* March 20, 2006 (www. consulted on 15/01/07).
9 SEN – Special Education Needs. It should be noted, however, that this term covers an extremely diverse range of learners, all with very different needs. Globe Education must take great care to ensure Globe Education Practitioners have appropriate skills to meet the particular needs of learners in their group. In addition to work with Gosden House School, Globe Education also works with Keith Park in association with SENSE.
10 See Tim Carroll chapter 2, 'Practising Behaviour to His Own Shadow', p. 40.
11 E. Turner and I. Stronach cited by David Oddie and Garth Allen in *Artists in Schools: A Review* (London: The Stationery Office, 1998), p. 5.

CHAPTER THIRTEEN

RESEARCH AND THE GLOBE

Martin White

ARCHITECTURE AND GLOBE RESEARCH

Today, there are ten reconstructions (to different degrees of accuracy) of Elizabethan public playhouses around the world. As Franklin Hildy has pointed out in chapter 1 in this volume, these are mostly replicas of, or inspired by, the Elizabethan Globe, 'Shakespeare's Globe', such as the one placed unexpectedly in the gardens of the Villa Borghese in Rome, or the one planned for Staunton, Virginia (where there is already a replica Blackfriars). Elsewhere, other playhouses have provided the model: the skeleton Fortune at the University of Western Australia in Perth, for example, or the proposed reconstruction of the Rose in Lenox, Massachusetts.

The Globe in London (Globe Three as I shall call it) is the result of collaboration between craftspeople, scholars and theatre artists that has produced the largest timber-framed building on a circular plan to be erected in England since before the Civil War, and represents probably the largest arts and humanities interdisciplinary research project ever undertaken in the UK. I want to focus on two connected aspects of the project: the research into experiments in our understanding of past performance practices that the reconstruction has enabled, especially – though not solely – through productions guided by what the Globe calls 'original practices'; and the ongoing research on the building itself.

A couple of health warnings need to be issued. To begin with, it is important to underline that there is a high level of speculation about the physical nature of the building itself, as the main sources for a Globe reconstruction are even sparser than for many other contemporary playhouses: only a small part of the foundations (which lie under a terrace of listed Georgian houses) has been exposed, as opposed to the comparatively extensive archaeological remains of the Rose; no builders' contract survives such as that for the Fortune; no reliable image of the exterior or interior of the first Globe survives (Hollar's Long View of London being of the second Globe of 1614); no map that indicates with any certainty the size or ground-plan of the playhouse has been found; evidence from play-texts known to have been performed at the Globe, or the surviving accounts of those who visited it to see such plays are often fragmentary and contradictory. The reconstruction is in many ways, therefore, in the honest and straightforward words of Andrew Gurr, a 'best guess' at interpreting the surviving evidence.[1] In addition, there is a danger that a reconstruction, by its very physical presence, can tempt us to think that its features are somehow more correct, its discoveries more solid, than they might in fact be. If one writes a book and subsequently something new emerges, not much is lost. A second edition can update the information, or a new book can supersede it. That is less easy where a multi-million-pound building is concerned. But it was part of Sam Wanamaker's vision that the Globe's structure should be kept constantly under review, and that in the event of new historical evidence emerging (such as the Rose excavation), or radical and convincing reinterpretations of existing evidence being put forward, the Shakespeare Globe Trust would endeavour to make any alterations that were practicable. Research into Globe architecture is overseen by the Architectural Research Group (ARG), which is made up of theatre practitioners, theatre historians (including historians of performance), architects, builders and archaeologists.

As I write, the ARG is focused on three main issues concerning the building. First, the columns that support its galleries of seating are square. The Fortune contract, however, draws specific attention to the fact that its own columns were to be 'square and wrought pilasterwise' which would make them *different* from the 'principal and main posts' at the Globe.[2] This suggests that the Globe reconstruction has got this element of the structure wrong. Square posts for a square playhouse might suggest round ones for a round playhouse. But, of course, we cannot infer from the evidence that the Globe posts were cylindrical and research is under way to explore examples of the shapes of posts in a wide range of surviving timber buildings. The cost of replacing them at Globe Three may be prohibitive, but the ARG sees this kind of investigation as of potential benefit to other future reconstructions.

The second key issue that is under scrutiny is the height of the lower gallery from the yard. It was agreed from the outset of the Globe project that the experience of those using the playhouse, as practitioners or audiences, should be analysed as evidence on which changes might also be considered. Consequently, we are revisiting the original scheme concerning the height of the lower gallery above the yard. The decision to sit the timber frame on four courses of brick was based on both the builders' contract for the Fortune Theatre of 1600 and on the supposition that the ground was originally flat. The result was that the first row of audience in the lowest gallery can barely see over the heads of the spectators standing in the yard.

For their part, the actors have found themselves playing either to the yard, which merges with the lower gallery, or to the upper galleries, as none of the audience members are at the actors' eye level, which is a common feature of subsequent playhouses. It has recently been suggested that when the original Globe was built, it may have been shaped with shovels to give a dished depression for the yard with a raised 'ring' on which the foundations for the galleries were laid, placing them higher above the yard. For the 2007 season the research group instigated an experiment with a temporary revision of the two bays of the lowest gallery nearest to the stage, raising them level with the stage and making the rake of the bench seating in them steeper. Apart from improving the view and creating a distinctive difference between sitting and standing, this brought the configuration of the lower gallery more in line with the two galleries above, doing away with the blank space of wall currently above the heads of the back row that forms a band of white wall round the playhouse at the lower level. If, in the view of the performers and spectators (whose opinions are sought through questionnaires), and of the Architectural Research Group, this experiment is judged to be an improvement, a decision may be taken to see if it is possible to raise the remaining bays.

A knock-on effect of that change would be to alter how the audience accesses the lowest gallery. The evidence for how spectators made their way to different vantage points in the open-air playhouses is contradictory, and so open to different interpretations. The work to the lowest gallery would mean that audiences headed there would go via the stair-towers rather than, as now, first entering the yard. A further development (fire regulations permitting) might be that the number of entrances into the yard might be reduced from four to two creating a more satisfying, less 'broken' line of the lowest gallery and more closely following the line of the galleries above.

The final issue of concern for the interior of the building is the question of decoration. At present, the highly decorated *frons* (rear wall) of the stage and underside of the canopy, with the stage posts painted to look like marble, are in strong contrast to the plainness of the oak and lime-washed plaster in the rest of the auditorium. Painting the balusters that run round the front of the middle and upper galleries in a red ochre has helped, but it is generally (though not unanimously) agreed by the ARG that the remainder of the auditorium should be itself decorated to create a harmonious, coherent space rather than, as at present, having the stage and auditorium in distinct styles. However, what is harder to determine is exactly what that overall decorative style should be: vernacular (perhaps more in common with styles of the late 1590s) or a more neo-classical aesthetic that might fit more closely with the later years of the Globe's life.

ARCHITECTURE AND THEATRE PRACTICE

I want to turn now to ways in which reconstructions of playhouses, from any period, can be used to investigate past theatre practices. There are different views on the methods and potential of reconstruction, seen, for example, in the projects either realised or proposed by Robert K. Sarlós of the University of California at Davis and Alan Woods at Ohio State, or those undertaken some years ago by Tom Lawrenson at the University of Lancaster. Professor Sarlós aims to 'transport viewers and listeners . . . into a past age', and to this end he suggests that:

all conceivable theatrical and non-theatrical elements of make-believe should be employed. Noises, scents, and other stimuli external to the work itself, but characteristic and evocative of the place and time, should be courageously, imaginatively, and forcefully recreated and exploited.

He wishes to produce:

the kind of experience that, by means of consequent contemplation, leads to a new, more complete, and more enlightened narrative. Minimally, it ought to result in a sophisticated summing up of intuitive insights into sensual and emotional aspects of theatrical style, derived from the performance.[3]

Rather than pursue this experiential (and I think unachievable) aim, I see the research into past theatre practices as akin to a series of laboratory experiments in which one seeks to identify and test assumptions or discoveries about particular texts and implications for their performance in a way *simply not possible* without the reconstruction. This work is based on the axiomatic link between stage languages (physical and verbal) and the performance space in which those languages are articulated. This is particularly relevant in the case of Elizabethan and Jacobean playwrights, whose plays were increasingly tailor-made to suit the particular company who commissioned them: the opportunities offered by the performance space and the talents of the actors who would be likely to be cast in particular roles. As the Printer of *The Two Merry Milkmaids* (1619) reminds us: 'Every poet must govern his pen according to the Capacity of the Stage he writes to, both in the Actor and the Auditor.' Although any performance at Globe Three might provide insights, research has focused particularly on 'original practices' productions, which include dressing the actors in clothes that are historically accurate (including appropriate materials and methods of construction), all-male casts (though the female roles are played by young actors – rather than boys – with older men for certain parts), historically accurate props, and music played on replica instruments (even if the music is not period, but simulated by modern composers). On two occasions, performances have explored the use of reconstructed Elizabethan English. These productions have led to a whole range of discoveries, well documented in the Globe's own Research Bulletins.[4] One of the most productive areas has been the exploration of those signature elements of the Elizabethan stage that are often acknowledged in discussion – pillars, 'discovery space', upper level, etc. – but the implications of which, in practice, are not always fully understood. Even serious, stage-centred commentators can overlook what have turned out to be problematic issues. J. L. Styan's 1967 book, *Shakespeare's Stagecraft*, is rightly acknowledged as a pioneering work. In it, however, he makes only two brief references to stage pillars, and sums his view up thus: 'The stage posts . . . do not call for more than cursory reference.'[5] None of his diagrammatic illustrations of staging includes pillars. In practice, their size, position and impact on performance for actors and audiences continue to prove the knottiest item on the Globe stage, and it is unlikely they would now be ignored in any academic study.

THE USES OF RECONSTRUCTION-BASED RESEARCH

But what can we not recover through reconstruction-based research? Professor Sarlós, Alan Woods (in his experiments with Italian Renaissance tragedy) and George Pierce Baker also have attempted to recreate acting style. This is, in my view, too elusive a quarry. But what *can* be explored are the material factors that would have shaped the style of performance in Elizabethan and Jacobean playhouses, as they do the work of all actors in all periods, foremost of which is the physical environment. Within this scheme, actors can explore actor/actor and actor/audience relationships (particularly the proximity and location of the spectators in what is a theatre-in-the-round, if an unevenly distributed one); the nature of the lighting (natural and artificial); the use of music to underscore the action; positioning of actors (i.e., blocking); conventions of gesture; staging set-pieces such as duels, dumb shows and banquets; the question of sightlines and other, often more contentious issues, such as the use of the yard in performance. From the outset, for example, actors recognised the challenge set by the Globe to activate and energise the whole playhouse, quickly identifying the quirks and strengths of the playhouse, and how the texts of Shakespeare's plays responded to the structure. Soliloquies appeared to 'work' in particular places on the stage, and playing quickly helped keep the audiences focused, for example. At the same time as the excitement of acknowledging the presence of the spectators, actors (and audiences) discovered opportunities for self-absorption in the action, as clearly their Elizabethan counterparts did too. In Thomas Heywood's *A Woman Killed With Kindness*,[6] the suspicious husband, Frankford, with his servant Nicholas, returns unannounced in the middle of the night to his house to see if his fears of his wife's fidelity are justified. The combination of stage-whispering and appropriate action (Nicholas's line 'I will walk on eggs this pace' (XIII.21)) gives us a very clear idea of the implicit performance, matched by the audience's engagement, and can create perfectly the appropriate mood and atmosphere. Indeed, Frankford's line 'A general silence hath surprised the house' (XIII.22) may well describe the tension in the playhouse during the scene.

This pattern of shifting between moments of 'detached self-awareness' and 'engagement' suggests to me a depth and intensity of contrast similar to the striking *chiaroscuro* of Renaissance painting. I believe this pattern offers a clue as to how Elizabethan actors – partly by shifting the 'depth of focus' – sought to control audience response, something their modern counterparts confront.

Audiences present other issues. In 1895, George Pierce Baker, preparing a production of Jonson's *Epicoene* at Harvard, saw one of his tasks as being to recreate an Elizabethan audience, training his students to represent fops, gallants and citizens, in carefully choreographed sequences of loitering, even fighting. When Theatre Studies Departments (Theaterwissenschaften) were first founded in German universities in the 1920s, reconstructions of past theatres and performances were rapidly developed as a means of investigation. Opposition to this method, however, focused on the fact that as theatre is essentially a two-way relationship between stage and audience, and as the historical audience cannot, by definition, be reconstructed, such an approach was fundamentally flawed. Clearly, we cannot expect modern audiences (nor would one want them to) to imitate their predecessors (the episode of *Dr Who*, set at the original Globe and filmed at the reconstruction, was the only time I have seen an audience perform in this way there). But the *presence* of the audience can illuminate the crucial relationship between text and playhouse architecture. Derek Peat, for example, working on the Fortune reconstruction in Perth, observed how the repetitions within longer speeches allowed the actor to direct them to different sectors of the audience. Much more needs to be done to explore the relationship between playhouse and text. Early modern play texts also imply a receptive audience, able and ready to respond to the provocations of the play and assumed by the playwrights to be capable of entertaining irreverent attitudes and sceptical opinions. For example, in *King Lear*, Lear speaks the dangerous lines: 'See how yond justice rails upon yond simple thief. Hark, in thine ear: change places, and, handy dandy, which is the justice, which is the thief?' (4.6.151–6). In the modern theatre this line must remain an intellectual idea. At the Globe in 1606, however, with its heterogeneous audience distinguished not only in their dress but by their location in the playhouse, the identification of 'thief' and 'justice', underlined by their very distinct, *physical* 'places' – lords' room and yard – and the ability of the whole audience, watching in daylight, to see each other, would have been especially potent. We may not be able to recover that entirely – though there are padded chairs in the gentlemen's rooms and standing only in the yard – but in a playhouse like the Globe it reminds us of a dynamic in Elizabethan theatre to exploit faction rather than assume a shared, homogenous response, and to play it out in the full glare of day, not to spectators seated safely in a darkened auditorium. For me, the most striking aspect of performances at Globe Three, which distinguishes performances there from all other venues (many of which share many of the Globe's physical characteristics), has been the impact on performers and performances of a standing audience. This has released a sense of audience energy, mobility and involvement more akin to that experienced at a football match – or, perhaps, Brecht's boxing match. Indeed, watching the moving mass of this audience from the vantage point of an upper gallery, I have been repeatedly struck by the sense of a crowd with the power to shape and influence the action on stage, a trace, perhaps, of the popular force that the Elizabethan and Jacobean authorities were fearful the playhouses could incite.

Trying to draw these two key drivers of theatrical performance together, Mark Rylance, as Artistic Director and leading actor (a very Elizabethan combination), is clear that the relationship between actor and audience at the Globe is 'genuinely unique and awakening'. He explains:

The contrast between presentation and play, between showing something and playing it, is another feature that attracts me to experimental work at the Globe. It will be very difficult to 'present' a play there, to present a 'solution' to a play. An audience responds to playing. The idea of the word 'playing', and a space that demands play, could be very beneficial to the acting profession. To create a space like the Globe, where playing is all, will I hope benefit and refresh theatre performance generally.[7]

PUTTING RESEARCH INTO PRACTICE

The unique exploration and the discoveries the Globe reconstruction makes possible are clearly of considerable value, but we must remember that they are also highly speculative. Just as building a physical reconstruction might convince us that its solutions are therefore more solid, so we must beware of believing that Globe performances provide a similarly reliable window into past practices. When, for example, a director (itself an invention of the late nineteenth century) chooses not to stage a particular moment in the large recess at the rear of the stage as the sight-lines are poor, we need to remind ourselves that Shakespeare's company might have had very different views on who could, or should, see what. Our experience might suggest that the downstage corners of the stage are particularly potent positions, but we must be wary of deducing that they were similarly viewed by Elizabethan actors. In other words, we must be cautious of writing – or performing – new theatre history that creates its own notions of past practice.

For example, although billed in some places as being 'presented in Renaissance style', the 2007 *Merchant of Venice* was not an 'original practices' production (costumes were mixed in style and materials, the *frons* of the stage was altered with the addition of flats, the lateral doors were removed, extra stages erected in the yard, Perspex plinths held the caskets, and so on).[8] Nevertheless, Alistair Smith in the *Stage* (27 June 2007) wrote of the set, 'spreading out into the yard via a suitably Venetian bridge, allows the action to spill out into the audience in true period fashion', an assumption he was not the only critic to make.

CONCLUSION

And finally, what of future research at the Globe? Like all research, its process is iterative, and much will comprise reworking and re-examining the kinds of issues I have touched on above. The most significant new development will be the construction of the interior of an indoor playhouse to stand alongside the Globe, providing two spaces that will reflect those the original company had once they acquired the Blackfriars for their own use in 1609. The shell of the building has already been built, to the dimensions shown in a set of seventeenth-century drawings of an unidentified playhouse. There is a host of questions posed by these plans, and there is no space to explore them here. Once completed, the new theatre will allow the exploration of all the performance practices issues undertaken at the Globe but in the very different context of the smaller, indoor space with all its audience seated – a totally different experience for actors and audiences alike. It will also enable two new areas in particular to be researched: the use of candlelight (about which we know precious little) and the intriguing question of the transfer of plays between the outdoor and indoor spaces. Title pages of plays frequently tell us that plays, such as Webster's *The Duchess of Malfi*, for example, were 'presented privately at the Blackfriars and publicly at the Globe'. How, theatre historians have pondered, could one play fare in such totally different theatrical environments? I hope we may soon have the opportunity to try to answer that question.

I am grateful to members of the ARG, and to Iain Mackintosh and Jon Greenfield in particular for their help, especially with the issues surrounding the lower gallery. Some aspects of this paper appeared in my articles for the Globe's journal, *Around the Globe*, in 1999.

NOTES

1 For example, the dimensions of the stage at Globe Three are based on the measurements given in the Fortune contract, which states that it was to be 47 foot 6 inches across, and to reach to the middle of the yard. As the Fortune's yard was to be a 55 foot square (the Fortune was built on a square plan) it is assumed the stage there was to be 27 foot 6 inches in depth.

The Globe reconstruction is, like its original, built on a circular plan (in fact, a twenty-sided polygon – that number being reduced from an earlier figure of twenty-four sides following the excavation of a small part of the foundation I referred to above). Its overall diameter is 99 foot, its yard around 70 foot in diameter (dimensions considered too large by a number of theatre historians). The stage of Globe Three is 44 foot wide and, stopping slightly shy of the 'middle' of the yard, 25 foot deep. The result is a rather shallower stage than I had myself envisioned, one that spreads across, rather than juts out into, the standing spectators.

2 The Fortune Contract, in *Henslowe's Diary*, ed. Reginald Foakes, 2nd edition (Cambridge University Press, 2002).

3 Robert K. Sarlós, 'Creating Objects and Events: a Form of Theatre Research', *Theatre Research International*, 5, 1 (1979–80), 82–8. Alan Woods describes his work in 'Reporting Performance Research', *Theatre Survey* 6 (1989), 171–6.

4 *Research Bulletins* were created by the early research team at Shakespeare's Globe. They document the rehearsal process at Globe Three and contain interviews with actors and directors; these bulletins only go up to 2002.

5 J. L. Styan, *Shakespeare's Stagecraft* (Cambridge University Press, 1967), p. 18.

6 Thomas Heywood, *A Woman Killed With Kindness*, ed. R.W. Van Fossen, Revels Plays (London: Methuen, 1961).

7 Mark Rylance, 'Playing the Globe: Artistic Policy and Practice', in *Shakespeare's Globe Rebuilt*, ed. J. R. Mulryne and Margaret Shewring (Cambridge University Press, 1997), pp. 169–76, p. 171. This book overall provides the most comprehensive study of the processes and decisions taken in constructing Globe Three.

8 Mark Rylance's successor as Artistic Director, Dominic Dromgoole, is dedicated to the research activity that the Globe pursues, but has decided not to put 'original practices' at the heart of his artistic policy.

PART III

RESEARCH IN PRACTICE: PRACTICE IN RESEARCH

INTRODUCTION

Christie Carson and Farah Karim-Cooper

Criticism of the reconstructed Globe on Bankside has often centred on the perceived de-aestheticising of Shakespeare's plays as performed in a popularised, tourist-oriented heritage site. Dennis Kennedy notably states:

When Wanamaker announced the project in 1973, his goals were carefully worded so that the first priority was 'to reclaim Southwark's Thames bank' and then to redevelop the area for 'culture, education and entertainment.' ... No doubt he intended these social and civic concerns to give the scheme gravitas; in reality they brought him even closer to Walt Disney, who saw his parks as models for urban planning and even as experiments for the future, like the EPCOT Center in Orlando.[1]

In this statement Kennedy aligns Wanamaker with Disney because of a perceived vision of a Globe Centre which encapsulates a world view that is geared towards influence extending beyond its own boundaries. This vision, according to Kennedy, places Shakespeare's Globe in the fundamental position of cultural theme park, providing what Disney executives referred to as 'edutainment'. Kennedy goes on to imply that there is an inevitability to this approach: 'whether you like it or not, Disneyland is the most logical model of how to present a culture of pastness in a global economy'.[2]

It must be noted that Kennedy's comments were written in 1997, during the Theatre's first real season on the stage, from a careful critical distance which does not acknowledge the engaged, and at times disharmonious, work of this theatrical and educational centre. Patrick Spottiswoode argues that although the project 'grew on the back of the heritage industry, it is not part of the heritage industry at all'. While there is a sense that the Globe appears to be presenting a 'culture of pastness' (to use Kennedy's phrase), Spottiswoode argues that 'we are nevertheless interrogating the past; we are not eulogising it, not describing it; we explore it and we make use of the theatre space as a way of interrogating the present'.[3]

W. B. Worthen, writing more recently, provides a more complex view of this theatre's social position and its interaction with the scholarly world. The Globe, he says, 'is sort of authentic, sort of theme park, tourist dependent, mediated, a Polonian early modern–modernist–postmodern event: In other words, it is our Globe, necessarily part of how we imagine the great (w)hole of history'.[4] What is interesting to interrogate here is the return of the personal pronouns 'our' and 'we', replicating both the pre-theatre critical response to the Globe project and Spottiswoode's view from 'inside' the current working centre. Worthen in his comments conscientiously uses this personal approach to acknowledge that it is the possibility of external involvement in the process of meaning-making that provides the crucial difference between the Globe Theatre and one of Disney's theme parks: 'theme parks tend to construct their visitors more passively as consumers rather than producers ... in this sense the explicitly theatrical function of the Globe marks a remove from the total institution of theme park'.[5] What Worthen suggests is that theatrical productions at the Globe are not re-enactments of 400-year-old performances; they are contemporary performances in a present, living theatre, regardless of the style in which they are presented. What he does not say is that the theatre is part of a centre and therefore part of a meaning-making process that extends beyond theatrical practice alone. This assertion may appear to swing dangerously close to the Disney/Wanamaker claims about cultural redevelopment. However, instead, what it tries to acknowledge is that the Globe is a multifaceted organisation which should not be contained by a debate that considers only one aspect of its activities.

At Shakespeare's Globe the Theatre and Education departments are separate but complementary entities that grew out of the ideals of Sam Wanamaker's project. The original project had invested in it the hopes of a range of academics on both sides of the Atlantic. Inevitably, the practical articulation of those ideals has dis-appointed some. The first ten years of activity on the reconstructed stage, equally inevitably, brought some teething problems. But these growing pains also helped to develop an experimental methodology which has allowed these two departments to develop quite separate activities based on the founding principles. The Theatre during this period was defined by the concentrated work of a group of theatre artists working together on a collective research project which they named 'original practices'. This concentration of activity allowed for a practical exploration of the period that is unprecedented. Dominic Dromgoole describes this project as 'prob-ably the most consistent, thought through and intelligent approach to producing Shakespeare since Peter Hall at the RSC in the early 1960s'.[6] Equally, Globe Edu-cation has established an innovative programme of projects, events and courses based around Wanamaker's original plans and the expertise of its ever growing staff.

Interestingly, what Dromgoole's comment points out is not only the achievement of the theatrical project but also the context in which that achievement has been judged. The performances at Shakespeare's Globe have been seen in the light of prevailing expectations of Shakespearean performance and placed within a continuous progression of theatrical history that has often been seen as the preserve of the Royal Shakespeare Company. But, as Mark Rylance points out in this volume, the approach taken by this creative team has as much in common with the experimental and physical theatre movements of the 1990s as it has with the prevailing attitudes and approaches to Shakespearean performance. The aim of the theatrical experimentation project articulated in Part I has been to ignore (some would say refute) the established Shakespearean tradition in favour of approaching the building as the primary resource, an instrument to be tested. This instrument was then 'played' in a way that drew on a great deal of scholarly research into the music and dress, as well as the visual culture and material practices of the Renaissance period, articulating in practical terms the aims of cultural-materialist criticism.

Before the theatre was up and running, Globe Education had already begun a series of radical programmes that engaged in a process of questioning and destabilising the centrality of Shakespeare in the curriculum and on stage. The involvement of scholars and actors in the *Read Not Dead* readings helped to form links with research practices and to question current theatrical practices from the outset. This process established specific links with specific scholars working in particular institutions. This may seem to support the notion of an exclusive club of insiders, another criticism often levelled at the Globe, but the gathering of dedicated experts is also a traditional model for developing a specialist research area as well as a necessary practical step in developing a new theatre company.

One outcome of this study has been to confront misconceptions about the work of the theatre but also it has tried to highlight the extensive resources available to investigate the 'original practices' production project. The work undertaken during this initial period of development by Jenny Tiramani, Claire van Kampen and Mark Rylance must be seen as a valuable resource for future scholarship. But further work on this period and this project must be undertaken if scholars are to answer the question: can a practical approach to cultural production of the Renaissance period contribute to an understanding of that period for scholars and audiences? The limitations of current critical practices have been highlighted by this new kind of work just as starkly as the limitations of modern acting and audience expectations and yet scholars have not adapted to these new conditions as quickly or as well as audiences and creative practitioners. What this volume has pointed out is that a more rigorous approach to criticism of the 'original practices' aesthetic, which takes into account its full developmental process, is needed to gain a greater understanding of this phase of the Theatre's development.

Looking at how meaning is generated in the present moment from the coming together of the plays and the architecture, it is useful to speculate about the future in order to approach the recent past. As articulated by each of the members of the creative team, the architecture of the building has had a profound impact on the work that has been possible in it. The actors as well as the audience have had to relearn their roles, and new conventions of communication with the audience have been devised. Performances at the Globe developed over the ten-year period in question a series of conventions that were the result of a compromise between the practitioners, the audience and the physical space. The plays took on new meaning in this space through the reanimation of the role of the audience after several centuries of passivity.

This aspect of the theatrical experience is being taken up by the new Artistic Director in an interesting way. Dromgoole, with his new writing projects and his extensive (and some argue) 'inauthentic' use of the yard, as well the approach taken to hybrid costuming, illustrates an emphasis on a presentist position for the new artistic policy. This shift in the use of the space, to be primarily concerned with the present moment, may help to highlight aspects of the 'original practices' approach that so far have gone unnoticed. Therefore the crucial critical question of how we make meaning in the space today must be posed continually. The relationship between artistic policy and the discoveries that are possible in the space must be acknowledged. Mark Rylance in this section expresses his concerns about the conflicting pressures and opposing pulls of the roles of Artistic Director and actor on the Globe stage. He acknowledges this conflict as a form of creative tension but one that ultimately made it difficult to sustain an entirely consistent approach to 'original practices'.

The commercial pressures on the Theatre have grown with its success and this, ironically, has made it more difficult to present the audiences with radical experiments. However, it is interesting to consider the extent to which bowing to the exigencies of a commercial theatre is itself an 'original practice'. Shakespeare was writing for a particular company of actors who had very conventional and, in all likelihood, habitual performance styles. The development of a 'house style' at the Globe Theatre under Mark Rylance's directorship can be seen to be a particularly appropriate 'original practice', which upsets current ideas about the extent to which an actor should lose him or herself in the role. Reinvention was not the norm in the Renaissance period; convention almost certainly ruled the creative practices on stage.

This section of the volume looks at the outcomes of the experiments of practitioners on the Globe stage and combines this with a pragmatic scholarly approach to the lessons learned to date. A great deal more could be said critically about the conventions developed through the 'original practices' project and this section of the volume aims to map out some productive territory for further investigation. To date no in-depth studies of the acting practices or performance styles developed at Shakespeare's Globe have been undertaken, yet materials available to facilitate this kind of study have been carefully accumulated. Therefore, the three chapters in this section aim to encourage scholars to look more closely at the discoveries of this period in order to engage scholarly debate in the wider ongoing theoretical questions addressed at Shakespeare's Globe. The first chapter in this section draws together a pragmatic discussion of authentic sound in the commercial theatre by Claire van Kampen with the accounts of Keith McGowan and William Lyons, two musicians who have trained in early music but have come to learn about the acoustic challenges faced in the Globe Theatre through their experience of playing in the space and through audience responses. The work of these musicians in the theatre, as active members of the company appearing on stage, goes against the traditions of modern theatre, where musicians are often hidden, and concert performances, where musicians are usually seated and still. The experiments undertaken by these musicians have led them to want to work more in this environment to develop a greater understanding of the music of the period that accommodates a spirit of compromise.

The second chapter in this section combines a discussion of the developmental approach taken to creating the repertoire by Mark Rylance with two accounts of the challenges of acting on the stage by Globe actors Yolanda Vazquez and Paul Chahidi. These actors, who have both worked at the Globe Theatre for a number of seasons, share their knowledge of the demands of the performance space and their understanding of the strengths and weaknesses of the 'original practices' approach to create accounts that illuminate Mark Rylance's initial discussion of principles of selecting repertoire. These two performers have also both worked as Globe Education Practitioners creating again the link between these two departments. Being forced to reflect on their work to explain it to student groups has helped these actors both to articulate and to view their own working practices in new ways.

The section ends with a 'rule book' for directors developed by Ralph Alan Cohen out of his experience directing at the Blackfriars Theater in Virginia, as well as his ongoing involvement in the Globe project. This chapter offers a spirited practical approach to the outcomes of research in a reconstructed theatre and demonstrates, through a series of concrete examples, the productive nature of experiment-led work of this kind. Together these three chapters help to illustrate the nature of the outcomes that can be gleaned from practical research in this area, reinforcing Fiona Banks's idea that 'The practical and academic are less frequently seen as opposites and there is growing recognition that rigorous academic understanding can arise from, and be part of practical exploration.'[7]

This final section of the volume therefore points out areas for potential further research which usefully reanimate the problematic questions initially posed: who can claim ownership of the outcomes of the first period of experimentation and who will direct the future of those experiments? This volume documents the extent to which the creative energy that has fuelled these experiments must be credited to the theatre artists involved. However, it must also be acknowledged that these experiments came out of ideas that were instigated by scholars. It seems sensible, then, to suggest that scholars have a responsibility to examine the results of these experiments in detail in order to make suggestions for the future. This is not to say that the Artistic team cannot learn their own lessons or that scholars know best; rather it suggests that scholarly practice looks for different outcomes and very little work has gone into determining what can be said about these experiments in terms of what they offer scholarship. The creative team will invariably carry on utilising the lessons learned in this theatre in other spaces and with other kinds of theatrical production (for example, Tim Carroll and Jenny Tiramani recently directed and designed *Dido and Aeneas* at the Queen Elizabeth Hall).

Dominic Dromgoole, as the new Artistic Director, may well repeat lessons learned in the early days of practical experiments on the stage. However, for scholars the change in artistic leadership presents a renewal of the experimental process in that this change of artistic perspective will help to highlight what, if anything, was special and unique about the 'original practices' period of performance. It will be important to chart which aspects of the present conditions of performance and reception, and the audience's new-found comfort with the Globe Theatre's demands, will be challenged by this new artistic environment. The fundamental relationship between the play texts, theatre architecture and audience reception is being explored in a very different way by Dromgoole, but it is a way that might prove equally illuminating. If scholars are to make best use of the outcomes of the research to date it is possible that existing models of criticism will prove insufficient and new kinds of scholarly approaches, such as the one put forward by Cohen, will need to be developed.

NOTES

1 Dennis Kennedy, 'Shakespeare and Cultural Tourism', *Theatre Journal* 50, 2 (1998), 183.
2 *Ibid.*, p. 178.
3 Patrick Spottiswoode, interview with the editors, 30 October 2007.
4 W. B. Worthen, *Shakespeare and the Force of Modern Performance* (Cambridge University Press, 2003), p. 103.
5 *Ibid.*, p. 97.
6 Dominic Dromgoole, interview with the editors, 24 May 2007.
7 See Fiona Banks, 'Learning with the Globe', p. 157.

CHAPTER FOURTEEN

PERFORMING EARLY MUSIC AT SHAKESPEARE'S GLOBE

Claire van Kampen, Keith McGowan and William Lyons

CLAIRE VAN KAMPEN ON CREATING A WORKING DEFINITION OF 'AUTHENTICITY'

On my arrival at the Globe Theatre I was immediately bombarded with a wave of scholarly theories about the performance of period music within Shakespeare's plays, theories that had been garnered from academic research but had not been put to practical application in a reconstructed Elizabethan playhouse.[1] The word 'authenticity' had been bandied about in connection with musical performance and period production, but what did this actually mean?

My conclusion about the term 'authenticity' meant that no matter how we addressed the desire to be 'authentic', such a term, if we were to employ Renaissance music, was actually meaningless. Shakespeare's company used modern instruments, tunes, clothing and texts. To be truly 'authentic', we would have to recreate an entire 1590s culture, including audience, acting company and musical band, and somehow contrive this to 'speak' for our own twenty-first-century society, to feel 'modern' and 'topical', as Shakespeare's work certainly did in his own period. This is obviously impossible.

One way of addressing the issue of 'authenticity' could perhaps be achieved by having the actors playing in twenty-first-century dress to their modern audience, with music played on modern instruments; but we then have the issue of Shakespeare's text, which is now very far from our contemporary speech and includes many period references to clothing, music and custom, all of which must become more of a metaphor in a 'modern' production to make sense. Together with the difficulty of actors playing in modern dress in front of a sixteenth-century highly decorated *frons scenae*, the modern-dress solution did not seem to answer the question of 'authenticity' satisfactorily. Our response to the question was to create a selective approach; we decided that what we were ultimately searching to find was

13 Musicians, *Edward II* (2003), Shakespeare's Globe

accuracy of character detail created through careful attention to the text and stage directions.

It is interesting to speculate about the ambient sound levels in London in the early modern period. One would imagine that without overhead aircraft, honking river boats and the incessant background hum of traffic, that Bankside in the 1600s would have been a tranquil environment for the actors' sound-waves to make their trajectory through the Globe's auditorium. However, when I reconstructed a basic 'Elizabethan soundscape' to create a context for the opening track on our CD set of music and speech from our former productions,[2] I found the opposite to be true. The clunking of oars and the continual cries of ferrymen, street traders, cattle and sheep being driven to market, dogs, birds, carts on cobbles and above all, church bells from more than 100 churches in one square mile created an atmosphere outside the playhouse that must have been high on decibels and multilayered in texture. Once within the playhouse, 3,000 people were packed together, possibly standing even in the galleries, playing cards and dice in the lords' rooms, eyeing prostitutes, buying beer and food. Against all this, 'soft music' would have been used very sparingly.

An interesting scholarly belief in 1996 was that the first Globe had a 'house band' based around the instruments in a 'broken' or mixed consort of flute, violin, lute, cittern, bandore and bass viol. We know from Henslowe's papers that actors owned instruments such as lutes and viols. Rather than jump to the conclusion that these instruments were performed by their actor owners in the Rose and Globe amphitheatres, we should rather look at the acting companies' need to sustain patronage, in the way the present Globe companies do now, by sonnet readings at corporate events, and the like, and the amount that the companies took their plays on tour, often playing in indoor spaces.[3]

It is possible that when the plays were performed in the Globe theatre, the audience of the day would have been content with much less musical representation and iconography to help delineate different worlds, and the subtle differences in character status and hierarchy that our audiences expect today. The 'original practices' approach we developed to address the question of 'authenticity', then, can be described as exploratory, using methods that were rigorous yet practical for a contemporary commercial theatre.

KEITH McGOWAN: GLOBE MUSICIAN

APPROACHING 'ORIGINAL PRACTICES' IN MUSIC

The Shakespeare's Globe experiment with recreating early theatrical performances is pioneering in its field, but Wanda Landowska and Arnold Dolmetsch began exploring the potential of historical musical instruments about a century before the *Festival of Firsts*,[4] and the historical performance movement in music has achieved a great deal of maturity. I bring this up because musicians may have sold LPs in the seventies on the promise of 'original instruments' in 'authentic performances' that would clean up the old masters, but these days period orchestras are more modest in their hopes of recreating past musical experiences. 'Period instrument performance', or 'historically informed performance' (HIP) are common credos now, for ensembles that subtly distance themselves from the expectations of recreating 'the original'. I think the change in stance helped stem the antagonism between modern orchestras and the once-maverick period bands, and signalled a greater level of co-operation between the two in recent years.

Over the years I have grown to believe that our approach to putting music into an 'original practices' production must be more compromising. For example: the trumpet fanfares that we use are based on research from original sources, and relate to the six 'poynts of warre' which were the signals that every soldier would have to know to be able to perform properly on the battlefield. Knowing your calls could be a matter of life and death, so when the Tudor theatregoers heard these calls it was not simply as if they heard a trumpet fanfare; the alarum was a highly charged signal that would create an immediate physical response. This repertoire of trumpet calls would evoke powerful memories for many Elizabethan and Jacobean men. There is no way you can recreate that response for a modern audience using only 'historical' resources. I am coming more and more to the idea that we have got to try and add something extra to an 'original practices' performance to try and get that same emotional, and even physical, response.

I fear that the expectation from 'original practices' performance is for something that is elegant, and essentially 'safe', when we know that the theatres of Shakespeare's Bankside could be places of riot and sedition. I believe that to achieve that historical sense of danger we need to broaden our understanding of 'authenticity'.

COLLABORATION WITH DIRECTORS

The musical experience of most directors, and indeed of many composers, is mediated through a mixing desk alongside the lighting cues, technology which has not been extensively employed at Shakespeare's Globe. A mixing desk would be very basic equipment in any other theatre, and while the Globe remains a champion of live acoustic music the issue of sound engineering is frequently discussed. A director may hear in his or her head a kind of cinematic soundtrack which could be realised in a tech-ready darkened theatre, but recreating those effects and details in an acoustic space can often fall short of expectations, which can be a cause of frustration on both sides.

Working with Tim Carroll was a notable exception in this regard, as he is comfortable with period music and musicians, I guess because of his experience in directing opera. In his production of *Twelfth Night* (2002) the musicians were encouraged to remain in view, even when we were not playing, which did help to make music a part of the drama. *Measure for Measure* (2004) was John Dove's first experience of 'original practices' performance at the Globe and some of the music ideas we presented him with were rather unusual, even in the field of early music. Although a soundworld of jew's harps, dulcimer, viol and triangle was not what he (or anyone else) had in mind the combination justified itself to the extent that John has since used the viol as a reference point in subsequent discussions about scoring for other work.

One of the things that attracted me to early music is the level of contribution an individual can make to the interpretation and even creation of a score. As a composer I like to build in opportunities for the musicians to develop and explore their musical role, although in the theatre this level of musical autonomy often has to be reined in to remain true to the world the director has in mind.

With *Edward II* (2003), director Tim Walker had very clear ideas about what he wanted, though his reference points were Richard Wagner's *Siegfried* and the film *Monsoon Wedding*. While this music was a long way from the resources of an 'original practices' brief, I could imagine the atmosphere he wanted and I developed an understanding of the pathos of the piece that he was after, and we managed to interpret that in a very integrated way that supported the action, remained perfectly within the historical framework and satisfied Tim.

PERFORMING AT THE GLOBE THEATRE

One of the things that immediately emerged was that the florid style that we use in concerts is not always appropriate here. It would be fair to say that in certain styles of pre-classical music it would be wrong to perform without embellishment. But we found when we came to the Globe that embellishment got in the way of the impact of the music, and everything had to be much clearer and bolder.

Subtle changes in instrumental timbre and melodic character do not have the same impact in an outdoor space that they would in a darkened theatre, where lighting can call for an audience's hushed attention. This is particularly true of afternoon performances at the Globe when the sun and city noises are at their height. As composer on a production I try to find a group of musicians who, by complementary instrumental skills and much doubling and even trebling, can provide a very broad palette of musical timbres, from very gentle sounds (lute, viol, flute) to a big noise to accompany dancing (shawms, percussion). This emphasis on musical variety was the very essence of the waits' ensembles, the groups of professional musicians that provided music for the London theatres, and who prided themselves on their versatility. In this way melodic variation can be cued by a significant change in instrumental timbre, so that the music will support stage business like characterisation, or a change in location.

AUDIENCE RESPONSE TO MUSIC

I play for all sorts of audiences, from a drinks party at an army base to Southbank recitals. I am quite used to walking up to someone and trying to engage them in what I am doing, one to one. Before I worked at Shakespeare's Globe my aspiration was, like most classically trained musicians, focused on interpreting sophisticated concert repertoire. It happens that most of the music that has survived from the time of Shakespeare is from the sophisticated repertoire because it was only the literate stratum of society that was inclined to put its music on paper. There is a vast amount of earlier music of more popular appeal that either retains a shadowy presence or is entirely lost. This imbalance is particularly unfortunate in relation to 'original practices' at the Globe where we have, for instance, no reliable English source for military music of the period (all our tuckets and alarums are German, French or Italian) and the earliest source of popular dance tunes was not published until 1651. In scoring the music for *Twelfth Night*, for example, I wanted to try and recreate the sound of a sixteenth-century English shawm band, realising that almost no contemporary sources survive expressly for an ensemble that committed its material to memory or relied on improvisatory skills. You can picture the problem if you imagine what we would know of the music and technique of a modern player such as Charlie Parker were it not for his recordings. The resolution of the problem, for better or worse, was to play from printed sources while encouraging experienced musicians to be playful with their notated part.

Given the comparative paucity of suitable musical sources it would be easy for productions always to draw on the same resources, so that 'original practices' productions could begin to sound all the same to a modern audience. This, of course, would not be a problem for Shakespeare's groundling, who would welcome hearing his favourite tunes on the stage. That familiarity is not there for us, and I feel that if a production is to be located in its own particular world the composer has to offer more than might have been historically sufficient.

When I present my talks to Globe Education groups about theatre music in the time of Shakespeare I characterise what we do in 'original practices' productions at the modern Globe as more like the sort of rich musical experience you might have got at an indoor theatre but played in an outdoor auditorium. There would probably have been little time for music as part of the short afternoon performance permitted by the city authorities, a scant two and a half hours that does not even allow time for act breaks, and Henslowe's accounts do not suggest any regular musical participation in the Rose. A modern audience would probably feel cheated at the breakneck pace of a show in the Globe in 1600, but can relax in the expectation of music before the play and in the act breaks, as seems to have been the custom for a whole evening's entertainment in one of London's indoor theatres.

WILLIAM LYONS – GLOBE MUSICIAN

THE ROLE OF MUSIC IN THE THEATRE

From my point of view 'original practices' means considering very carefully what instruments were available, who would have played them and how in a historical context music would have been used in the play. We know very little about non-melodic sound effects. We know they used cannon, trumpets and drums, but other than that, the way the music worked is unknown.

You often find that the use of music in conventional theatre is very filmic. My great bugbear is the little 'sting', as we call it, at the end of the scene. A piece of music gets cut down and cut down, and it always ends up being four bars long, which is like the advert break or the scene swizzle hidden in the TV or film production. You will have trouble finding a director who would think of other methods than that traditional way of producing cuts between scenes. That is not to say that it did not happen, it may well have been like that in Shakespeare's day. But I think a lot of that music is just filler and it certainly does not serve a musical purpose. It is just an aural distraction to take the audience's mind off the fact that nothing is happening. I think the fear of silence is all pervasive.

PERFORMING AT THE GLOBE THEATRE

On a very basic level, playing out in an open space completely affects how the instruments sound, how they carry, what sort of resonating surfaces there are. We found that it is quite interesting with wind and string instruments how they react differently and how the various climactic influences can affect how the music resonates around the building depending on how big the audience is. On a wet day, the instruments carry in a probably easier, but less resonating way; they carry but they do not feel as if they go very far. The instruments do like being up in the gallery; when we use them in other places, you can tell that acoustically they do not carry as well. Certainly it is a fact that even quieter instruments such as lutes and viols work very well up in the gallery. There is something about the forward projection of the roof that directs the sound down; whereas on the stage, it can often get quite lost among all the action, falling into the yard.

AUDIENCE RESPONSE TO MUSIC

I have seen audiences focus their attention on the quietest instruments. In some of the productions in which we have employed 'original practices' when you have had just a lute or a viol playing, audiences will pick up on that pretty quickly. I suppose it is part of retraining them to appreciate non-amplified sound. Audiences will adapt to that very rapidly, although sometimes that has not been allowed to happen. Music has not been allowed to take the time to settle in. Often it is because the production needs to have a certain dynamic in itself and an internal tempo. Directors often want to segue very quickly between things, so if there is a song, they often think, 'We can't have this song taking over the whole scene so we want something else going on in the time'; whereas my feeling is that a song came up because theatre, masque and spectacle were very much tied together. I think that the audience would have sat back and listened to a song quite happily. When we tried that in the plays, such as with Feste in Twelfth Night (2002) and Autolycus in The Winter's Tale (2005; see figure 8, p. 116), I think the audience have loved it even as an interlude in the action; it does not matter that the narrative thread is not carried on at that point, because quite often the songs have some relevance to the action. Audiences should not be underestimated and productions do not have to fill every gap with effect.

I think we establish a good rapport with the audience: there is always a rousing cheer at the end of a production. When we go out and do pre-show music on the stage or in the yard, they are very appreciative. I think they like seeing live musicians on the stage; they do not want to experience what you get in conventional theatres where they do not know whether or not the music is live, it is just pumped through speakers. At the Globe there is immediacy. There is also the rather pleasant matter of people seeing us actually playing the instruments, especially historical instruments that they do not often see. Without exception, the audience seems to have really enjoyed the musical contributions here, whether 'original practices' or not.

THE RELATIONSHIP BETWEEN THE MUSICIANS
AND THE ACTING COMPANY

There is a great sense of inclusiveness, the shared dressing rooms and the non-hierarchical structure of the company has worked very well, and people tend to accept willingly the other disciplines that are going on around them and make friends easily. Having said that, it does depend on the dynamic of the company that you are working with; in some companies it takes a long time to feel like you are a part of it. As musicians we always have that slight stigma attached to us that we are only here for the money and we are not really interested in anything to do with the dramatic side of it. It may be an exception here, but every musician I have worked with here has embraced the theatrical side of their role and the whole process of blending in, being on stage and being part of the scene, reacting to what is happening around us. It is when we are pushed away and the director does not really want to know about the band, that is when a certain divisiveness happens. But in general, actors are pleasantly surprised that musicians are willing to take part.

WORKING AT THE GLOBE VERSUS OTHER THEATRES

I work in lots of different areas, I am involved in film music and I compose and work with smaller chamber groups and conduct research into early music. I have worked at the National and the RSC, but I have to say, that this is the place where I have done most of my growing up in the theatre. I started off in 1998 coming in as a player for productions that had people writing music for them and some of them were using period instruments and mixing and matching, and it really helped my knowledge of how to apply music to theatre. It has been a wonderful experience. I think that this is a very special space but it presents its own problems, problems which occur more when you try and impose a closed-theatre mentality on this open space. That is when you find the productions that are not successful in my view; they try and take away what the theatre actually is; they cover it up or put massive banks of scenery to cover up the façade at the rear of the stage. I think the best productions do not need to do that; they let the performance work and the music speak for itself.

CREATING A MUSICAL ENVIRONMENT AT THE GLOBE

The audience embrace the performances at the Globe wholeheartedly; we all have imaginations; we all have pictures in our heads that the words give us. We do not need a great deal more. That is the whole point of the underscore. By underscore I mean the music that underlies the text and has an influence on the emotional direction of that text for the audience. You can create a sinister underscore or you can create a delicate underscore, and one thing we worked at quite a lot with Claire van Kampen, which I thought was a great idea, was creating other worlds off stage. You could hear a life carrying on inside a Venetian house or on the streets outside a palace or music outside Richard II's cell and by using the various spaces around the Globe without any avocation you can create that effect. In *Coriolanus*, you have marching and drums in the distance and trumpet calls nearby. I think music can really develop those layers of understanding and layers of reality for an audience.

APPROACHING 'ORIGINAL PRACTICES' IN MUSIC

The trouble with being a purist is that you do not actually know what happened in the theatre. So I would like to think that there could be a production that really used music, not necessarily as integrated into the action as it sometimes is. I think quite often music can almost be a separate entity. We have got quite close to that here. The ideas of sound effects and underscoring are modern and overdone. We lose sight of the likelihood that in the early modern theatre instrumentalists would have stood up and played a piece of music that was well known to everybody. Perhaps in strict performance practice the company would play their own instruments and only on special occasions would they have hired the City Waits and the military trumpeters for particular plays. It does seem significant that a lot of the cues call for wind instruments such as cornets and hautboys and trumpets, which probably means that musicians were brought in from the outside. Stage directions do not often say that the lute accompanies a song or the cittern is played for ribald songs; it sometimes says 'soft music on recorders'. Shakespeare knew that he would have musicians coming in and he would have to designate what instruments he wanted at that point. So, in a way, he is being very specific because he is directing what the sound should be but not the actual music.

I think that you end up compromising a lot of the original material. We know that music was being written for masques and other entertainment. Just because music was not written down for theatre, apart from some of the songs which have survived, it does not mean that people were not composing for the theatre; it just means that it has not survived. I would love to see what they were doing and I cannot quite extrapolate from any surviving sources how music would have been used in theatre.

COLLABORATION WITH DIRECTORS

When I worked in collaboration with Claire van Kampen, it was very often that she would meet with the director and say, 'We're thinking of this here and this there, and what have you got?' What you come up with first of all is location; the period does not really matter, because that is another modern theatrical idea that you set something geographically and you set something in its time. In Elizabethan London you would have heard Elizabethan music from London; there was not that idea of suggesting Sicily or Verona or Poland or far-off lands like Illyria. The temptation now is to turn everything into a sort of world music fest, and I think that is absolutely fine but I cannot imagine that Londoners were totally insular, they were part of a cosmopolitan environment. I do not know whether they would have had that mind-set to have thought: 'Here comes the Prince of Morocco' and had suitable music. They might have had some clashing cymbals or something like that for effect.

The role of music is to paint a colour on to a scene. In 'original practices' we tried to stick very much to the music of early modern London. If there is a play that is set in Italy and you want to use Italian music that is fine because there would have been a lot of Italian music in England at the time, but when productions were set in Vienna, for example, we would try to find sounds that resonated with Viennese traditional music. Maybe I am being totally unfair to Elizabethan musicians, but I cannot imagine that they would have tried to achieve the same level of geographical specificity when providing music for a play. Often I think the musicians were providing mood music rather than location music.

The singers of songs were street performers and court fools, the sort of person who would sing a song to which everyone would know the tune. The audience would get the references, verses and jokes. I am sure there were so many layers of references, misquoted proverbs that would have had audiences in stitches. I do not know if we will ever fully capture that ethereal idea of what music meant to the first Globe audiences.

NOTES

1 This chapter combines conversations between the editors and Keith McGowan (9 February 2007) and William Lyons (12 June 2007) conducted at Shakespeare's Globe Theatre with a written contribution by Claire van Kampen.

2 *Celebrating Shakespeare: This World's Globe, with the Musicians and Actors of Shakespear's Globe Theatre London* (2006).

3 It is entirely possible, as with the Globe's 2007 touring production of *Romeo and Juliet*, that the actors supplied their own accompaniment to songs, and indeed, until the growth of competition between the public indoor theatres, this was probably entirely adequate.

4 The *Festival of Firsts* was a celebration to commemorate the opening of Shakespeare's Globe. It consisted of *Henry V*, *The Winter's Tale* and 'Triumphs and Mirth', which was a specially prepared performance to celebrate the completion of the Globe.

CHAPTER FIFTEEN

DISCOVERIES FROM THE GLOBE STAGE

Mark Rylance, Yolanda Vazquez and Paul Chahidi

MARK RYLANCE ON HIS ROLE AS ARTISTIC DIRECTOR AND THE GLOBE REPERTOIRE

CC: We were curious about your two roles as Artistic Director and as actor. How did you balance those two roles within the building?[1]

MR: Eventually, not effectively enough for me to be able to stay, I got overwhelmed, really. I think actor-managers you find who have the energy for being artistic directors are a very good thing. The really core place for a theatre is on the stage, what is happening between the actors and the audience, because if that goes down, then really everything goes down. Artistic Directors must remain conscious of that core. My time here was very Shakespearean in a way, someone who was sitting at the highest, most removed and protected level of Boardroom decision-making was also out in the most visceral, rainy, afternoon matinees. When things went wrong I was with the other actors, saying, 'We've got to do this, we've got to do that. I'm going to try, follow my lead. I don't succeed every time, so don't blame yourself if you don't succeed', and that was much more comfortable than when I was a director rather than an actor on the one show I directed, *Julius Caesar*.

CC: How did you approach developing the repertoire for the theatre? What motivated your choices?

MR: At first, I chose the plays to fulfil the mission of exploring a reconstructed amphitheatre. I also tried to link each season with a topical theme. I understood my job to be the creation of a theatre community, artists and audiences, who would rediscover how Shakespeare's amphitheatre worked. Perhaps the first of the 'original practices' I tried to follow was my understanding that Shakespeare and his company responded to the topical issues of the Elizabethan and Jacobean audience. They were not just putting on plays to make money. The Globe experiment could not just be about itself. To be a theatre our plays had to reflect the world outside. In the first season, *Henry V* (1997) was about a group of people earning a new land for themselves with words, encountering the fate they have inherited and risking everything, and *The Winter's Tale* was about the rebirth of something that had been lost. These ideas coincided with both the reopening of the Globe and New Labour returning to power. They were hopeful days. From the start I also wanted to explore amphitheatre plays by Shakespeare's contemporaries, so we also produced *The Maid's Tragedy* and *A Chaste Maid in Cheapside* that year. I imagined a theatre space, as it was originally, for other writers, especially those writing about the city just across the Thames.

The second year the theme was Justice and Mercy, fathers and daughters. We used 'original practices' [OP] clothing again and tackled Middleton and Dekker as well as Shakespeare. There were actresses and actors in all of the productions, as well as international and multicultural casting. *As you Like It, The Merchant of Venice, A Mad World My Masters, The Honest Whore* were the productions that made up the 1998 season.

I remember after the second season feeling that we should begin to explore tragedy, and so we moved again into all-male OP productions of *Antony and Cleopatra* and *Julius Caesar* (1999), in the Roman, Four-hundredth Anniversary season. A 'free-hand' *Comedy of Errors* also featured that season, with Marcello Magni and Katherine Hunter, two of the founders of Complicite Theatre. I wanted plays that would reveal different things about the place and test us, the actors and audience, as we learned how to listen and act in a completely new way. So in 1999 we also produced our first new play, commissioned especially for the Globe: *Augustine's Oak*, a verse play by Peter Oswald about the clash of Roman and Celtic Christian faith. I always felt it would be wrong if the space was only used to challenge and grow actors, directors and designers, that it was a writer's space most famously, and modern writers should be writing for it.

I had been trying to develop an ensemble of players in the central core of the company as I had initially thought that it would be easy to get lead players, because it would be such a thrilling challenge to come and play here. It seemed to me that a great company was not to do with its lead players, who would come and go as their careers dictated, but to do with the ensemble who were there regularly supporting the lead players. I had focused on things to develop that ensemble and added even more skills development to rehearsals in 1999.

In 2000, choosing *Hamlet* and *The Tempest, The Antipodes* and *Two Noble Kinsmen*, I came to see that the most difficult thing, actually, was the challenge of getting the established classical actors to come and take a risk. Leading on the Globe stage was exhausting and actors felt extremely vulnerable. Most of the actors I asked were too frightened or just not interested. Some never came during the whole of my ten years here, even to see the place. I realised I had to choose some productions, as I was doing at times for myself, with the lead actor as the starting point, for example Vanessa Redgrave or Jasper Britton, who played Caliban in *The Tempest* and was wonderful in the space. *Macbeth* (2001) came out of me asking him what he would like to do the following year; would he like to play Macbeth, who would he like to direct? In 2000, the casting of Vanessa as Prospero arose from my concerns about all-male productions denying actresses parts. We all loved the imaginative nature of single-gender work but we could achieve this as well, in our 'free-hand' work, if we did gender-blind productions and moved towards the all-women's company. Vanessa coming and playing Prospero with all her awareness of exile and injustice was the first step in our main productions towards that. (Actually way back in 1996 we did our first all-female production of a source play for *The Two Gentlemen of Verona*.)

As I have said already I offered directors two modes of approach to the stage: (1) a disciplined, faithful exploration of as many original playing practices as possible or appropriate; (2) a 'free hand' to explore the space with any and all of their modern theatre instincts, except electric lights and sound. Up until 2000 each season had been a mixture of these approaches, but in 2001 it was all 'free-hand', with *King Lear*, *Macbeth* and *Cymbeline*, exploring RSC, East European, and Shared Experience techniques. We cut back that year and only did three productions. I said 'Let's not do more work; let's mount these plays and re-rehearse them while we play them in the Globe.'

After the 2001 'free-hand' season we swung very heavily back towards 'original practices' in the season of Cupid and Psyche, with *Twelfth Night* (2002 – although it was originally produced for the Middle Temple Hall). We also did *A Midsummer Night's Dream* that year, which was 'free-hand', and we did *The Golden Ass*, a big new play by Oswald that combined both companies. So that was as much a development of our new writing that year as it was a development of 'original practices'. I was starting to try to hold on to directors, Tim Carroll, Mike Alfreds, which is eventually the only way you build a regular ensemble of actors. Directors have to have the right to cast who they want. A real ensemble of experienced actors was emerging. People Like Liam Brennan, Colin Hurley, Patrick Brennan, Terry McGinity, Bill Stewart, Geraldine Alexander, John McEnery, Jules Melvin, to name a few of the strong-voiced, committed company players.

I suppose it was after the success of *Twelfth Night* that the following year (2003) was all 'original practices', the season of regime-change. That was the year the war in Iraq began, and I was increasingly angered by what was happening in the world around us. So we staged an all-male production of *Richard II* (Middle Temple Hall again), *Richard III* with Katherine Hunter leading the first all-female company, *Dido, Queen of Carthage*, the first time we did a Marlowe play, *Edward II*, and *The Taming of the Shrew*. That first female company was very exciting. *Twelfth Night* had been very successful because Tim Carroll had said, 'Let's push the OP experiment even farther.' We found it was what audiences wanted and they continued to come with us as we demanded more and more of their imaginations.

In 2004 it was the season of star-crossed lovers, when we linked with the Samaritans and our whole programme partnered a particular movement in society. *Much Ado About Nothing, Measure for Measure, Romeo and Juliet* (2004) were all 'original practices' that year too, but the casts were all-female and two mixed-genders, no all-male. So we were always mixing things up a bit. That was the year we also tried original pronunciation for the first time since Tim [Carroll] added that experiment over one weekend with *Romeo and Juliet*.

The next new thing we wanted to try to do was a whole production of original pronunciation, which we did with *Troilus and Cressida* in 2005 as part of the World and Underworld season; my final season which also included our three-actor *Tempest*, a very 'free-hand' flying *Pericles*, an OP *Winter's Tale* (see figure 14), a third new play from Oswald, an adaptation of Plautus called *The Storm*, and one of my favourite pieces, an original devised mask play by Jack Shepherd, *Man Falling Down*. Jack was the first actor/director to join me way back in 1996 with *Two Gentlemen of Verona* and he made our first jig, a masked rap by Lennie James and the company.

That completes the list of our productions but it is important not to forget all the fascinating International productions that we invited from South Africa, Cuba, Japan, India, Brazil. They always taught us things we did not know. Also I would like to point out the impact of our two tours to Japan where the surviving seventeenth-century, traditional, all-male Kabuki theatre inspired us all. The visits to other period architecture such as the Middle Temple Hall, Hampton Court and the Teatro Olimpico in Italy were very important to our development. And touring to America, which we did three times, also gave us confidence that we were creating a way of acting Shakespeare which was different and survived even in modern thrust and proscenium spaces.

YOLANDA VAZQUEZ: ACTOR AND GLOBE EDUCATION PRACTITIONER

PERFORMING ON THE STAGE FOR THE FIRST TIME

Initially, the first time I worked here in 1999, as we were coming out to do the very first performance of *The Comedy of Errors*, I was petrified. In a darkened space you pretend that the audience is not there and you bring them in like a fly on the

14 Yolanda Vazquez as Hermione in *The Winter's Tale* (2005), Shakespeare's Globe

wall to listen to the story. I thought, 'Whether I like it or not, this is in daylight and therefore I am going to see faces and it is frightening.' From that fear I came on to the stage and realised that people when they come to see a play come to be entertained and not to judge. What a joy that was to be able to say, 'Actually, I've got a really good story and you're going to enjoy this.' I felt like I had a gift that I could give the audience and at the same time they were giving me a great gift by listening and being attentive and enjoying the story as it went along.

Two things happened to me there: first, I realised that what I had done as an actor in a darkened space was make the audience into a monster that was there to judge rather than to receive and to enjoy, which I suppose says a lot about me. But the other thing was I found it wonderful to play with an audience and how much that helped with the development of the story on stage and how that sort of playing became very satisfying as an actor. It is much more exposing than any other stage that I have worked on in that sense.

I think that having Mark here as an actor and also Artistic Director worked because he was so open to seeing how the space could work. It helped the rest of the actors on that stage because he was very generous about sharing his discoveries and discussing how we were developing or could develop on the stage. He instinctively knows how to use the space and he worked on passing that knowledge on, which to me meant that the work on a play was continuous, new discoveries could be brought in and experimented with. It is a freer way of working than in other theatres and I enjoyed the challenge.

AUDIENCE ENGAGEMENT

Two of the things I have noticed about this theatre are how quickly the audience respond and how quickly they are up for using their imagination. I find it interesting that when the audience is given the power to use its imagination it responds very quickly. People will comment on what they have experienced and where they have been in their heads during a show, which might have little to do with what they have actually seen. The language and the playing transport them. I think that is fantastic.

One of the things I have thoroughly enjoyed is when I have seen big groups of kids of about eleven or twelve years old standing at the front or around the sides who have got so involved in the story that they are suddenly laughing out loud and I think, 'Oh my goodness, they're not laughing at slapstick, they're not laughing at a visual joke, they're laughing at the language!' If you were to tell them that they would say, 'No, no, Shakespeare, I don't understand it', but there they were really guffawing and interacting with what they would have seen as this ancient language. I am sure they would have said to their teachers, 'I don't wanna go to see a Shakespeare play!' and yet they were involved. It is an intelligent space and the plays become accessible within it.

HOW THE GLOBE DIFFERS FROM OTHER THEATRES

Before coming to the Globe I had worked in many different theatres and with lots of different companies. Primarily, I suppose, I worked for the Citizens' Theatre in Glasgow and for the RSC. I had been working with brilliant directors, some who are extremely visual and who like to have a very strong idea of how a production should look and should be played but who would leave the characterisation, relationships and what we wanted within the story, up to the actors. So I suppose I had always been told where to stand and where to speak from, not completely, but in a little bit more prescriptive way. I really enjoy that way of working, but the difference between that and then coming to the Globe, where there was more freedom to say, 'What do I want? Where do I want to take this? How do I have to use this stage?' was quite liberating. To be able to think for myself in the sense of 'OK, I think it will work if I do this', not having a director that was saying, 'Please stand there and don't move until ...', but just saying, 'Let's work the scene and see what happens'.

Maybe that is the reason why a lot of directors think twice about working here, because they are aware that this is an actor's space. I know some directors have said, 'I don't think I can direct there because the work I do includes so much else, I don't think I'd be able to work just with the actors and the text.' I think the actor really does take over in this space.

WORKING IN 'ORIGINAL PRACTICES' COSTUMES

As Beatrice in *Much Ado About Nothing*, at certain times when she was becoming a little bit more passionate, in the rehearsal room I would be able to breathe easily through a phrase, but when the corset arrived and the dress and the overcoat, I realised I could not quite breathe in the same way on lines. I had to rethink it and feel where the breath had to be taken and how many lines I could get through. Once that technicality had been taken care of it was fine and the more I got used to the clothes the easier it became. Initially it is always a bit of a shock.

Sometimes if we were wearing these clothes that had been so beautifully made, we would feel like we had to show them off, so suddenly, instead of wearing them as characters, we began to show off the costume, walking like, 'Isn't this fantastic? Look at me, I've got a beautiful, lovely dress on!' Glynn MacDonald (Head of Movement) was very good at saying to us, 'Don't stand in that weird manner, how would you stand normally? How would you walk normally?' She had to make us aware of this, because you do feel very special and amazed by the amount of work and the beauty of the materials. You have to get over it, though, and start treating it like normal everyday clothing, then it is fine.

There were certain restrictions in 'original practices', things which on a practical level you could not do. We used to have rain cover stand-bys at the entrances and exits as you could not get the costumes wet. So 'original practices' kept you farther away from the audience. When we were in modern dress, you could have a more physical connection to the audience in the sense that, for instance, in *The Comedy of Errors*, we used the yard as the sea. We would now and then jump into the yard and we would fly around with the audience in our costumes and we were not worried about them. You could really be in contact with the audience, physically, and I suppose, with the 'original practices', we did not tend to do that, mostly because we did not use the yard. Which is more, possibly, like the practices of Shakespeare's time. I loved the detail that went into the 'original practices'.

USE OF THE YARD

Sometimes it is very exciting as an actor to be able to use the yard, I think the use of the yard in *Titus Andronicus* (2006) was fantastic. I loved the way it was used and in other productions in the past. I loved being able to go through the audience in *The Comedy of Errors* and beg at the beginning of the play, and then being able to use the audiences as fish or the sea. It was quite exciting and you can get away with a lot. You can push audience members around and play with them and see what their reactions are going to be, which can be fun. I think the audiences really enjoy it, but of course that just happens in the yard, the other audience members are sitting down and cannot join in.

In one of the 'original practices' productions, *Richard III* (2003), we did try to use the yard a couple of times as an entrance. In the second half I came in through the yard as if going towards the Tower, and it was really, really hard. It was packed; people had placed their bags on the ground and it is like an obstacle course trying to get on to the stage. People had their backs to you, as they were facing the stage, so I spent most of the time saying 'Excuse me, excuse me' to try and get through before going up the stairs on to the stage, and by the time I got there I was thinking, 'Was that worth it? Wouldn't it have been better to use the side entrance and go round the pillar?' It would have been the same journey, more or less, and in fact when we did rain cover, that is exactly what we did.

ALL-FEMALE COMPANIES

We did two plays initially with an all-female cast, the first being *Richard III* where I played Queen Elizabeth, which was female, obviously, then *Taming of the Shrew* (2003) where I played Hortensio and I became a gentleman. Now, we had decided to work both plays completely differently, the first play, the director and the cast had decided that we were going to look at characters and not stereotypes or characterisations. So all the girls playing boys really just looked at the characteristics and how we related to them in order to play them. We looked at how they would move, at the difference in movement between the genders and we did a lot of work again with Glynn MacDonald. Women walk with parallel feet and men walk with one foot in front of another.

But then when we worked on *Taming of the Shrew*, we decided that we were going to do caricatures of these men. We were going to think as women and see what we could bring out. I looked at Hortensio and had to make a judgement about him, to decide how I perceived him; what were his characteristics? I thought he was fantastic and I loved to play him, but I then judged him on these characteristics and then played with that in mind, and as it was a comedy, it worked for me. I had a lot of fun doing it. One of the things that I think we all realised as an all-female cast was the amount of energy needed, physical energy, to be these men in *The Taming of the Shrew*. We were all exhausted and would always say, 'I don't want to be a man!' The idea of showing the exterior, of having to be these cockerels most of the time, because that is what most of us, as men, were within the play, was exhausting. I saw Hortensio as quite a sensitive guy but who was trying to impose upon himself the idea of a man's man, one of the lads who wants lots of ladies when in fact that is not who he is. But if I played it as me, Yolanda, with female sensitivity, it did not work. So I had to play him at what we call 'Level Ten' physicality and energy, and, within that, find his sensitivity.

ORIGINAL PRONUNCIATION

I thought the original pronunciation rehearsals and performance was a great experiment, to hear how these plays have changed in sound. I know that some people thought it was a waste of time and thought, 'Why bother?' but it was brilliant for a company to be able to say, 'Let's have a go and see what happens!' That is what this space should be about – discovery, about seeing how these plays may have worked in the past, how we can learn from that, what we can do with them now and how we can go forward. Then it does not become a museum or archaic; it is something fruitful and in the moment.

As I say, with the original pronunciation, I found it *fascinating*, we did *Troilus and Cressida* (2005) and that was very strange as we rehearsed from the very beginning in original pronunciation. It had happened before on *Romeo and Juliet* (2004), which was rehearsed normally then the original pronunciation was added on to it. We worked with David Crystal and he made us phonetic scripts and went through what the phonics were, and how we should use them. He went through all the sounds with us. I am really useless when it comes to accents; I think it is because English is my second language. I can do them in Spanish, but I have to work really hard to do them in English, so I was petrified to begin with. I was playing Agamemnon. I thought the best thing would be to dive headfirst into it and see what happened. So from the very first day, I decided to do original pronunciation whatever came out of my mouth. This caused much hilarity because apparently I sounded Jamaican! But what was interesting is that David Crystal said, 'Well, why not, because Jamaica was one of the places where possibly this strand of accent went to', and he was so sweet about it and gave me a lot of encouragement and by the end of it, I really loved it. I loved trying to work out all the speeches.

I think people that came to see it, whether out of interest or to learn something, would have got a lot out of it. Personally, I found it fascinating, and learned from it. I realised that within the accents, even if we cannot be 100 per cent sure of the accuracy, I could hear every strand of English spoken in other places round the globe. I could hear South African, Australian, Irish, certain North American dialects, and I began to understand it as a mixture of sounds that travelled and survived as something different. And that really made me feel connected. I loved it.

INVOLVEMENT WITH THE EDUCATION DEPARTMENT

I got involved with the education work through *Adopt an Actor*, which I thought was a fantastic programme that Globe Education ran. From the very first day that I joined I liked the sound of it, I thought it was very funny, so I said, 'Can you adopt me, please?' and I became an adopted actor. Every time I came to work here I was asked and I accepted. Then I met Chris Stafford (Projects and Development Manager) when I was doing *Richard III* and we used to chat about the goings-on in the rehearsal room and I thought, 'God, the kids must be getting so bored with just listening to me gabbing on.' So I started setting up exercises for the kids to do online so they could do them in their classrooms and give me their response. It was quite selfish really, as I could get a lot of good ideas in return which I could use in my work. Chris told me that this was basically what they did in the Education department, and asked me to come and join. So I did and have carried on doing it; now I work in all areas of Globe Education: *Lively Action*, community, higher education, projects and research. I do the whole gamut.

I see myself as an actor/educator now. I think that is what is extraordinary, I have not been involved in any other theatre's education department, I know that the National has a big education department and so does the RSC, but I believe that Globe Education has fantastic working actors who are doing an immense amount of good acting work, then coming back and sharing their experiences with the students. I do not know how often that takes place elsewhere.

PAUL CHAHIDI: ACTOR AND GLOBE EDUCATION PRACTITIONER

SPEAKING TO THE AUDIENCE

The fundamental area in which this theatre reveals so much is in the symbiotic relationship between the words of the playwright, the actor, the audience and the architecture of the building, which are all intrinsically linked; you cannot separate one from the other. And where I had a sort of epiphany, when I started to get slightly bigger parts here and I started to talk to the audience, was with the soliloquies. It just became so obvious and so beautifully simple, and so clear what the relationship between the actor and the audience should be, and what you should be doing when you are speaking a soliloquy, which is holding a conversation with the audience. And that is something that has been lost with proscenium-arch theatres, speaking into the darkness, and a certain style of acting has come up from that architecture.

This whole approach of what you might often get in a proscenium-arch theatre is a scatter approach where you just throw it around and think you are taking everyone in, whereas in fact, as we found at the Globe, if you pick one specific person, and maybe not do the whole speech to them, but do at least a few lines to them and make it real that way, you can bring it right down and make it almost conversational. As long as you are supported and heard that will have the effect of making everyone else included far more than if you scatter it round. That was the fundamental discovery for me, and from that flowed lots of other discoveries, but it gave me the self-confidence to eyeball the audience and to just talk to them and not be afraid of that.

As someone who does a lot of comedy, it is brilliant for comedy. It really hones your skills. Always the danger at the Globe is not to get too seduced by the groundlings who are so up for a good time. I have never in my life come across an audience like the one at the Globe, where so many people really want to enjoy themselves, because they have already arrived there in a state of wonder at how beautiful the building is. That is the other thing, as an actor, you have to realise; you have to flex all your acting muscles in a way you definitely would not have to in a conventional theatre. Because you do not have lighting to help you and tell the audience where to look, you just have some other actors, the costume and the music, and then you have to learn how to use that space. It really forces you to work out your techniques, your voice production, the way you would use an audience, how you would stop yourself from tipping over into going for out-and-out comedy each time. The audience are so ready to laugh, and you have got to try to bridle and control that, because it can hijack a play; it can hijack the whole story.

THE GLOBE THEATRE AS AN ACTOR'S THEATRE

It is such a democratic space and the spoken word becomes even more important. Therefore, as an actor, it is even more important that you can be heard, while retaining subtlety, but also that you absolutely understand what you are saying. Because it is a very unforgiving space if you are unclear about what you are doing. You have to come in with a clear and interesting intention, even if you have got nothing to say, because otherwise they will lose interest in you very quickly. If you do not have clear intentions and do not understand the words completely yourself, the building will upstage you. Because I think every actor has to remember that the building itself is to some extent the star of any show. You have to respect that, while at the same time using that to tell your story. I think the Globe encourages generosity in actors. You can be anywhere on stage, and everyone will get your back at some point, but backs are good and reactions are as interesting as the person speaking. I think it is a really great leveller and a way of encouraging actors to think about the story first.

The Globe is definitely more an actor's theatre than a director's theatre. But I think it is a musician's theatre and a costume designer's theatre too. I think for a lot of directors it is a bit intimidating because I think they feel their craft is not recognised enough in that space. However, the reality is you need a bloody good director to make that space work; especially if you are going to do a tricky play. Which is why I think someone like Tim Carroll is just amazing, a genius really. But I think that the director's craft in that space is not acknowledged enough by critics.

COMEDY IN THE PLAYS

The Globe has made the plays fun, but the trouble is by using the word 'fun' it lightens what I am trying to say. I feel like it is bringing Shakespeare's plays, or any classical plays, back to audiences, to see them performed. They were scripts to be performed, not texts to be studied. Yes, of course they must be studied, there is so much value in that. But it is also just as important that particularly young people, who would not normally go and see a play, let alone a classical play, have an exciting, interesting, thought-provoking, moving time. Audiences have changed, they have different expectations, and we are in an age when different styles of acting are more

15 Paul Chahidi as Maria in *Twelfth Night* (2002), Shakespeare's Globe

acceptable and are perceived as more truthful. I just think that that kind of general wash of tragic tone to a tragic play is just death for any production, and if you do not find the humour in it, then you are not really exploring the play properly. And I do think that some people think that comedy is less profound than tragedy, but I would say the opposite. Because comedy, when it is done well, is deadly serious.

'TWELFTH NIGHT': MOVING FROM MIDDLE TEMPLE TO THE GLOBE STAGE

We did Twelfth Night (2002) in Middle Temple, and we extended it and then did it again at the Globe. Because Middle Temple was a traverse stage with audience on either side, Tim Carroll would encourage us to keep it fluid. He said as long as you are not throwing each other off kilter completely and putting each other off in some way, keep it fluid and move to different positions each night. But Middle Temple was a smaller space – not more intimate, because the Globe is very intimate. At the Globe we got so used to moving and adjusting to each other, and at least half had worked there before, we found that it was really easy to adjust, because you trusted them, and you knew that they would adjust to you, so it would be very fluid. And the response is always slightly different from an audience each night.

Moving to the Globe we had to restage certain bits; that was a fact because it had to include an audience on a thrust stage. To begin with it felt like we had lost so much, it felt small and jewel-like in Middle Temple, and it was a wonderful place to perform it, but pretty soon you found a different way of being intimate with the audience when you needed to be. The comedy was very robust; it was a very robust production. It is a very robust play. So we changed the staging, and then you adjusted your performance levels a bit, but I do not think it has to be a huge difference to go from the Middle Temple Hall to the Globe. Yes, you have to be heard, but it does not mean you are booming everything. It was just as truthful and detailed, I think. You just got this huge response on the laughs, which was a bit more polite at the Middle Temple Hall. You had to learn how to deal with that as it went along.

PLAYING A WOMAN

What happened with Twelfth Night, we had a session with Sian Williams, our chore-ographer, where Mark, myself, and the Viola actor (Michael Brown) talked about, in very basic terms, the different physiognomies of men and women, how that affects their movement. We observed her and another woman in a room moving, and aped it. It felt very crude, but the hips are different, the pelvis different and it affects the way you move. In theatre we learn that very stereotypical male movement occurs in straight lines and angles, but – and this is something Mark would always talk about – women move in curves on stage. This theory is so generalised that I always have to preface it by saying that it is not so cut and dried, but if you want to it is a very simple and perhaps crude way of thinking about masculine and feminine movement. Not only the curves, but the way you use your hands to gesture can be quite female. We did that and I did not think about it very much – we had rehearsal skirts on, but not the full costume. I have to say, my approach to playing a woman was always 'this is just another character that I am playing, who happens to be a woman'. What I cared about is what she cared about, what she wanted from the scene. That is all you have to worry about as an actor – you should not worry about the sex, because that will come later – it is just another role. The audience will accept that you are a woman – you look like one, maybe a slightly butch one. They are accepting so much in the Globe that they will make that imaginative leap immediately.

When it came to the costume it was a massive revelation. The corset which I had to be put into, it gave you a posture – with the skirt, the shoes and the hard-shelled wig – you had to move in a certain way. You had to be very upright in your carriage. There are some extant texts about lady-like deportment. My character was Maria – who is often played as a saucy milkmaid but is actually from a very good background and also brought up as a lady (see figure 15). We had read about the upright posture and smooth deportment, but actually, it was impossible to do anything else in that costume, you would fall over otherwise. It was duck-like – smooth and serene on top, but moving furiously underneath. Rolling your hips, just the way Sian had always told us to do. Otherwise, there was the danger of looking like a man in drag making fun of the character and that was the one thing that I did not want to do. I did not want to make it funny because I was a man playing a woman. I wanted it to be truthful and real, for the audience to forget that the actor was a man.

There was tittering at first, when you come on as a woman. But the building encourages people to use their imaginations. You do not have the luxury of the set, but that luxury can lead to a lot of lazy theatre. From the initial imaginary leap, it is one small extra step to believe that it is a woman. Once they have settled down, which does not take long, there is total acceptance. It was an advantage that we got used to the costumes in Middle Temple Hall. But you should wear the clothes; they should not wear you. It is not your costume; it is your character's clothes. I did not want to feel like I was just displaying the costume. In that way, I approached it as with any role.

USE OF VOICE ON STAGE

Watching Mark is an education in itself. Seeing how quietly he can speak and how he draws an audience in. How effective it can be if you are supported in your voice, you know what your intentions are and the meaning of the words – you can bring it right down. The levels are interesting. Your first impression is that you will have to be loud and you will never achieve the subtlety that you had in other theatres, but it is just not true. Actors learn not to shout. It is a question of choosing which level to speak at for which moment. You can grab an audience by the scruff of the neck when speaking, or you can beckon them in – you need both. It has taught me how to give focus to other actors; it has encouraged generosity. It has shown me the importance of diagonals and the intimacy they create. It allows the audience in, when you have the space between actors, giving them your back from time to time. I think every actor should turn their back on the audience during the show.

I worked in the main house in Stratford before I came to the Globe – very small roles. I did not go back there for ten years, when I did *Taming of the Shrew* with Jasper Britton, who is also a very seasoned Globe actor. Cicely Berry, Head of Voice there, said she could tell we had worked at the Globe, because we were not afraid of the audience. She admitted that it was not her taste to see actors going up to the audience and talking to them. This is fine, of course, but after she had seen *Cymbeline*, where I was playing Cloten, and I did a lot of that (which will always displease *some* people), she thought that it worked very well. I think directors on the whole are grateful for actors who can relate to an audience like that, particularly in clown roles. You need to reach out in proscenium-arch spaces even more. But it is amazing how many actors can be very unyielding and afraid of an audience.

AUDIENCE ENGAGEMENT

I think it is a much more excited and engaged audience than anywhere else, without a doubt, because they are not slumped in their seats being passive – they are an active part of the process of telling the story. You are so intimate with everyone in the house, more so when it is full, and it is like an electric current running through everyone – the words through the actors through the stage and the building, the groundlings and all three levels, a sea of faces. When you hold that many people's attention, it is incredible and it is unlike anything else. The most exhilarating experience you can have as an actor is at the Globe. You must not go out there feeling that they are the enemy in some way; they are there to embrace you. The fact is, they might not concentrate all of the time, but that is true about any theatre, it is just that you see it more at the Globe. And all it makes you do is try harder to tell the story. Naturalism is merely another style; it does not equal truth. Truth comes in all sizes and is all that matters; style is irrelevant. If naturalism is right for the Globe, then you do it; but naturalism is a style which is definitely not right for the space. Shakespeare writes naturalistically within a verse format: you will spend your life trying to crack that one. The Globe has taught me to realise that you can be very heightened and yet just as truthful.

I think this is a place that encourages experiment, and it encourages you to be daring, because you have an audience that are open to a new experience, and it is a totally different space from anywhere else. Immediately, as an actor, when you walk into that building, it is all new. On the whole, most actors rise to that challenge. Sometimes you meet actors who come away having done one season who hated it, and I think that is about control. You do not have as much control as you are used to in a conventional theatre. It makes you go back to the basics, to the basic principles of the language. At least it should do. I think if an actor does not go back to the basics, then he or she is missing a vital tool and risks losing the audience's attention and being upstaged by the building. Ultimately, the space forces you to use the language as your main tool.

INVOLVEMENT WITH THE EDUCATION DEPARTMENT

I have never been in a theatre which has such a close relationship with academics and the Education department. It is usually a separate world. But because education was one of the founding pillars it has been an integral part of the Globe's development, which I think has been an inspiration to lots of other theatres. I had never done workshops in my life until I came here. It started with me being an adopted actor and talking to students, and for me that was scary; I was not used to it. It is amazing how intimidating that can be. It made me think about what elements go into performance and what it means to be working on the Globe stage. It made me more articulate, I think, about my thoughts on acting and it was just hugely rewarding to see the way that I could get through to students and get them excited and on stage and into acting. They will perceive theatre as something enjoyable and not just as something they are doing for an exam. That is where the challenge lies; if we do not attract the young audiences, we have had it. We have to both attract and inspire them. The geography and the pricing system of the Globe both play their part: five pounds for, without a doubt, the best place to see the play in the house. I have seen children and 80-year-olds standing throughout the performance in the yard. I have not seen that in any other theatre.

NOTE

1 This chapter is drawn from conversations between the editors and Mark Rylance (17 April 2007), Yolanda Vazquez (2 February 2007) and Paul Chahidi (16 February 2007), all conducted at Shakespeare's Globe.

CHAPTER SIXTEEN

DIRECTING AT THE GLOBE AND THE BLACKFRIARS: SIX BIG RULES FOR CONTEMPORARY DIRECTORS

Ralph Alan Cohen

Shakespeareans looking back at the present century will note that it began with the recreation of the two theatres for which Shakespeare wrote his plays: Shakespeare's Globe (London, England, 1997) and the Blackfriars Playhouse (Staunton, Virginia, 2001) (see colour plate 8). Doubtless they will find in those two projects much to say about the popularity of Shakespeare at the turn of the century, about interest in early modern theatrical context, about tourism and nostalgia, and even about the marriage of arts and economic development. The question, however, is whether scholars and practitioners in the future will be able to say anything about how these two buildings influenced the performance and production of Shakespeare or, beyond that, theatrical performance and production in general. The harshest critics saw the Globe as little more than a Disneyfication of Shakespeare, but even the critics most sympathetic to the building of the Globe for reasons of historical interest were dismissive of its potential to make important theatre. The consensus was – and largely remains – that the best one can hope for from productions at the Globe is well-executed museum theatre, with the corollary that any other more significant production will be at odds with the building itself. This view of working in these two theatres not only makes it difficult for the Globe and the Blackfriars to position themselves as serious contributors to the progress of theatre, but it also creates a vicious cycle in which talented directors are hesitant to work in what they view as the constraints of the two theatres.

And on one level they are right. These theatres – like all theatres – are the expression of a set of expectations and values in the staging of plays, and, as such, have their own theatrical imperatives. Since these particular theatres are about the expectations and values of Shakespeare and his contemporaries, they naturally push performances away from the last 375 years of technological changes. The argument of this chapter is that in doing so the two theatres – and any future recreations of early modern theatres – are not only pushing theatre backward, they are also pushing theatre forward. The editors invited me, as a director and a scholar of early modern theatre, to contribute a chapter suggesting the 'pros and cons' of a rulebook for directors who work in early modern spaces. The 'cons' of such a rulebook are fairly obvious – constricting ingenuity, petrifying performance, ensuring sameness, putting museum into museum theatre and so on. The 'pros,' however, may not be so obvious. The rules set forth here for directing on early modern stages look two ways at once: micro-theatrically, they look backward to an understanding of how the text and the stage worked together when the plays were first performed (and thus how they might work together today); macro-theatrically, they look forward to a theatre freed of the nineteenth- and twentieth-century developments that in many ways have fettered it and its audiences.

When Shenandoah Shakespeare,[1] the touring company that predated the theatre, moved into the Blackfriars Playhouse in 2001, we found it easier to attract talented people to direct for us than it had been when we were simply a travelling troupe, but we discovered, as Shakespeare's Globe had, that directors came into our space trying to figure out how to fix it. For these directors, their understandable defence against museum theatre is to use the theatres in ways we know they were not used, ways we know Shakespeare did not imagine using them. The opportunity to recover the original stagecraft of the play appears a way back rather than a way forward, an expression of the old rather than of the new, and an imposition on rather than an opportunity for their own art. My own experience as a director makes me sympathetic to these directorial concerns; after all, good productions of classic plays are productions that feel as if they are new. My experience, however, as a director at the Blackfriars Playhouse and as a frequent audience member at Shakespeare's Globe, makes me believe that directors for whom the main goal is to make a great play live can achieve that goal directing on the stage at the Globe or the Blackfriars. Beyond that, directors who pay attention to the stage and the stagecraft of Shakespeare and his contemporaries will find that in doing so they will be freeing the plays from the accreted technological conventions that have substituted for their strongest dramatic energies. In particular, such directors will find themselves returning to the plays the two elements most crucial to the future health of theatre: the performer and the audience.

What follows, then, are 'rules' for directors who would work in the Globe or in the Blackfriars. In the comments that accompany the micro-theatrical specifics, I give justifications based on early modern practices – the 'this is how they were' argument. Beyond that, however, I hope to suggest the macro-theatrical objectives a director can achieve, the ones that have to do with the argument of how to make the play – and plays – 'better'.

BIG RULE I. HAVE ACTORS ATTEND STRICTLY TO THE WORDS

Good productions of Shakespeare give primacy to the words of the plays. John Barton and others have taught us that, and it is a lesson all the more necessary on the bare stages of the Globe and the Blackfriars. In fact, one major advantage of such stages is that they minimise the distractions from the words at the heart of these plays. The audience that latches on to the words will go on the imaginative journey that language and good acting inspire. No audience can latch on to the words if the actors themselves are not fastened to the words or when the actor or director has made a choice that distracts from the words.

Though scholars can debate the extent to which metrics, rhetorical figures and even orthography may have signalled acting choices to early modern actors, all agree that with little time for rehearsal and with sides instead of scripts Shakespeare's actors relied more heavily on clues in the text than modern professional actors are accustomed to do. For that reason, the culture of performance at the Globe and the Blackfriars needs to raise awareness of the text. I am not arguing here for a particular system in approaching the text; I am arguing only that a system be in place and that directors are stringent in having actors apply it. Great acting is specific acting, and any system that forces an actor to make choices about the text as specific as a syllable or a punctuation mark raises the level of the acting and signals to the audience's collective subconscious that those choices need their attention. For this reason, we require that our actors have a thorough understanding of their words, their punctuation and their metre.

HAVE THEM PARAPHRASE WORD FOR WORD

To help assure that the actors know the meaning of each word and grasp the reasons for the syntax, our policy is that all actors will arrive at the first rehearsal having found synonyms for all nouns, verbs, adjectives and adverbs. We allow them to use the same proper nouns and prepositions as in the text. Finally, we require that they use the same syntax as the original. In our table work, the actors read their paraphrases while we listen for the rare moment in which they have chosen the wrong translation. Our experience is that each of our twelve actors on average will have mistaken only two words. While that does not sound like much, it means that twenty-four times in a two-hour production – or once every five minutes – the audience would have heard the play go slightly off track, and twenty-four times actors will be working through mistaken intentions.[2] The temporary result of these word-for-word replacements is that the actors' paraphrases often sound as if they had been compiled by a robot who had eaten a thesaurus, but the object is not to find playable text but (1) to be certain that the actors understand precisely what each word means, and (2) to help actors understand how the thought generates the syntax and thus the order of the words.

HAVE THEM SCAN ALL VERSE ALOUD, AND REVIEW IT WITH THEM

We also require that actors scan each line and read it aloud with emphasis on the stresses.[3] For our veteran actors, this exercise is now second nature, and they need virtually no time to deal with verse. Actors unfamiliar with scansion shortly get the knack of it, and through their scansion work begin to learn lessons from the language that make their acting better.

CREATE MAXIMUM CLARIFICATION FOR AND MINIMUM DISTRACTIONS FROM THE WORDS

A director must know how to use blocking and gesture on a bare stage to assure that the language is doing all it can do. He or she must also know when other elements interfere with the language, when a blocking choice hides the speaker or the speaker's referent, when a gesture conflicts with or supports the words, and when sounds – intentional, such as music or vocal reactions, or unintentional, such as noisy soles on the stage or thigh slaps or hand claps – obscure the most important sounds of all: the language.

BIG RULE II. WHEREVER POSSIBLE EMPLOY THE STAGECRAFT OF THE AUTHOR

If a director at the Royal Shakespeare Company or at the Oregon Shakespeare Festival or at any of a hundred Shakespeare theatres staged a production in English of a Shakespeare play that used the plot but changed most of the words, it would create an outrage. Shakespeare's language is a cultural treasure, and we expect the institutions whose mission is to produce Shakespeare to be as faithful as possible to his wordcraft. By contrast, we seem not to care much about being faithful to his stagecraft. Why? We would never ignore the stagecraft of a Mamet or a Stoppard, so why do we hold in such low esteem the stagecraft of Shakespeare, a man of the theatre who was an actor and a sharer in his company? Certainly, one reason is that his wordcraft is fully preserved in the text, whereas we see his stagecraft only in glimpses. Those glimpses, however, are frequently quite clear in explicit stage directions and in embedded stage directions, and directors working on early modern stages ought to attend as carefully to those aspects of Shakespeare's art as to his language.

The tools we ask our directors to use in recovering the stagecraft are the stage directions that appear in the Folio and in the existing quartos of the plays (easily identifiable in conservative and well-annotated editions such as the New Arden).[4]

PAY ATTENTION TO THE ENTRANCES

A director must look first at Shakespeare's instructions for an entrance in answering the questions when? who? how? and where? Our experience is that if we start with the information in the stage direction it simplifies matters and frequently illuminates issues of character.

TAKE SHARED CUES AT FACE VALUE

When the speech prefix is 'all' or 'Lords,' have your actors respond on cue. The occasionally discordant or comic moment that emerges from this practice adds the dimension of theatrical self-awareness.

USE THE PROPS REFERRED TO IN THE STAGE DIRECTIONS OR IN THE TEXT

Even a cursory look at Philip Henslowe's inventory will disabuse the notions that the early modern theatre had little for the eyes, and Shakespeare's plays and those of his fellow playwrights are full of props that distil into visual terms the concerns and themes of the play. We ask directors to see how those props work before eliminating or substituting for them.

PLAY THE NIGHT SCENES INDICATED BY THE PROPS AND THE TEXT

One of the greatest joys of a theatre that 'does it with the lights on' is that it gives the audience extraordinary night vision. That is, while the characters have trouble seeing in the dark, audiences can simultaneously see the imagined darkness and exactly what is going on in it. Shakespeare and his contemporaries had three ways to create night: with props, with the text, and with acting. These three tools can spur the simultaneous vision of audiences. Over the last 150 years we have traded that dual pleasure for the compromised night-time that a lighting designer can simulate.

USE ASIDES SPARINGLY

Beware the tendency of editors to overuse asides. In all of thirty-six plays in the Folio, only four uses of the word 'aside' appear in a stage direction, yet editors have added that stage direction in hundreds of places in the text. Naturally, when the plot requires that one character on stage not know what the speaking character has done or is planning to do, the aside is necessary; but when the aside is primarily a matter of politeness it can drain the moment of the very dramatic tension it requires. Does Hamlet worry if his first line in the play – 'A little more than kin and less than kind' (*Hamlet* 1.2.65)[5] – offends Claudius? Does Enobarbus care if Cleopatra hears him say of Antony, 'Sir, sir, thou art so leaky / That we must leave thee to thy sinking, for / Thy dearest quit thee' (*Antony and Cleopatra* 3.13.63–5)? I think that the answer to both these questions is 'no'. Directors should consider that the source of these asides, these significant blocking choices, are normally editors for whom a guiding principle is propriety and should deal with those moments accordingly.

BIG RULE III. DO NOTHING TO LENGTHEN THE PLAY

What was the playing time of early modern plays? Shakespeare twice mentions two hours (*Romeo and Juliet* and *Henry VIII*), and Ben Jonson in *Bartholomew Fair* says two-and-a-half hours. Some argue that Shakespeare, not having a minute hand, would have called any play that ran from two o'clock in the afternoon (the normal starting time for plays) until something before five o'clock 'two hours'.[6] Shakespeare's shortest play, *The Comedy of Errors*, is 1,700 lines long and his longest play, *Hamlet*, is just over 4,000. In today's pronunciation of English, it takes an actor one minute to read twenty lines of a Shakespeare play – a little less for verse and a little more for prose. The average length of a play is fewer than 2,700 lines. At a normal reading pace, it would take contemporary actors two hours and fifteen minutes to say the words of the average Shakespeare play in their entirety. David Crystal's experiment at the Globe with original pronunciation further indicates that original pronunciation would take another ten minutes off the total playing time.[7] Thus, assuming that there were no pauses in the speaking of the lines, the average Shakespeare play took Shakespeare's actors two hours and five minutes to say their words – or just five minutes slower than the two hours' traffic that Shakespeare mentions in the Prologue of *Romeo and Juliet*. In short, the empirical evidence is that – if actors spoke the lines without pauses – early modern plays could certainly have been two-hour entertainments.

To understand what these numbers represent, consider *Macbeth*. At 2,200 lines it would require only one hour and fifty minutes to say all the words (or no more than an hour-and-three-quarters in original pronunciation). So what takes up the extra time in a contemporary production of the play lasting two-and-a-half hours? Some of that time, of course, will be for combat (though an entire round of boxing takes only three minutes) and some for whatever witch-like choreography the director decides to do (though the longest Fred Astaire and Ginger Rogers dance number in *Top Hat*, 'Cheek to Cheek', takes just five minutes and seven seconds). Allowing one hour and fifty minutes for the words and ten extra minutes for combat and for witch business, what is happening in the other thirty minutes of a two-and-half-hour production of Macbeth? Productions that take that much time are either devoting it to a director's concept (to which I will return) or to actors' pauses.

In short, how much did actors pause in their speech on the early modern stage? I believe that the conditions of performance for Shakespeare and his fellows militated against pauses. In an open-air theatre on a stage surrounded by a milling audience, whose attention will always be ambient, an actor crossing the stage without speaking would be inviting trouble.[8] Challenging sight lines and 360 degrees of visual distraction put a premium on sound; it was the necessary current of the play. To get an idea of what the effect of a five-second pause might have been during a performance on the Globe or Blackfriars stage, imagine five seconds of complete silence on the radio when the stream of sound stops. And those seconds add up. Shakespeare's plays average roughly 100 entrances and exits. If each entrance or exit is accompanied by just three seconds of silence, the pauses to enter and exit will add 300 seconds or five minutes to a show.

Those five minutes of needless silence are a waste of an audience's time, and by the end of the show, even a seated audience will inevitably feel the effects of the extra five minutes. All directors want to put 'bums on seats'; good directors concern themselves with the restlessnesss of those bums once they are in the seats and want to make sure that they get bums out of seats in a timely manner. Here are some ways to do that.

HAVE ACTORS PICK UP – ALMOST JUMP – THEIR CUES

In practice this means that actors should act while they are speaking. If they are making a cross, they should do their lines while they cross. If they want to laugh at the line to which they are reacting, they need to laugh in the line they are saying. If they are astonished by something someone says, they must show that astonishment as they speak. Such an approach is more natural than the pauses we so frequently hear in over-long productions. People in real life are eager to speak, and the most realistic dialogue is that in which characters almost jump their cues. Actors must not, however, confuse the instruction to be quick on their cues for an order to rush their lines. Character and intention alone should dictate the pace of the speaking. Having to listen is part of the collaborative enterprise of good theatre, and the goal for the actors should therefore be a comprehensible pace that never lags.

WEIGH CAREFULLY THE VALUE OF ANY PRODUCTION BUSINESS REQUIRING THE CESSATION OF WORDS

We rarely complain that a two-hour production should be longer; we frequently find ourselves wishing it would end sooner. By the end of a show the minute or two of added business that seemed like a good idea at the time can seem an indulgence. So a director with a good idea for business should both make as much of the added business as possible a part of the ongoing flow of language and/or restrict it to its essentials. If, for example, the business is an added song, can the words be from the text? Or if the added business is a dance, can the dance take place while the words are going on?

I do not want to leave Big Rule III without emphasising that the value of the rule is not merely to avoid tiring an audience. Consider the energy and efficiency of a full-text production of *Macbeth* that takes only two hours to perform: it will appear tighter and more charged than a production that takes thirty more minutes. Beyond that increased energy, as in any enterprise that involves rehearsed performers moving adroitly in concert, a good pace gives audiences the experience of expertise and of ensemble. Those are qualities we value in any theatrical work.

BIG RULE IV. ACKNOWLEDGE AND COLLABORATE WITH THE AUDIENCE

This essay began by asserting the potential of the work on recreated early modern stages to look forward as well as backward and even the potential of such work to free Shakespeare, and indeed theatre, from nineteenth- and twentieth-century conventions that may have sapped some of its fundamental power. Without any doubt, the added convention that most transforms – in my view, disfigures – Shakespeare is the banishment of the audience behind the proscenium's fourth wall and their visual erasure in darkened auditoria. The darkening of the audience had begun in Italy as early as Brunelleschi, but in England the audience stayed in the light until the middle of the nineteenth century, when theatres slowly began to turn out the house lights.[9] The subsequent rise of the popularity of film and the theatre's struggle to compete as a medium selling visual illusion assured that audiences at establishment theatre would stay in the dark. This shift to an invisible and thus anonymous audience essentially sacrificed its power to confer on an audience the pleasure of acknowledgement, the sense of being recognised as a part of the proceedings.

Closely connected to the joy an audience can take in acknowledgement is the joy of collaboration. Neither of these pleasures are antique; they are as much the future of the theatre as they are the past. Original staging returns power to the audience by relying on them for collaboration, and audiences called upon to work in conjunction with the play will invest themselves in the task. This investment is an overlooked dynamic of the fundamental theatrical transaction. To see this transaction at its most basic, its most challenging, and – when it works – its most impressive, observe it in a stand-up comedy routine. The comic stands before a paying audience using only his voice and his body to establish an entire world. At stake for the audience is the cost of their admission, and although their predisposition for the first few minutes will be to like the show, their laughter at first is tentative and far from unanimous. You can hear the beat between the joke and the response as they make the connections the comic wants them to make and as they accustom themselves to his persona. They are in the process of accepting or rejecting the collaboration, subconsciously deciding whether or not to work with the comic. Comics understand this fundamental partnership, which is why when one of them struggles he pleads, 'Work with me, people.'

This transaction is precisely the one at the heart of Shakespeare's text, a text written for the early modern theatre wholly dependent on a collaborative audience – on a collective make-believe. To spur that transactive dynamic of theatre we ask that our guest directors use the universal lighting to include an audience in their productions in all of the ways that the text allows.

USE SOLILOQUIES TO CAST THE AUDIENCE AS A WHOLE IN A GROUP ROLE

Such moments as Antony's funeral oration, King Henry exhorting his troops at Agincourt, and Claudius addressing the court at Elsinore are obviously moments in which Shakespeare has transformed the house into a part of the play. All of his plays have such public moments that transcend the bounds of the stage to include the world inside the theatre. Directors should look for those moments and have their actors address their speeches specifically to the audience and not, as Patrick Spottiswoode describes it, 'to the exit light'.

MILK INSULT SPEECHES THAT CAST CERTAIN MEMBERS OF THE AUDIENCE AS INDIVIDUALS

Many speeches in Shakespeare's works refer jokingly to characters that are not in the cast. In The Merchant of Venice, Portia's description of her suitors is a series of amusing insults aimed at the Neapolitan Prince, the Count Palatine, Monsieur Le Bon, Baron Falconbridge, and the Duke of Saxony's nephew – none of whom are in the play. In Measure for Measure, Pompey's list of the inmates in his prison is a roll call of the men he used to see in Mistress Overdone's brothel, none of whom are in the play. The Porter's speech in Macbeth, which merely names professions, works in the same way. In a darkened proscenium theatre, where the audience is to imagine that those being named are simply in the off-stage fictional world of the narrative, these passages may amuse. But the same material is hilarious when an actor points to a member of a visible audience and casts him or her as one of the people in the list. Directors should use moments such as these to alert and amuse the audience and to enlarge the play.

HAVE ACTORS USE THE TEXT TO CAST THE AUDIENCE AS CONFIDANTE, JUDGE, FRIEND, OR FOE

The corollary to this rule is that an actor could bring the audience in at any time – including moments that to our cinematically conditioned minds are 'private'. Imagine, for example, that Hamlet, while he is ranting at his mother about her sex life (surely a private conversation, especially with Polonius now dead), appeals to the audience when he says,

> Nay, but to live
> In the rank sweat of an enseaméd bed,
> Stewed in corruption, honeying and making love
> Over the nasty sty.
>
> (*Hamlet* 3.4.82–5)

This moment can be more, not less, intense, if Hamlet delivers it to the audience, because the actor playing Gertrude has to deal with the embarrassment of having her sex life 'outed' by her own son.

ALL METATHEATRICAL MOMENTS ARE A SHARED JOKE WITH THE AUDIENCE

Any time Shakespeare calls attention to the theatrical process at hand, he gives a wink and a nudge to the audience. When Fabian says, 'If this were played now upon a stage, I could condemn it as an improbable fiction' (*Twelfth Night* 3.4.114–15); when Cassius asks 'How many ages hence / Will this our lofty scene be acted over?' (*Julius Caesar* 3.1.112–13); when Biron complains, 'Our wooing doth not end like an old play' (*Love's Labour's Lost* 5.2.851); when the first Cleopatra, a prepubescent boy, objected to seeing 'some squeaking Cleopatra boy my greatness / I' the posture of a whore' (*Antony and Cleopatra* 5.2.216–17); when Macbeth tells us that life is 'a poor player / That struts and frets his hour upon the stage' (*Macbeth* 5.5.23–4); and when Hamlet, surrounded by hundreds of audience members, says, 'I am alone' (*Hamlet* 2.2.526), these moments are a joke shared with the audience, a joke about the collaborative work of making believe. Directors should look for and cherish these opportunities to let the audience into the play.

At the same time, directors should be aware of two dangers in including the audience – first, making the audience uncomfortable with an audience contact moment and second, keeping the play in front of the audience.

AVOID AUDIENCE CONTACT THAT MAKES THE AUDIENCE INDIVIDUALLY OR COLLECTIVELY UNCOMFORTABLE

Actors should not address the audience members in a way that is hurtful, obliges them to do or say something, and makes no sense of the language. They should also avoid physical contact.

1 If an actor indicates that a plain woman in the audience is ugly, or a fat person fat, or an old person wrinkled, the effect is to alienate the audience rather than to bring them in. Our experience is that men do not mind being called ugly, that bald guys can deal with being called bald, and that kids do not mind being called kids. We have also found that if the allusion is absurd – for example, calling a young girl a wrinkled, old hag, that too is okay.

2 Except on the rarest of occasions, actors should not address audience members in ways that oblige them to say or do something. Either, as is usually the case, the audience member will sit there confused and thereby slow down the show and make the rest of the house feel embarrassed for the victim. Or the audience member will say or do something and force the actor(s) to deal with it – usually at a cost to the moment. Thus, actors should pose their questions to the audience in a way that makes clear either that the question is rhetorical or that immediately dismisses the possibility of an answer. The big exception to this rule is when the director or actor *wants* some response or action from the audience, but such choices should be made prior to a performance – not during one.

3 Any reference to the audience and any personification of the audience should make sense. The actor who points at an individual in the audience and says, 'This castle has a pleasant seat', may get a laugh from the 'unskilful' but will make the 'judicious grieve' (Hamlet 3.2.23–4).

4 Actors should be careful never to touch an audience member. Audience contact is a mental and not a physical thing, and no audience member should have to deal with an actor touching him or her without permission.

KEEP THE PLAY IN FRONT OF THE AUDIENCE

Audience contact should be a way to make that story come alive for the audience; it should never replace the story. In short, use audience contact judiciously and purposefully. The trick is to remember that audience-contact moments should be part of something larger than themselves. When an actor chooses to acknowledge the audience, to anchor that moment to the play the other actors on the stage must act in the context of that choice. Actors who are in contact with the audience must always stay in character, serve the story, and listen to their fellow actors. In short, audience contact is a reason for actors to employ more rather than less of their traditional skills.

Directors at the Globe and the Blackfriars have a remarkable opportunity to advance the art of theatre by reminding the world of the pleasures of being included in the world of the play, of having their presence matter as it never will at a movie. The future of theatre lies not in the ways it can imitate film but in the ways in which film can never imitate theatre. Directors at the Globe and the Blackfriars can and should be leaders in that movement.

BIG RULE V. PLAY THE MOMENT, NOT THE PLAY OR ITS SUPPOSED GENRE

Much Ado about Nothing is a comedy in which the innocent ingénue is slandered and 'dies' in the fourth act. *Hamlet* is a tragedy in which two clowns enter in the last act. *Antony and Cleopatra* is a tragedy in which a clown enters in the last scene and does a duet of risqué jokes with the Queen of Egypt about 'the pretty worm' (*Antony and Cleopatra* 5.2.238). The French have been complaining since the seventeenth century about Shakespeare's lack of 'decorum', his disdain of a unified tone. They are right. Shakespeare obviously thought little of the dictates of genre, or, if he did think about them, he must have thought that tragedy and comedy thrive best next to one another. The director who sees the script, and the actors who act their parts, through the lens of genre will suffocate the play.

'Exit Antigonus pursued by a bear' (*The Winter's Tale* 3.3.57): directors worried about genre – even those who recognise that *The Winter's Tale* is a tragicomedy – resist this stage direction in the prescient fear that a bear entering at this moment will make an audience laugh. After all, an old man is abandoning the infant child of a wronged queen, presumably to certain death. What can be funny about that? Perhaps something more than funny: perhaps it is a great ursine release after the horrific first three acts in Shakespeare. Certainly productions that follow Shakespeare's stage direction inevitably shock and delight an audience in a way that frees them from the accumulated tension of the first three acts and readies them for the humour of the Clown, who will enter twenty lines later. Directors should trust Shakespeare's instincts about such moments and welcome the opportunity to challenge their audiences. This advice brings us to the final Big Rule.

BIG RULE VI. CHALLENGE YOUR AUDIENCE AND DO NOT BE AFRAID TO MAKE THEM WORK

When it was first clear that Sam Wanamaker's plans for the Globe included an open roof and an audience standing in the yard, the reaction was a unanimous scoff.

People, said the scoffers, would not stand for three hours of Shakespeare (or even two); people would certainly not stand in the rain. What we have learned since then is that the standees enjoy the show at least as much as those with seats.[10] We have also learned that when rain falls on the standees, they respond with laughter and with an increased determination to enjoy the show, a determination that communicates itself to the actors, who raise their games in appreciation. Twenty years ago, when the Shenandoah Shakespeare Express first started touring and left the house lights on, audience members would look around the house to see when the lights would go off. We had to add a pre-show speech explaining why we were 'doing it with the lights on'. Today, many in our audiences come to the Blackfriars *because* we leave the lights on, and they have learned to prefer 'lights on' Shakespeare.

In this way and many others the Blackfriars and Shakespeare's Globe are changing the future of theatre. An architectural survey of new Shakespeare theatres opened or opening or dreamed of in Chicago, in Washington, DC, in Stratford-upon-Avon, in New York City and in Staunton, Virginia, suggests that Sam Wanamaker's much debated project has already changed the shape of theatres – literally – as all of them move from the model of a proscenium to something much more like an arena. But the work that goes on in the Blackfriars and in Shakespeare's Globe can have more far-reaching effects on the ways that audiences experience theatre. It can challenge the very notion of what it means to be a member of an audience.

Six years ago in our first production of *The Winter's Tale*, the issue arose of how to reveal the statue of Hermione at the Blackfriars Playhouse. If we merely opened the curtains of the discovery space, then audience members sitting near the *frons scenae* would not be able to see Hermione; if we pushed the platform and the statue out, then we could make no sense of Paulina's threat to 'draw the curtain' (5.3.68) since that would no longer conceal Hermione. Knowing that Shakespeare wrote the play with the Blackfriars in mind and having no evidence of a moving platform, we decided to reveal Hermione in the discovery space and let her stay there. Perhaps, we thought, it was true that early modern audiences came to hear a play, not see a play, and that our audience would be content to do the same. They were not. Instead, what happened at our production was that audience members too far upstage to have a view into the discovery space so wanted to see the statue Paulina revealed that they stood and moved to a better vantage spot. At first, when Paulina says, 'Behold and say 'tis well' (5.3.20) they craned their necks, but when Leontes began to speak three lines later – 'her natural posture!' (5.3.23) – and then began to comment so specifically on the age represented in the 'statue', as many as twenty of them, well-dressed people, pillars of the community, some of them sitting in our lords' chairs on the side, would finally get up and move down the aisle behind the gallery seats to see. Their curiosity simply overwhelmed their conventional theatre behaviour. Then came the best part: they stood watching to see if Leontes or Perdita would touch the statue, while Paulina threatens all the while to close the curtain. Every evening, about fifty lines later, a few of those who had stood would start to return to their seats, but Paulina's line 'if you can behold it, / I'll make the statue move indeed' (5.3.87–8) would stop them, and Paulina would take the next lines, 'It is required / That you do wake your faith. Then all stand still' (5.3.94–5) first to the seated audience and then to the standees. Leontes would second her, 'Proceed' (5.3.97), and direct his next order to the standing audience members above and below: 'No foot shall stir' (5.3.98). It was as though the playwright had anticipated the way an audience would respond to the architecture of the Blackfriars. It seemed to answer simultaneously the questions, 'How did the play work?' and 'How do we make the play work better?'

Above all, it gave us a glimpse of the ways in which audiences are both resilient and educable. They welcome a good production that pushes them out of their comfortable ideas of crushed-velvet theatre, sometimes even at the cost of their physical ease. In this respect, directing for an early modern stage presents some of the same hurdles and opportunities that directors find in working on the most contemporary productions, such as environmental theatre or promenade productions. Good directors want to direct plays that challenge the intellectual assumptions of their audiences, frustrate their normal expectations, and force them to see anew. Directors at the Globe and the Blackfriars have that opportunity and more: they can challenge the very behaviour of an audience and expand the idea of what being at a play means. By looking past the nineteenth- and twentieth- century conventions that have dictated that theatre should be film manqué, they can lead the way to a reinvigorated contemporary theatre practice. They need only look for their inspiration to the theatres' buildings themselves and take seriously and gratefully the stagecraft of Shakespeare and his fellow playwrights. In Mark Rylance's words:

It always seemed to me logical that a theatre artist as great as Shakespeare was probably going to have a pretty great theatre. And if you could find out honestly and faithfully what it was like, you were probably going to be on the winning side.[11]

NOTES

1 In 1988, Jim Warren and Ralph Alan Cohen formed Shenandoah Shakespeare Express, a professional travelling troupe.

2 We learned this procedure from Murray Ross of Colorado Springs's TheatreWorks. See Stephen Booth's article, 'The Best Othello I ever Saw', Shakespeare Quarterly 40, 3 (Autumn 1989), 332–6.

3 The best book on the subject is George T. Wright's Shakespeare's Metrical Art (Berkeley: University of California Press, 1988).

4 Scholars debate how many of the stage directions in the Folio and the quartos are Shakespeare's as opposed to a stage manager's, but the fact is that all of those stage directions

represent at the very least the product of his collaboration with production. We urge our directors to consult Alan Dessen and Leslie Thomson's indispensable book, *A Dictionary of Stage Directions in English Drama 1580–1642* (Cambridge University Press, 1999), which alphabetises every word of the stage directions of the period and gives every use of it available in the printed plays.

5 *The Norton Shakespeare*, ed. Stephen Greenblatt *et al.*, eds. (New York and London: W. W. Norton 1997). All subsequent references are to this edition.

6 For two opposing views of this matter see A. Hart's article, 'The Time Allotted for Representation of Elizabethan and Jacobean Plays', *Review of English Studies* 8, 32 (October 1932), 395–413; and David Klein's response thirty-five years later, 'Time Allotted for an Elizabethan Performance', *Shakespeare Quarterly* 18, 4 (Autumn 1967), 434–8.

7 American Shakespeare Center stage manager Mary Coy, who had worked with David Crystal, conducted a similar experiment with the closet scene in *Hamlet*. She had our actors do it once in contemporary pronunciation and a second time in original pronunciation and found that the original pronunciation was three minutes shorter.

8 I recently saw again Ernst Lubitsch's brilliant 1942 film *To Be or Not to Be*, in which Jack Benny plays a hammy Polish actor ('what you are I wouldn't eat', says a Jewish fellow-actor) in the role of Hamlet. When he enters for the title speech, his slow, silent cross to down centre and then his long pause before beginning his speech lampoon the artistic self-indulgence lurking in every pause.

9 A. M. Nagler, *A Source Book in Theatrical History* (New York: Dover, 1952), pp. 41–4.

10 I have taken many groups to the Globe and invariably they enjoy the play more when they stand.

11. Mark Rylance, Interview, 'Re-creating Shakespeare', PBS: 27 December 2005. News Hour.

CONCLUSIONS

Christie Carson and Farah Karim-Cooper

In order to think about the next phase of critical engagement with this theatre it is useful, taking Cohen's approach, to look backwards in order to look forward. Charting briefly the development of close scholarly involvement, it is important to remember that a great deal of the original investment in the ideals of the project originated from American universities. The first programmes delivered to university groups by Patrick Spottiswoode's department were devised for American students. The later interaction with the University of Reading through Andrew Gurr, and the increasing engagement of Globe Education with Southwark Community, has instigated a process of negotiation with the structures and practices of the British university system and the national curriculum. The relationship established with Reading University was, after the retirement of Andrew Gurr, seemingly replaced by, although not limited to, a relationship with King's College London through the development of two MA programmes. This structural integration of full-time students at the university level in the Education programme was further supported by the employment of the Globe's first full-time Lecturer. However, the difficulties of maintaining a programme of research generated from outside the centre were hard to overcome. The increasingly demanding nature of academic life has meant that the original optimism about the complete integration of academics and practitioners was virtually impossible to achieve for much of the first decade of the project's life.

The 'we' and 'our' of W. B. Worthen's recent criticism has come up against significant practical hurdles in execution, making the 'we' of Spottiswoode's comments about the work of the Globe appear to be both exclusive and restrictive. However, the advent of the Arts and Humanities Research Council and its increasing shift in funding towards practice-based research and collaborative endeavours, as well as the Knowledge Transfer Partnerships programme, are helping to address these structural barriers. Globe Education now has two collaborative PhD students, one working jointly with a colleague at King's College London and the other working jointly with a colleague at Queen Mary, University of London, who both form part of the Globe Research team. This model of collaborative research with a range of academic departments and institutions provides a wealth of opportunities for the future of research at the Globe. However, now that formal structures are in place to help achieve greater integration of scholarship in the daily activities of Shakespeare's Globe, a more practical discussion about the form that integration should take must be addressed.

A research methodology is emerging from this discussion which centres on a systematic comparative approach that aims to track the development of discoveries in the Globe and other reconstructed spaces over an extended period of time. Again, it is interesting to look at existing critical practice in order to determine an approach that might usefully be employed. Jean Howard, speaking of the way that literature is analysed by new historicist critics, provides a potential model for the analysis of the current work of the Globe:

> I would argue that a new historical criticism attempting to talk about the ideological function of literature in a specific period can most usefully do so only by seeing a specific work relationally – that is, by seeing how its representations stand in regard to those of other specific works and discourses. A work can only be said to contest, subvert, recuperate, or reproduce dominant ideologies (and it may to any of these) if one can place the work – at least provisionally and strategically – in relation to others.[1]

This volume has attempted to move towards this kind of relational model of criticism. Interestingly, the practitioners at the Globe have themselves discovered the limitations of a purist and isolated approach to the practical application of cultural materialist criticism. The movement of *Twelfth Night* from indoor performances at Middle Temple to the outdoor performances at the Globe highlighted how a fruitful new approach to the relationship between text, architecture and audience might work practically. Perhaps the most important lesson of the first ten years of experimentation has been the discovery of how lopsided our perceptions of the period and the plays have become. Through an immersion in the period, its writers and its theatrical, visual and musical practices, the practitioners have begun to develop a multilayered context for Shakespeare's work. This practical work is helping to develop new insights into the way we approach thinking about the past.

The ethos of always learning through experimentation is what unites the Theatre with Globe Education. The experimental and critically informed practical approach mapped out in the second section of the book helps to articulate how the creative methods of practical experimentation can be usefully employed in an educational environment. The expansion of the canon suggested by the *Read Not Dead* series of readings has been facilitated by the quarto editions of some of these plays published by the Globe but also by the increasing availability of these texts online. Academic and theatrical tendencies to stick to a narrow band of acceptable Renaissance texts can now be challenged. The participatory nature of the *Lively Action* programme and the innovative ways in which school children are engaged in the plays present interesting lessons for university pedagogy. The involvement of practitioners as teachers developing practical collaborative projects in the classroom suggests ways in which scholars might also use practical experimentation in our teaching as well as our research. Above all, the linking together of the teaching and research roles in this environment is a stark reminder of how often these two areas of endeavour are pushed apart under the pressures of modern academic life. Spottiswoode's insistence on the Globe centre's 'maverick' identity is central to his department's working practices. Globe Education has demonstrated that theatre education departments can be autonomous agents working collaboratively, and even selectively, with the theatres to which they are attached. Not only this, theatre education departments like Spottiswoode's can provide an environment of critical enquiry and self-reflection for practitioners, educators and scholars alike. As Dromgoole pushes the Globe stage farther into the twenty-first century by challenging contemporary playwrights to fashion new drama that would suit the space, Spottiswoode envisions a new education centre that would provide a 'training ground for actors and academics'.[2]

The conclusion of this collection must therefore be that despite the existence of a great deal of writing critical of the Globe, much of the practical work produced in this initial crucially important ten-year period has not been thoroughly or rigorously interrogated, although the Theatre has given unprecedented access to its own creative processes. This book provides a framework for discussion of this formative period in this influential Theatre and Education centre and suggests a collaborative and systematic methodology for future consideration. But hopefully this book also provides insight into the connections between the way we research and the way we teach. The Globe model shows how creativity and rigorous critical enquiry can serve and enliven each other. The work of Shakespeare's Globe helps to break down the unhelpful divide between creativity and critical analysis, while maintaining the productive divide between the outcomes of a commercial theatre and a self-sustaining Education department. Scholars can and should be creative and practitioners can and should be critical. An understanding of the methodological approaches of these two disciplines can help to enliven and interrogate the work of both of these areas of endeavour. According to Dromgoole this theatre is 'teaching people new ways of enjoying each other, congregating and being alive together'.[3] It may also help to re-establish the interdependence of scholarship and creative practical experimentation at an important moment when new creative modes of critical thinking are developing more widely.

Shakespeare's Globe has challenged accepted assumptions through its architecture, its location and its activities. The working practices of the theatre have destabilised established hierarchies in the theatre and presented challenges to current actor training. The additional engagement of the audience at the Globe has influenced all areas of performance, as well as the approaches used in the Education department. One point which this volume makes clear is that a key relationship between the Theatre and Education departments has been through the people involved. As Spottiswoode has pointed out, the splitting of the use of the theatre between a theatrical season and an educational season allows for a change of roles in the building. Increasingly, and importantly, some of these roles are being filled by the same people, illustrating quite clearly the fact that it is the methodology and the outcomes of the activity undertaken rather than the people engaged in the work that differentiates a theatrical and an educational approach. Taking on the self-reflexive position of educators has helped to change the practitioners' views of their working processes as well as their relationship to the theatre space.

The Rylance years in this theatre established an artistic team that were experts themselves in the practices of the Renaissance period. Dominic Dromgoole is taking a different approach, drawing on research provided by the Education department to inform the work in the building but steering away from direct experiments in 'original practices'. The fact that under both of these Artistic Directors the performative event includes the audience at all times cannot be ignored in this theatre. The open-door policy of the Theatre, while financially driven initially, has produced an atmosphere of openness and accessibility (of a variety of kinds). At the Globe, actors, directors, musicians and education staff continue to conduct practical experiments with their audiences every day. Some of these experiments are influenced by research and by academic discourse but their work can also inform scholarly debate. At its best, Shakespeare's Globe works to contain and to combine expertise from a range of sources. In order to re-establish the importance of scholarship in this process, academics must be willing to become more fully integrated in the collaborative process of discovery and reassessment that Shakespeare's Globe demands.

NOTES

1 Jean Howard, 'The New Historicism and Renaissance Studies', in *Reconceiving the Renaissance*, ed. Ewan Fernie *et al.* (Oxford University Press, 2005), p. 91.
2 Patrick Spottiswoode, interview with the editors, 18 May 2007.
3 Dominic Dromgoole, interview with the editors, 24 May 2007.

AFTERWORD

Gordon McMullan

'Releasing original Shakespearean meanings': William Worthen's words for the desire embodied in the Globe are provocative words, words fraught with difficulties. Words matter a great deal at Shakespeare's Globe, of course – not only when they are spoken by actors but also when they are spoken by others (perhaps the latter is the case more than in any other contemporary theatre). The building is a 'reconstruction', not a 'replica', we are reminded; certain Globe productions seek to reproduce 'original', not 'authentic', practices; and words such as 'experiment', 'laboratory', 'translation', 'testing ground' have been variously deployed, alongside political terms such as 'radical' or, by contrast, 'reactionary', to describe the space and its impact. Other less welcome words have been used too, the derogatory 'Disneyland' being the most obviously antagonistic (underlining the anti-Americanism implicit, as both Franklin Hildy and Christie Carson observe, in attacks on the Globe). Perception matters as much as practice, it seems, when it comes to debate about the Globe.

Questions of perception as well as of practice are of course unavoidable in any critical account. The Globe project has made very clear the faultlines not only between theatre practitioners and scholars but also between different manifestations of scholarly endeavour or commitment: literary criticism, performance studies, theatre history, archaeology. The gulf between theatre historians and literary critics, for instance, sometimes seems broader even than that between critics and theatre practitioners: the place of interpretation is contested persistently across these borderlines. The Globe has also foregrounded certain very basic questions of taste: simply put, some people prefer doublet-and-hose productions, others white-box minimalism. I have always leaned to the latter myself, as it happens, which has meant that my own engagement with the Globe over the last decade has been a curious two-headed beast, a blend of enthusiasm and resistance, not unlike Dr Dolittle's Pushme-Pullyu. Perhaps this is inevitable with a project of this kind – and is arguably at its most apparent in the history of the attitude to the Globe of the local borough council whose turf it has been so instrumental in transforming.

For academics who have spent time there, the impact of the space has been substantial and not by any means always consciously so. I now have a very clear vision of the tiring house, of the lords' room, of the galleries, of the physical existence, in other words, of the first Globe theatre, and I am unlikely ever to shrug off that vision because I have walked in and on it, through it and around it, enough times for it to be ingrained on my mind in scale, dimension, feel, aural quality – as an experiential reality, in other words. Yet it might be misleading, this space, as a range of scholars and theatre practitioners have suggested. I have stood in the damp, cramped space of the excavated Rose and have been shocked by how tiny it is, and I am aware that, as Hildy reports, the reconstructed Globe may itself be a size or two overscale. A visit to the Rose probably ought to be obligatory for everyone who attends a Globe show or takes a Globe tour: the contrast, not only of scale but also of light and dark – the darkness enforced both by the excavation's situation in the foundations of an office block and by the exigencies of preservation, which makes its small size still more impressive even as it makes it impossible to imagine the original open to the sky – is instructive, even slightly intimidating, since it insists that we continue to wonder and imagine rather than accept that we now know what there is to know. Essentialism threatens constantly to seep into the Globe experience – perhaps essentialism, in the end, *constitutes* the Globe experience – and correctives are needed. The question is the extent to which this essentialism can be perceived and held under scrutiny – and of course the observer is always complicit in the observation, as I am in commenting on a theatre with which I have built up a series of institutional and personal links over ten years and more.

I also by now have (or think I have) a clear sense of how audiences respond to the Globe space and I am unlikely to shrug off my lack of conviction about the possibility of projecting 'original practices' on to new audiences. My gut feeling is that the kind of audience interaction provoked in the new theatre's Prologue Season, and sustained in various forms subsequently, has little to do with the experiences of those attending plays in a not dissimilar theatre just round the corner between 1599 and 1613. I cannot easily put my finger on why, except that every time I read a Jacobean play I find myself more and more aware of the theatrical knowledge assumed on behalf of the audience by the playwrights, knowledge that can only have been gained by regular, repeat visits to the same space to see an evolving series of plays negotiating generic, stylistic, linguistic and personnel change. This kind of knowledge is matched in today's audiences, not by an ingrained understanding of theatrical performance in an early modern amphitheatre space or by the kind of limited, if eager, engagement available to the hard core of repeat Globe playgoers invoked by Claire van Kampen in her chapter, but rather by their deep awareness of the genres, forms, parodies, inversions and reinventions of Hollywood cinema. The upshot is a displaced Globe audience, one self-consciously *playing* at being a Globe audience, performing, in a certain way, no less than are the players they are watching (Tim Carroll writes of 'the audience's ability to play the role required of it' (see p. 43), as if he were directing everyone in the theatre, not just those on the stage), and forced by the wishes of the institution (because, after ten years, that is inevitably what the Globe has become), as Catherine Silverstone has rightly observed, to 'exhibit a range of responses from complicity to resistance' – complicit and resistant as the first audiences were, but in markedly different ways.

What becomes clear above all, perhaps, is the disjunction between the perceptions of Shakespeare's Globe of those of us fortunate enough to live and work within range of the Globe or to those who have spent sustained time (on research leave, say) in proximity to the Globe and those whose engagement with the building is necessarily limited to the occasional visit to see a production. It is hard now for me to imagine thinking of the Globe solely as a theatre; it is Globe Education which has, if I am to be honest, had by far the more marked impact on my own development as a scholar of Shakespearean drama – by way of the Globe Quartos series of editions of uncommercial early modern plays, of the *Read Not Dead* series of staged readings, of the constant stream of visiting lectures, seminars, workshops and book launches by many of the most significant scholars in the field, and of the sheer energy, openness, pedagogical curiosity and generosity of Patrick Spottiswoode and his steadily increasing team (several of whom have, as it happens, passed through the MA programme run collaboratively by my university, King's College London, and Globe Education). One Globe Education resource in particular seems to me worth highlighting, though it has only been very occasionally deployed by researching scholars, and that is the series of Winter Playing workshops that take place on the out-of-season Globe stage, at which actors make themselves available to academics for controlled experimentation with the reconstructed space: this has involved, for instance, trying out options for the use of the upper gallery for certain scenes in *Henry VIII* (which helped me tangibly in creating the commentary for my edition of the play) or seeing whether both chess 'houses' in *A Game at Chess* might have fitted on to the stage for a given scene. This is, in a way, the theatre-as-laboratory which the Globe's originators imagined; at the same time, its discoveries can only be discoveries about the new space and thus only secondarily or displacedly, if at all, about the original: additional material for interpretation, not demonstrable objective evidence.

As for the theatre itself, it will surely take three or four artistic directorships before a clear trajectory emerges. Mark Rylance's extraordinary charisma shaped the inception of the Globe Theatre from before the building was even built, his engagement with the location initiated and completed through *Tempests* with a tangibly shared DNA. Dominic Dromgoole has begun, in turn, to carve his own path, championing new writing for and in the space and looking on benignly at the reconstitution of 'original practices' on the model of intellectual property as something external to, independent of, the Globe, despite its origins as a series of counterpart practices to the reconstructed architectural space (as Jenny Tiramani's numbered explanations of the logic of OP clothing make clear – see p. 43). The nature of Globe experimentation will inevitably change with changes of regime, and scholars may be dismayed as they see practices which were close-but-not-close-enough replaced with those they see as still-farther-away. But as Worthen observes in the quotation which prefaces this collection's introduction, 'Globe performativity' is something new, something that has emerged from a decade in a new theatrical space, which draws on both early modern and postmodern practice in uneven, serendipitous and frequently uncomfortable ways and which is thus arguably the most fascinating product of the entire experiment.

There is always, then, the risk that, as Franklin J. Hildy phrases it in chapter 1, performance at the Globe might turn out to have 'nothing to do with Shakespeare's actual stagecraft and everything to do with what we want that stagecraft to have been' (p. 14), but this has surely been, and continues to be, a risk worth taking. More than that, it can be seen to be not a risk at all, but rather both an inevitability and a productivity of a kind unenvisaged by any of the proponents of a new 'Elizabethan theatre' from Poel to Wanamaker – not a recovery of things lost but a genuine, even an authentic, invention.

GLOBE THEATRE AND 'ESSENCE OF GLOBENESS' PROJECTS SINCE 1970

Franklin J. Hildy

1971   The Globe Playhouse, '99-seat half-replica' West Hollywood, California.

1975   'Globe Theatre', Busch Gardens 'Europe', Williamsburg, Virginia. Although originally advertised as a reconstruction, the plan was changed and it is now a modern facility.

1976   St George's Shakespearean Theatre, Tufnell Park, London. Built by St George's Elizabethan Theatre Trust, founded in 1968.

1986   The Swan Theatre, Stratford-upon-Avon.

1988   The Tokyo Globe. Later called the Panasonic Globe.

1988   The Globe Theatre, Rheda Wiedenbrueck, Germany. Moved to Neuss, Germany in 1991.

1992   The Globe Theatre, Hotel Esplanade, Berlin.

1996   The Black Rose Theatre 'replica Elizabethan indoor playhouse', Emory University, Atlanta, Georgia.

1997   Globe stage, Shakespeare Country Park, Maruyama-machi, Japan.

1998   The Globe Theatre, Lichtensteig, Switzerland. Small-scale version of Shakespeare's Globe, sold to Europa Park, Rust, Germany, where it reopened in 2000.

1999   The Globe Theatre, Prague, Czech Republic.

1999   The Chicago Shakespeare Theatre at Navy Pier, modelled after the Swan Theatre, Stratford-upon Avon.

2000   The Haller Globe Theatre, Schwäbisch Hall, Germany. Inspired by the Prague design, this is a sixteen-sided Globe built to be movable.

2001   Staunton, Blackfriars Playhouse (reconstruction of 1597 indoor theatre), Staunton, Virginia. Home of Shenandoah Shakespeare's American Shakespeare Center.

2003   Globe Theatre, Villa Borghese, Rome, Italy, modelled on Shakespeare's Globe.

2003   Ice Globe, Jukkasjärvi (on River Torne), Sweden. Built for three winter seasons ending in 2005.

2004   Curtain Theatre, Coldwater Canyon, Austin, Texas; inspired by Shakespeare's Globe.

2004   Rose of Kingston (modern version of Rose Theatre II of 1592), Kingston, England.

2007   Elizabethan stage, the Palm Beach Shakespeare Festival, Carlin Park, Jupiter, Florida. Amphitheatre with stage 'modelled after the Globe Theatre in London'.

2007   Elizabethan Stage, Curtain Call Theatre, Stanford, Connecticut. Shakespeare on the Green 'the company's outdoor theatrical festival celebrated in a recreated stage of the famed Globe Theatre'.

APPENDIX TWO

A DRAFT ARTISTIC POLICY – 1988

The policy of every company is circumscribed by the physical plant it operates and the income it receives. Some willingly add to their constraints (the English National Opera sings only in English, for example), so the chosen constraints of the Globe project, plus the expectations of its public and its backers, must be reflected in its policy:

1 The purpose of the project is to present the plays of Shakespeare in the building for which he wrote many of them.
2 At least one play each season should be presented as authentically as possible.
3 The repertoire should include plays by other writers and of other periods.
4 No production should alter or damage the fabric of the building.
5 The audience–actor relationship created by these sixteenth-century conditions should be explored.
6 Natural light should be the rule. Artificial light, if needed at night, should be general enough to cover both players and spectators.
7 No modern sound amplification should be used.
8 The experience and discoveries of the Globe should be recorded and transmitted by all modern methods.

NOTE

Two versions of an Artistic Policy were tracked down in the Shakespeare's Globe Archive to an uncatalogued file labelled 'Theatre Committee Correspondence 1984–1988' (MB/10.8.88). The surrounding papers would suggest that the MB that appears on this draft is Michael Birkett.

Michael Birkett is the theatre producer and director Lord Birkett of Ulverston, who oversaw the creation of the Artistic Directorate and appointment of Mark Rylance.

TEN COMMANDMENTS FOR THE NEW GLOBE BY ALAN C. DESSEN, 1990

1 Thou shalt sidestep modern editions (and the entire eclectic editorial tradition since the eighteenth century) and rather mount any experiments on the basis of the relevant quarto and Folio scripts.

2 Thou shalt honour and respect the original stage directions as precious evidence (as opposed to the casual treatment often given these signals by modern editors), including where such signals are positioned in the original printed editions.

3 Thou shalt not retreat from (apparent) anomalies in the early printed editions but shalt be open to the possibility that what may seem strange to us today may in turn provide a window into what was distinctive or taken for granted then.

4 Thou shalt strain mightily to transcend, as the be-all and end-all in the interpretive process, various manifestations of 'realism' (whether psychological, geographical or narrative).

5 Thou shalt start afresh in the new Globe with as few preconceptions as possible about the *aside*, the soliloquy, and other forms of direct address to (and eye contact with) the audience (and rethink which speeches *are* asides and how they should be signalled).

6 Thou shalt reject as a false god variable lighting (or any equivalent) and all the anachronistic thinking it inevitably (and sometimes disastrously) brings with it. Only the rare theatrical professional can resist the siren call of variable lighting if it is available in *any* form.

7 Thou shalt avoid as another false god Designer's Theatre or Director's Theatre and all the 'concept' thinking that goes with it and instead explore the Elizabethan/Jacobean sense of design (e.g. *their* rationale for costumes and properties).

8 Thou shalt eschew intervals–intermissions so as to eliminate the anachronistic single fifteen-minute break that changes the rhythm and dynamics of performance. Without such breaks, seeing a play at the new Globe will be a different

experience from seeing a play elsewhere in London (and the added momentum–continuity will help the standees).

9 Thou shalt never forget the watchword of the faith enunciated in the choric speeches of Henry V (e.g. 'piece out our imperfections with your thoughts' or 'eke out our performance with your mind') and therefore always keep in mind the pivotal role of the playgoer's imagination in the unspoken contract assumed between the original players and their audience.

10 Above all else, thou shalt trust the scripts (and, as a corollary, the actors and play-goers), for the surviving scripts (as reflected, however accurately or inaccurately, in the early printed editions) are our *only* evidence. These scripts (not scholarly formulations, directorial concepts, or actorly ingenuity) must therefore drive or control *all* experiments or tests. Without sufficient trust in these documents, the process will be tainted.

(Shakespeare's Globe Archive, Northwestern Conference papers; also found in *New Issues in the Reconstruction of Shakespeare's Theatre: Proceedings of the Conference Held at the University of Georgia, February 16–18, 1990* (New York: Peter Lang, 1990), ed. Franklin J. Hildy)

SHAKESPEARE'S GLOBE PRODUCTIONS 1996–2007

KEY

MD	twentieth-/twenty-first-century dress
SP	clothing and properties of a specific period
MW	clothing and properties of a mythic world
RP	Renaissance period
OPMG	'original practices' approach to period clothing/mixed gender
OP	'original practices'/all-male cast and OP approach to period clothing
OPF	As OP but with all-female cast
EMS	early modern speech (original pronunciation)
MM	modern music score
SM	specific-period music score
RM	Renaissance music score
MRM	mixture modern/Renaissance-period music score
INT	international production
Y	frequent/remarkable use of the yard as well as the stage

Play	Perf. type	Author	Dates
The Prologue Season 1996			
The Two Gentlemen of Verona	MD/MM	Shakespeare	21 Aug.–15 Sept.
The Opening Season 1997			
Henry V	OP/MRM	Shakespeare	14 June–21 Sept.
The Winter's Tale	MW/MM	Shakespeare	19 June–18 Sept.

Play	Perf. type	Author	Dates
A Chaste Maid in Cheapside	RP/MRM/**Y**	Middleton	19 Aug.–20 Sept.
The Maid's Tragedy	MD/MM	Beaumont / Fletcher	20 Aug.–16 Sept.
Umabatha – Zulu Macbeth	INT (Zimbabwe)	Adaptor: Welcome Msomi	4–9 Aug.
Season of Justice and Mercy 1998			
As You Like It	RP/RM/**Y**	Shakespeare	19 May–20 Sept.
The Merchant of Venice	OPMG/MRM/**Y**	Shakespeare	20 May–19 Sept.
The Honest Whore	MD/MM	Dekker	1 Aug.–18 Sept.
A Mad World, My Masters	MW/MM	Middleton	2 Aug.–19 Sept.
Otra Tempestad (Tempest)	INT(Cuba)	Adaptor: Raquel Carrio	21–6 July
Venus and Adonis (opera) semi-staged concert	MD/RM	Shakespeare	14 June
The 400th Anniversary Season/Roman Season 1999			
Julius Caesar	OP+MD/ RM/**Y**	Shakespeare	15 May–21 Sept.
The Comedy of Errors	MW/MM/**Y**	Shakespeare	28 May–25 Sept.
Antony and Cleopatra	OP/RM	Shakespeare	24 July–26 Sept.
Augustine's Oak	MW/MM	Oswald	6 Aug.–24 Sept.
Kathakali King Lear	INT(S. India)	Adaptor: David McRuvie	6 July
The Hercules Season 2000			
The Tempest (female Prospero)	MW/MM	Shakespeare	12 May–10 Sept.
Hamlet	OPMG/MM	Shakespeare	28 May–24 Sept.
The Two Noble Kinsmen	MW/MM/**Y**	Shakespeare/Fletcher	29 July–23 Sept.
The Antipodes	OPMG/MM	Brome	12 Aug.–22 Sept.
Romeu e Julieta	INT(Brazil)	Trans.: Onestaldo de Pennafort	11–23 July
Celtic Season 2001			
King Lear	MW/MRM/**Y**	Shakespeare	12 May–21 Sept.
Macbeth	MD/MM	Shakespeare	27 May–22 Sept.
Cymbeline	MW/MM	Shakespeare	30 June–23 Sept.
Umabatha	INT(Zimbabwe)		18–22 Apr.

Play	Perf. type	Author	Dates
Kyogen of Errors	INT(Japan)	Adaptor: Yasunari Takahashi	18–22 July
Cupid and Psyche Season 2002			
Twelfth Night	OP/MM	Shakespeare	6 May–28 Sept.
A Midsummer Night's Dream	MD/MM	Shakespeare	26 May–27 Sept.
Golden Ass	MD/MM	Apuleius/Oswald	3 Aug.–29 Sept.
The Season of Regime Change 2003			
Richard II	OP/RM	Shakespeare	8 May–27 Sept.
Richard III	OPF/RM	Shakespeare	25 May–27 Sept.
Dido Queen of Carthage	MD/MM	Marlowe	6 June–18 Aug.
Edward II	OP/RM	Marlowe	20 July–26 Sept.
The Taming of the Shrew	OPF/RM/**Y**	Shakespeare	10 Aug.–28 Sept.
The Season of Star-Crossed Lovers 2004			
Romeo and Juliet	OPMG/EMS/RM	Shakespeare	7 May–26 Sept.
Much Ado about Nothing	OPF/RM	Shakespeare	23 May–26 Sept.
Measure for Measure	OPMG/RM	Shakespeare	18 May–23 Sept.
The World and Underworld 2005			
The Tempest	OP+MD/MRM	Shakespeare	6 May–2 Oct.
Pericles	MD/MM/**Y**	Shakespeare	20 May–1 Oct.
The Winter's Tale	OPMG/RM	Shakespeare	4 June–1 Oct.
The Storm	MD/MM/**Y**	Plautus/Oswald	30 July–30 Sept.
Man Falling Down	MD/MM/**Y**	J. Shepherd/O. Cotton	15 Aug.–19 Sept.
Troilus and Cressida	MW/EMS/MM/**Y**	Shakespeare	24 Aug.–28 Sept.
Measure for Measure	OP/RM	Shakespeare	6–16 Oct.
The Edges of Rome 2006			
Coriolanus	RP/RM/**Y**	Shakespeare	5 May–13 July
Titus Andronicus	MW/MM/**Y**	Shakespeare	20 May–6 Oct.
Antony and Cleopatra	RP/RM	Shakespeare	25 June–8 Oct.
Under the Black Flag (World premiere)	SP/MM	Simon Bent	9 July–12 Aug.
The Comedy of Errors	MW/MM	Shakespeare	22 July–7 Oct.
In Extremis (World premiere)	SP/SM	Howard Brenton	27 Aug.–7 Oct.

Play	Perf. type	Author	Dates
Renaissance and Revolution 2007			
Othello	RP/MM	Shakespeare	4 May–19 Aug.
Love's Labour's Lost	RP/RM/Y	Shakespeare	1 July–7 Oct.
The Merchant of Venice	RP/MRM	Shakespeare	2 June–6 Oct.
In Extremis	SP/SM	Howard Brenton	15–26 May
Holding Fire	SP/SM	Jack Shepherd	28 July–5 Oct.
We, the People	SP/SM	Eric Schlosser	2 Sept.–6 Oct.

APPENDIX FIVE

'READ NOT DEAD' STAGED READINGS

Date	Read Not Dead Season	Play Title	Year	Author	Co-ordinator
21.05.1995	Re-Discovering Plays	Amends for Ladies	1611	Nathan Field	Mark Knight
04.06.1995	Re-Discovering Plays	Westward Ho!	1604	Thomas Dekker and John Webster	Samuel West
18.06.1995	Re-Discovering Plays	The City Madam	1632	Philip Massinger	Sheila Allen
25.06.1995	Re-Discovering Plays	The Island Princess	1621	John Fletcher	Mark Rylance
17.10.1995	The Year Before	Two Angry Women of Abingdon	1598	Henry Porter	Patrick Spottiswoode
29.10.1995	The Year Before	A Warning for Fair Women	1599	Anon.	Tom Morris
05.11.1995	The Year Before	Englishmen for My Money	1598	William Haughton	Ros King
26.11.1995	The Year Before	Every Man in His Humour	1598	Ben Jonson	Nick Hutchison
28.04.1996	The Bankside Playhouses	A Chaste Maid in Cheapside	1613	Thomas Middleton	John Tydeman
12.05.1996	The Bankside Playhouses	Bartholomew Fair	1614	Ben Jonson	Alan Cox
26.05.1996	The Bankside Playhouses	Orlando Furioso	1591	Robert Greene	Mark Rylance
09.06.1996	The Bankside Playhouses	The Malcontent	1604	John Marston	Timothy West
23.06.1996	The Bankside Playhouses	All is True	1996	Shakespeare and Fletcher	Gregory Doran
13.10.1996	Shirley and Lucrece	The Lady of Pleasure	1635	James Shirley	John Turnbull
20.10.1996	Shirley and Lucrece	The Witty Fair One	1628	James Shirley	Peter Benedict

(cont.)

Date	Read Not Dead Season	Play Title	Year	Author	Co-ordinator
27.10.1996	Shirley and Lucrece	The Humorous Courtier	1631	James Shirley	Paul Clayton
03.11.1996	Shirley and Lucrece	The Rape of Lucrece	1594	William Shakespeare	David Meyer
03.11.1996	Shirley and Lucrece	Tarquin Banished	1655	John Quarles	David Meyer
17.11.1996	Shirley and Lucrece	The Ghost of Lucrece	1600	Thomas Middleton	Claire van Kampen
24.11.1996	Shirley and Lucrece	The Rape of Lucrece	1608	Thomas Heywood	Sonia Ritter
23.02.1997	The Stage and Spain	Rule a Wife and Have a Wife	1624	John Fletcher	John Tydeman
02.03.1997	The Stage and Spain	The Spanish Gypsy	1623	Thomas Middleton and ?Samuel Rowley	Sheila Allen
09.03.1997	The Stage and Spain	The Spanish Curate	1622	John Fletcher and ?Philip Massinger	Peter Benedict
16.03.1997	The Stage and Spain	Alarum for London	1602	Anon.	Frank Stirling
23.03.1997	The Stage and Spain	The Noble Spanish Soldier	1634	?Thomas Dekker	Roger Moss
27.04.1997	The Stage and Spain	The Spanish Ladie	1640	James Mabbe (from Cervantes)	Charles Duff
20.07.1997	Shakespeare's Sources	Pandosto	1588	Robert Greene	Rosemary Linnell
17.08.1997	Shakespeare's Sources	The Famous Victories of Henry the Fifth	1588	Anon.	Geoffrey Towers
17.09.1997	New Play	Roaring Boy	1997	Rowan Joffe	Jane Lapotaire
02.11.1997	The Globe	Philaster, or Love Lies a Bleeding	1609	Francis Beaumont and John Fletcher	Alan Cox
09.11.1997	The Globe	Sejanus, His Fall	1603	Ben Jonson	Richard Cottrell
16.11.1997	The Globe	A King and No King	1611	Francis Beaumont and John Fletcher	Richard Olivier
23.11.1997	The Globe	The Miseries of Enforced Marriage	1607	George Wilkins	John Tydeman
07.12.1997	The Globe	The Devil's Charter	1607	Barnabe Barnes	Sonia Ritter

Date	Series	Title	Year	Author	Director
15.03.1998	Shakespeare and the Jews	The Custom of the Country	1620	John Fletcher and Philip Massinger	Jenny Eastop
22.03.1998	Shakespeare and the Jews	A Christian Turn'd Turke	1610	Robert Daborn	David Hunt
05.04.1998	Shakespeare and the Jews	The Whore of Babylon	1606	Thomas Dekker	Daniel Slater
19.04.1998	Shakespeare and the Jews	The Travailes of the Three English Brothers	1607	John Day, William Rowley and George Wilkins	Diana Devlin
03.05.1998	Shakespeare and the Jews	The Jew of Malta	1589	Christopher Marlowe	Joanne Howarth
07.06.1998	Shakespeare and the Jews	Selimus	1592	Robert Greene	Jenny Eastop
21.06.1998	Shakespeare and the Jews	The Innocent Child of La Guardia	?	Lope de Vega (trans. Michael Jacobs)	Colin Ellwood
28.06.1998	Summer Events	Rosalynd	1590	Thomas Lodge	Rosemary Linnell
02.08.1998	Summer Events	The Jews' Tragedy	1626	William Hemings	Graham Watts
17.08.1998	Summer Events	The Jews	1749	G. E. Lessing (trans. Noel Clark)	Peter Benedict
23.08.1998	Summer Events	The Necromancer	1504	Lodovico Ariosto (trans. Christopher Cairns)	Tristan Brolly
06.09.1998	Summer Events	The Honest Whore (part I)	1604	Thomas Dekker and Thomas Middleton	Alan Cox
13.09.1998	Summer Events	The Honest Whore (part II)	1605	Thomas Dekker and Thomas Middleton	Alan Cox
01.11.1998	Our Scene is London	The Three Lords and Three Ladies of London	1589	Robert Wilson	Heather Goodman
08.11.1998	Our Scene is London	Eastward Ho!	1605	George Chapman, Ben Jonson and John Marston	Kate Hall

(cont.)

Date	Read Not Dead Season	Play Title	Year	Author	Co-ordinator
15.11.1998	Our Scene is London	Ram Alley or Merry Tricks	1607–8	Lording Barry	James Wallace
29.11.1998	Our Scene is London	The Puritan or The Widow of Watling St	1606	'W.S'	John Tydeman
06.12.1998	Our Scene is London	The Fair Maid of the Exchange	1602	Anon.	Jenny Eastop
21.02.1999	Shakespeare and War	Edward III	1590	William Shakespeare and others	Clive Brill
28.02.1999	Shakespeare and War	The Lamentable Tragedy of Locrine	1590	Anon.	James Wallace
07.03.1999	Shakespeare and War	Soliman and Perseda	1592	Thomas Kyd	Nick Hutchison
14.03.1999	Shakespeare and War	Histriomastix, or the Player Whipped	1598	John Marston	Martin White
21.03.1999	Shakespeare and War	The Trial of Chivalry	1600	Anon.	Sonia Ritter
04.07.1999	Shakespeare in Rome	The Roman Actor	1626	Philip Massinger	Vivien Heilbron and David Rintoul
08.08.1999	Shakespeare in Rome	Messalina, The Insatiate Roman Empress	1634	Nathanael Richards	Graham Watts
15.08.1999	Shakespeare in Rome	The Inn at Lydda	1999	John Wolfson	John Tydeman
12.09.1999	Shakespeare in Rome	Valentinian	1610	John Fletcher	Matthew Smith
24.10.1999	In Shakespeare's Shoes	The Cobbler's Prophecy	1594	Robert Wilson	James Wallace
31.10.1999	In Shakespeare's Shoes	A Knack to Know a Knave	1594	Anon.	Alan Cox
07.11.1999	In Shakespeare's Shoes	The Politician	1639	James Shirley	James Wallace
14.11.1999	In Shakespeare's Shoes	The Weeding of the Covent Garden	1632	Richard Brome	Alison Skilbeck
28.11.1999	In Shakespeare's Shoes	George a Green	1599	Robert Greene	Sonia Ritter
19.03.2000	In Shakespeare's Shoes	The Shoemakers' Holiday	1599	Thomas Dekker	John Tydeman
26.03.2000	In Shakespeare's Shoes	A Shoemaker A Gentleman	1638	William Rowley	Nick Hutchison

Date	Production	Title	Year	Author	Performer
02.04.2000	In Shakespeare's Shoes	Tricks of Youth or The Walks of Islington and Hogsden with the Humours of Wood Street Counter	1641	Thomas Jordan	James Wallace
09.04.2000	In Shakespeare's Shoes	When You See Me, You Know Me	1605	Samuel Rowley	Alison Skilbeck
16.04.2000	In Shakespeare's Shoes	The Cobbler of Preston	1716	Charles Johnson, Christopher Bullock (2 different versions)	Charles Duff
25.06.2000	Words and Action	Hamlet (first quarto)	1603	William Shakespeare	Alan Cox
23.07.2000	Words and Action	The Tragedy of Hoffman	1602	Henry Chettle	Jenny Eastop
13.08.2000	Words and Action	The Sparagus Garden	1635	Richard Brome	Alison Skilbeck
27.08.2000	Words and Action	Antonio's Revenge	1600	John Marston	James Wallace
27.10.2000	Shakespeare Framed	Campaspe	1583	John Lyly	James Wallace
29.10.2000	Shakespeare Framed	The Wisdom of Dr Dodypoll	1600	Anon.	Helen Raynor
05.11.2000	Shakespeare Framed	The Picture	1629	Philip Massinger	Vivien Heilbron
19.11.2000	Shakespeare Framed	The History and Fall of Caius Marius	1679	Thomas Otway	Nick Hutchison
26.11.2000	Shakespeare Framed	The History of King Lear	1681	Nahum Tate	Vivien Heilbron
04.03.2001	Shakespeare and Gold	The Alchemist	1610	Ben Jonson	Joanne Howarth
11.03.2001	Shakespeare and Gold	Midas	1589	John Lyly	James Wallace
25.03.2001	Shakespeare and Gold	The Golden Age	1610	Thomas Heywood	Helen Raynor
01.04.2001	Shakespeare and Gold	The Devil is an Ass	1616	Ben Jonson	David Delve
08.04.2001	Shakespeare and Gold	Anything for a Quiet Life	1621	Thomas Middleton and John Webster	Thomas Hescott
24.06.2001	Words and Action	Lear	1971	Edward Bond	Barry Kyle
22.07.2001	Words and Action	King Leir and His Daughters	1605	Anon.	Jonathan Cullen
12.08.2001	Words and Action	The Late Lancashire Witches	1634	Richard Brome and Thomas Heywood	James Wallace

(cont.)

Date	Read Not Dead Season	Play Title	Year	Author	Co-ordinator
02.09.2001	Words and Action	The Mayor of Queenborough, or, Hengist, King of Kent	1615	Thomas Middleton and William Rowley	Nick Hutchison
04.11.2001	Shakespeare, Gresham and the City	The Wise Woman of Hoxton	1604	Thomas Heywood	Alan Cox
11.11.2001	Shakespeare, Gresham and the City	If You Know Not Me You Know Nobody (Part I)	1605	Thomas Heywood	Peter Lichtenfels
18.11.2001	Shakespeare, Gresham and the City	If You Know Not Me You Know Nobody (Part II)	1606	Thomas Heywood	Peter Lichtenfels
25.11.2001	Shakespeare, Gresham and the City	Sir Thomas More	1590–5	Anthony Munday, Henry Chettle, Thomas Heywood, William Shakespeare and Thomas Dekker	James Wallace
02.12.2001	Shakespeare, Gresham and the City	The Duchess of Suffolk	1631	Thomas Drue	Orla O'Loughlin
17.02.2002	Shakespeare and the Lawyers	The Devil's Law Case	1619	John Webster	Jenny Eastop
03.03.2002	Shakespeare and the Lawyers	Law-Tricks or Who Would Have Thought It	1604	John Day	James Wallace
17.03.2002	Shakespeare and the Lawyers	The Honest Lawyer	1615	'S.S'	Alison Skilbeck
24.03.2002	Shakespeare and the Lawyers	The Poor Man's Comfort	1616	Robert Daborne	Liza Hayden
07.04.2002	Shakespeare and the Lawyers	The Little French Lawyer	1619	John Fletcher and Philip Massinger	Vivien Heilbron

Date	Series	Play	Year	Author	Director
26.05.2002	Words and Action: Wicked Disguises	What you Will	1601	John Marston	James Wallace
30.06.2002	Words and Action: Wicked Disguises	The Grateful Servant	1629	James Shirley	Liza Hayden
21.07.2002	Words and Action: Wicked Disguises	John a Kent and John a Cumber	1590	Anthony Munday	Vivien Heilbron
04.08.2002	Words and Action: Wicked Disguises	Endymion: The Man in the Moon	1588	John Lyly	James Wallace
11.08.2002	Words and Action: Wicked Disguises	Loves Mistress or The Queen's Masque	1634	Thomas Heywood	Stephen Wisker
03.11.2002	Sonnets and Desire	Women Beware Women	1621	Thomas Middleton	Jenny Eastop
10.11.2002	Sonnets and Desire	The Insatiate Countess	1610	John Marston, William Barksted and Lewis Machin	Tony Bell
17.11.2002	Sonnets and Desire	Sappho and Phao	1584	John Lyly	James Wallace
24.11.2002	Sonnets and Desire	Venus and Adonis	1593	William Shakespeare	James Wallace
01.12.2002	Sonnets and Desire	The Labyrinth of Desire	?	Lope de Vega	Gerry Mulgrew
23.02.2003	Shakespeare: The King's Man?	Philotas	1604	Samuel Daniel	Tamara Harvey
02.03.2003	Shakespeare: The King's Man?	The Isle of Gulls	1606	John Day	Joyce Branagh
16.03.2003	Shakespeare: The King's Man?	The Second Maiden's Tragedy	1611	Anon.	Andrew Tidmarsh
30.03.2003	Shakespeare: The King's Man?	Sir John van Olden Barnavelt	1619	Philip Massinger and John Fletcher	James Wallace
06.04.2003	Shakespeare: The King's Man?	The Bondman	1623–5	Philip Massinger	Martin White

(cont.)

Date	Read Not Dead Season	Play Title	Year	Author	Co-ordinator
29.06.2003	Words and Action	Edward IV Part I	1599	Thomas Heywood and others	Tony Bell
20.07.2003	Words and Action	Edward IV Part II	1599	Thomas Heywood and others	Heather Davies
31.08.2003	Words and Action	The True Tragedy of Richard III	1591	Anon.	James Wallace
02.11.2003	Shakespeare Between East and West	Osmond the Great Turk	1622	Lodowick Carlell	Heather Davies
16.11.2003	Shakespeare Between East and West	The Renegado	1624	Philip Massinger	Tom Cornford
30.11.2003	Shakespeare Between East and West	The Turk	c 1607	John Mason	James Wallace
29.02.2004	Shakespeare and Islam	All's Lost by Lust	1619	William Rowley	Tom Cornford
14.03.2004	Shakespeare and Islam	Tamburlaine (Part I)	1587	Christopher Marlowe	Ellie Jones
28.03.2004	Shakespeare and Islam	Tamburlaine (Part II)	1588	Christopher Marlowe	Joyce Branagh
04.04.2004	Shakespeare and Islam	The Battle of Alcazar	1598	George Peele	Martin White
20.06.2004	Words and Action	The Fleer	1606	Edward Sharpham	Tony Bell
18.07.2004	Words and Action	The Unfortunate Lovers	1638	William Davenant	James Wallace
08.08.2004	Words and Action	Hyde Park	1632	James Shirley	Tom Cornford
03.10.2004	Shakespeare and Islam	The English Moor or the Mock Marriage	c. 1637	Richard Brome	James Wallace
10.10.2004	Shakespeare and Islam	The Emperor of the East	c. 1631	Philip Massinger	Vivien Heilbron
28.11.2004	Shakespeare and Islam	Lust's Dominion	c. 1599–1600	John Marston, Thomas Dekker and others	James Wallace
5.12.2004	Shakespeare and Islam	Othello (Q1)	1622	William Shakespeare	Tom Cornford

Date	Series	Title	Year	Author	Director
26.06.2005	Words and Action	The Faithful Shepherdess	1610	John Fletcher	Heather Davies
17.07.2005	Words and Action	The Enchanted Island	1670	John Dryden and Sir William Davenant	Ellen Hughes
31.07.2005	Words and Action	The Silver Age	1613	Thomas Heywood	James Wallace
07.08.2005	Words and Action	The Brazen Age	1613	Thomas Heywood	James Wallace
13.11.2005	Peace and Martyrdom	The Virgin Martyr	1622	Thomas Dekker and Philip Massinger	Tom Cornford
26.02.2006	Spring Events	Caesar and Pompey	c. 1605	George Chapman	Laura Baggaley
12.03.2006	Spring Events	Cornelia, or Pompey the Great and His Fair Cornelia's Tragedy	1594	Thomas Kyd	Crispin Bonham Carter
19.03.2006	Spring Events	If it be not Good the Devil is in it	1610/11	Thomas Dekker (and Robert Daborne)	Philip Wilson
02.04.2006	Spring Events	The Tragedy of Nero	1624	Anon.	Tom Cornford
02.07.2006	Summer Events	The Wounds of Civil War	1594	Thomas Lodge	[Cancelled]
16.07.2006	Summer events	Appius and Virginia	1624	John Webster and Thomas Heywood	Philip Bird
30.07.2006	Summer Events	The Tragedy of Claudius Tiberius Nero	1607	Anon.	Jason Morell
20.07.2006	Summer Events	The Menaechmie or The Twin Brothers	1595	Plautus, translated by William Warner	David Cottis
22.10.2006	Autumn Events	The Roaring Girl	1611	Thomas Dekker and Thomas Middleton	Antony Biggs
05.11.2006	Autumn Events	Old Fortunatus	1600	Thomas Dekker	Lucy Jameson

(cont.)

Date	Read Not Dead Season	Play Title	Year	Author	Co-ordinator
19.11.2006	Autumn Events	The Wits	1636	William Davenant	James Wallace
03.12.2006	Autumn Events	The Jews	1749	Gotthold Ephraim Lessing, trans. Noel Clark	Tom Cornford
18.02.2007	Shakespeare and Venice	Volpone Acts 1–3	1606	Ben Jonson	James Wallace
25.02.2007	Shakespeare and Venice	Volpone Acts 4 and 5	1606	Ben Jonson	James Wallace
11.03.2007	Shakespeare and Venice	Antonio and Mellida	1599	John Marston	Philip Bird
01.04.2007	Shakespeare and Venice	The Wonder of Women (Sophonisba)	1605	John Marston	Anthony Biggs
20.05.2007	Summer Events	Novella 7, Decade III of De Gli Hecatommithi	1565	Giraldi Cinthio	Tom Cornford
03.06.2007	Summer Events	The Gentleman of Venice	1639	James Shirley	Yolanda Vazquez
24.06.2007	Summer Events	Blurt Master-Constable	1601	Anon	Chris Rolls
01.07.2007	Summer Events	The Knave in Grain	1625	J.D.	Jason Morrell
21.10.2007	Young and Shakespeare	The Arraignment of Paris	1581	George Peele	James Chalmers
04.11.2007	Young and Shakespeare	Gallathea	1585	John Lyly	James Wallace
18.11.2007	Young and Shakespeare	The Wars of Cyrus	1588	Anon	Oliver Senton
02.12.2007	Young and Shakespeare	The Woman in the Moon	1593	John Lyly	James Wallace

GLOBE QUARTOS

The following titles were published by Nick Hern Books, 1998–2007:

The Antipodes, Richard Brome (ed. David Scott Kastan and Richard Proudfoot, 2000).

The City Madam, Philip Massinger (ed. Cathy Shrank, 2005).

The Custom of the Country, John Fletcher and Philip Massinger (ed. Nick de Somogyi, 1999).

The Devil's Charter, Barnabe Barnes (ed. Nick de Somogyi, 1999).

The Fleer, Edward Sharpham (ed. Lucy Munro, 2007).

The Honest Whore Parts One and Two, Thomas Dekker and Thomas Middleton (ed. Nick de Somogyi, 1998).

King Leir, Anon. (ed. Tiffany Stern, 2002).

A Mad World My Masters, Thomas Middleton (ed. Nick de Somogyi, 1998).

The Mayor of Queenborough, Thomas Middleton (ed. Howard Marchitello, 2005).

The Merry Devil of Edmonton, Anon. (ed. Nicola Bennett, 2000).

The Noble Spanish Soldier, Thomas Dekker (ed. Zachary Lesser, 2007).

The Poor Man's Comfort, Robert Daborn (ed. Jane Kingsley-Smith, 2005).

A Shoemaker, A Gentleman, William Rowley (ed. Trudy Darby, 2002).

The Wise Woman of Hoxton, Thomas Heywood (ed. Sonia Massai, 2002).

The Witches of Lancashire, Thomas Heywood and Richard Brome (ed. Gabriel Egan, 2002).

The Maid's Tragedy (ed. Nick de Somogyi, 1998).

BIBLIOGRAPHY

Appleyard, Bryan. 'History Rebuilds Itself, this Time as Farce', *Independent*, 9 August 1995, p. 13.

Auslander, Philip. 'Is there Life after *Liveness*?', in Susan Broadhurst and Josephine Machon (eds.), *Performance and Technology: Practices of Virtual Embodiment and Interactivity* (Houndmills: Palgrave Macmillan, 2007), pp. 194–7.

  Liveness: Performance in a Mediatized Culture (New York: Routledge, 1999).

Austern, Linda. '"Sing Againe Syren": the Female Musician and Sexual Enchantment in Elizabethan Life and Literature', *Renaissance Quarterly* 42 (1989), 420–48.

  '"Alluring the Auditorie to Effeminacy": Music and the Idea of the Feminine in Early Modern England', *Music and Letters* 74 (1993), 343–54.

Barish, Jonas. 'Is there "Authenticity" in Theatrical Performance?', *Modern Language Review* 89 (1994), 817–31.

Bennett, Susan. *Theatre Audiences: A Theory of Production and Reception* (London: Routledge, 1997).

Billington, Michael. 'The Final Curtain', *Guardian*, 28 February 2007.

Blakemore Evans, G. (ed.). *The Riverside Shakespeare* (revised edition), (Boston and New York: Houghton Mifflin, 1997).

Booth, Stephen. 'The Best *Othello* I ever Saw', *Shakespeare Quarterly* 40, 3 (Autumn 1989), 332–6.

Brenton, Howard. 'Playing to the Crowd', *Guardian*, Saturday 12 May 2007.

Brown, Howard Mayer. 'Pedantry of Liberation', in Nicholas Kenyon (ed.), *Authenticity and Early Music* (Oxford University Press, 1988), pp. 27–56.

Campbell, Margaret. *Dolmetsch: The Man and his Work* (London: Hamilton, 1975).

Capell, Edward. *Mr William Shakespeare, His Comedies, Histories and Tragedies* (London: 1790; New York: AMS Press, 1968).

Carlson, Marvin. *Theories of the Theatre*, expanded edition (Ithaca: Cornell University Press, 1993).

Carson, Neil. *A Companion to Henslowe's Diary* (Cambridge University Press, 1988).

Clapp, Susannah. 'Theatre Has Moved On – Whatever We Critics Think', *Observer*, Sunday 20 May 2007.

Clayton, Martin, Trevor Herbert and Richard Middleton (eds.). *The Cultural Study of Music: A Critical Introduction* (London: Routledge, 2003).

Conkie, Rob. *The Globe Theatre Project: Shakespeare and Authenticity* (Lewiston: The Edwin Mellen Press, 2006).

Crutchfield, Will. 'Fashion, Conviction and Performance Style in an Age of Revivals', in Nicholas Kenyon (ed.), *Authenticity and Early Music* (Oxford University Press, 1988).

Dessen, Alan C. '"Taint Not Thy Mind ...": Problems and Pitfalls in Staging Plays at the New Globe', in Franklin J. Hildy (ed.) *New Issues in the Reconstruction of Shakespeare's Theatre: Proceedings of the Conference Held at the University of Georgia, February 16–18, 1990* (New York: Peter Lang, 1990), pp. 135–58.

  'Recovering Elizabethan Theatrical Vocabulary: A Reconsideration of the Evidence' in Edward Pechter (ed.), *Textual and Theatrical Shakespeare: Questions of Evidence* (University of Iowa Press, 1966), pp. 44–65.

  Elizabethan Stage Conventions and Modern Interpreters (Cambridge University Press, 1984).

Dessen, Alan C. and Leslie Thomson. *A Dictionary of Stage Directions in English Drama, 1580–1642* (Cambridge University Press, 1999).

Dreyfus, Laurence. 'Early Music Defended against its Devotees: a Theory of Historical Performance in the Twentieth Century', *Musical Quarterly* 69 (1983), 297–322.

Duffin, Ross. *Shakespeare's Songbook* (New York: W. W. Norton, 2004).

Dunn, Lesley C. 'Ophelia's Songs in Hamlet: Music, Madness, and the Feminine', in Lesley C. Dunn and Nancy A. Jones (eds.), *Embodied Voices: Representing Female Vocality in Western Culture* (Cambridge University Press, 1994), pp. 50–64.

Escolme, Bridget. *Talking to the Audience: Shakespeare, Performance, Self* (London: Routledge, 1997).

Feldman, Donna Rose. 'An Historical Study of Thomas Wood Stevens' Globe Theatre Company, 1934–7' (PhD dissertation: University of Iowa, 1953).

Fernie, Ewan. 'Shakespeare and the Prospect of Presentism', *Shakespeare Survey* 58 (2005), 169–84.

Fox-Good, Jacquelyn. 'Ophelia's Mad Songs: Music, Gender, Power', in David C. Allen and Robert White (eds.), *Subjects on the World's Stage: Essays on British Literature of the Middle Ages and the Renaissance* (Newark: University of Delaware Press, 1995), pp. 217–38.

Gibson, Rex. *Teaching Shakespeare* (Cambridge University Press, 1998).

Gil Harris, Jonathan, and Natasha Korda. *Staged Properties in Early Modern English Drama* (Cambridge University Press, 2003).

Golub, Spencer. *Evreinov: The Theatre of Paradox and Transformation* (Ann Arbor: UMI Research, 1984).

Greenblatt, Stephen, Walter Cohen, Jean E. Howard, Katharine Eisaman Maus (eds.). *The Norton Shakespeare* (New York and London: W. W. Norton, 1997).

Gross Brockett, Oscar, and Robert R. Findlay. *Century of Innovation: A History of European and American Theatre and Drama since 1870*, 2nd edition (Englewood Cliffs, NJ: Prentice-Hall, 1991).

Gurr, Andrew. *Playgoing in Shakespeare's London* (Cambridge University Press, 1987).

  The Shakespeare Company 1594–1642 (Cambridge University Press, 2005).

  'Staging at the Globe', in J. R. Mulryne and Margaret Shewring (eds.), *Shakespeare's Globe Rebuilt* (Cambridge University Press, 1997), pp. 159–68.

Hart, A. 'The Time Allotted for Representation of Elizabethan and Jacobean Plays', *Review of English Studies* 8, 32 (October 1932), 395–413.

Haskell, Harry. *The Early Music Revival: A History* (London: Thames and Hudson, 1988).

Hawkes, Terence. *Shakespeare in the Present* (London and New York, Routledge, 2002).

Headlam-Wells, Robin. 'Historicism and "Presentism" in Early Modern Studies', *Cambridge Quarterly* 29 (2000), 37–60.

Henslowe, Philip. *Henslowe's Diary*, ed. Reginald Foakes, 2nd edition (Cambridge University Press, 2002).

Heywood, Thomas. *A Woman Killed With Kindness*, ed. R. W. Van Fossen, Revels Plays (London: Methuen, 1961).

Higgins, Charlotte. 'Praised and Confused', *Guardian*, 24 February 2007.

Hildy, Franklin J. 'Reconstructing Shakespeare's Globe Theatre', in Franklin J. Hildy (ed.), *New Issues in the Reconstruction of Shakespeare's Theatre: Proceedings of the Conference Held at the University of Georgia February, 16–18, 1990* (New York: Peter Lang, 1990), pp. 1–37.

  'Why Elizabethan Spaces?', *Elizabethan Performances in North American Spaces: Theatre Symposium* 12 (2004), 98–120.

  Shakespeare at the Maddermarket (Ann Arbor: UMI Research, 1986).

Howard, Jean. 'The New Historicism and Renaissance Studies', in Ewan Fernie et al. (eds.), *Reconceiving the Renaissance* (Oxford University Press, 2005).

Howard, Jean E., and Marion F. O'Connor (eds.). *Shakespeare Reproduced: The Text in History and Ideology* (New York: Methuen, 1987).

Hunter, L. and Peter Lichtenfels (eds.). *Shakespeare, Language and the Stage: The Fifth Wall: Approaches to Shakespeare from Criticism, Performance and Theatre Studies*, Arden Shakespeare (London: Thomson Learning, 2005).

Jorgensen, Paul A. *Shakespeare's Military World* (Berkeley and Los Angeles: University of California Press, 1965).

Joughin, J. 'Shakespeare now: an Editorial Statement', *Shakespeare* 1, 1 (June 2005).

Kahn, Jeremy. 'Imagining and Reimagining the Globe', *New York Times*, 13 January 2007.

Karim-Cooper, Farah. *Cosmetics in Shakespearean and Renaissance Drama* (Edinburgh University Press, 2006).

Kennedy, Dennis. *Looking at Shakespeare* (Cambridge University Press, 1993).

  'Shakespeare and Cultural Tourism', *Theatre Journal* 50, 2 (1998), 175–88.

Kegl, Rosemary. '"[W]rapping togas over Elizabethan garb": Tabloid Shakespeare and the 1934 Chicago World's Fair', *Renaissance Drama* new series 28 (1997), 73–104.

Klein, David. 'Time Allotted for an Elizabethan Performance', *Shakespeare Quarterly* 18, 4 (Autumn 1967), 434–8.

Levenson, Jill L. 'The Recovery of the Elizabethan Stage', *Elizabethan Theatre* 9 (1986), 205–29.

Lindley, David. *Shakespeare and Music* (London: Thomson Learning, 2006).

MacKinnon, Dolly. '"Poor Senseless Bess, Clothed in her Rags and Folly": Early Modern Women, Madness and Song in Seventeenth-Century England', *Parergon* 18, 3 (2001), 119–51.

Markham, Gervase. *The Souldier's Accidence* (1635), in Paul A. Jorgensen (ed.), *Shakespeare's Military World* (Berkeley and Los Angeles: University of California Press, 1965).

Marshall, Cynthia. 'Sight and Sound: Two Models of Shakespearean Subjectivity on the British Stage', *Shakespeare Quarterly* 51, 3 (Autumn 2000), 353–61.

Marston, John. *The Malcontent*, ed. Bernard Harris, New Mermaids (London: A. and C. Black, 1967, 1993).

Martin, Ralph G. *Jennie, Lady Randolph Churchill, the Dramatic Years, 1885–1921*, vol. II (New York: Signet, 1970).

McClary, Susan. *Feminine Endings: Music, Gender and Sexuality* (Minneapolis: University of Minnesota Press, 1991).

Menzer, Paul. 'Afterword: Discovery Spaces? Research at the Globe and Blackfriars', in Paul Menzer (ed.), *Inside Shakespeare: Essays on the Blackfriars Stage* (Selinsgrove: Susquehanna University Press, 2006), pp. 223–30.

Nagler, A. M. *A Source Book in Theatrical History* (New York: Dover, 1952).

Nelsen, Paul. 'Positing Pillars at the Globe', *Shakespeare Quarterly* 48, 3 (Autumn 1997), 324–35.

Nicol, David. '*Twelfth Night*, Performed by the Company of Shakespeare's Globe at the Middle Temple Hall, London, February 2002', *Early Modern Literary Studies* 8, 1 (May 2002), 1–23.

O'Connor, Marion F. *William Poel and the Elizabethan Stage Society* (Cambridge: Chadwyck-Healey, 1987).

Oddie, David and Garth Allen. *Artists in Schools: A Review* (London: The Stationery Office, 1998).

Paget, A. H. 'The Elizabethan Playhouses', *Transactions of the Leicester Literary and Philosophical Society* (London, 1891), 237–50.

Payne, B. Iden. 'Shakespeare at Work in his Theatre', *Educational Theatre Journal* 19, 3, Shakespearean Production (October 1967), 327–33.

Poel, William. *Shakespeare in the Theatre* (London: Sidgwick and Jackson, 1913).

Potter, Lois. 'A Stage Where Every Man Must Play a Part?', *Shakespeare Quarterly* 50, 1 (Spring 1999), 74–86.

Rawson, Christopher. 'Stage Review: Globe's *Twelfth Night* Shows Comedy, Heart', *Pittsburgh Post-Gazette*, Thursday 13 November 2003.

Richmond, Hugh. 'Techniques for Reconstituting Elizabethan Staging', in Franklin J. Hildy (ed.). *New Issues in the Reconstruction of Shakespeare's Theatre: Proceedings of the Conference Held at the University of Georgia, February 16–18, 1990* (New York: Peter Lang, 1990), pp. 159–83.

Russell Brown, John. 'Modern Uses for a Globe Theatre', in C. Walter Hodges, S. Schoenbaum and Leonard Leane (eds.), *The Third Globe: Symposium for the Reconstruction of the Globe Playhouse* (Detroit: Wayne State University Press, 1981), pp. 14–28.

Ryan, Jessica. *The 2002 Globe Season, The White Company: Twelfth Night, Globe Research Bulletin* 26 (July 2002).

Rylance, Mark. 'Playing the Globe: Artistic Policy and Practice', in J. R. Mulryne and Margaret Shewring (eds.), *Shakespeare's Globe Rebuilt* (Cambridge University Press, 1997), pp. 14–28.

Play – A Recollection in Pictures and Words of the First Five Years of Play at Shakespeare's Globe Theatre. Photographs: Sheila Burnett, Donald Cooper, Richard Kolina, John Tramper (London: Shakespeare's Globe, 2003).

Sarlós, Robert K. 'Creating Objects and Events: a Form of Theatre Research', *Theatre Research International* 5, 1 (1979–80), 82–8.

Schlueter, June. 'Michael van Meer's Album Amicorum, with Illustrations of London, 1614–15', *Huntington Library Quarterly* 69 (2006), 301–14.

Schutz, Chantal. 'Music at the New Globe', *Early Modern Literary Studies*, Special Issue 8 (May 2001), 1–36.

Silverstone, Catherine. 'Shakespeare Live: Reproducing Shakespeare at the "New" Globe Theatre', *Textual Practice* 19 (2005), 31–50.

Simpson, Claude M. *The British Broadside Ballad and its Music* (New Brunswick, NJ: Rutgers University Press, 1966).

Sinfield, Alan. '*Poetaster*, the Author, and the Perils of Cultural Production', in Lena Cowen Orlin (ed.), *Material London ca. 1600* (Philadelphia: University of Pennsylvania Press, 2000), pp. 75–89.

Smith, Bruce R. Shakespeare's Residuals: the Circulation of Ballads in Cultural Memory', in Stuart Gillespie and Neil Rhodes (eds.), *Shakespeare and Elizabethan Popular Culture*, Arden Critical Companions (London: Thomson Learning, 2006), pp. 193–217.

 The Acoustic World of Early Modern England: Attending to the O-Factor (University of Chicago Press, 1999).

Speaight, Robert. *William Poel and the Elizabethan Revival* (London: Heinemann, 1954).

Stern, Tiffany, '"You That Walk i'th Galleries": Standing and Walking in the Galleries of the Globe Theatre', *Shakespeare Quarterly* 51 (Summer 2000), 211–16.

Styan, J. L. *Shakespeare's Stagecraft* (Cambridge University Press, 1967).

Taruskin, Richard. *Text and Act: Essays on Music and Performance* (Oxford University Press, 1995).

 The Teaching of Shakespeare in Schools (English Association, 1908).

Tomlinson, Gary. 'The Historian, the Performer, and Authentic Meaning in Music', in Nicholas Kenyon (ed.), *Authenticity and Early Music: A Symposium* (Oxford University Press, 1988), pp. 115–36.

Vaughan Williams, Ralph. *National Music and Other Essays* (Oxford University Press, 1963).

Watt, Tessa. *Cheap Print and Popular Piety, 1550–1640* (Cambridge University Press, 1991).

White, Martin. *Renaissance Drama in Action* (London: Routledge, 1998).

 'William Poel's Globe', *Theatre Notebook* 53, 3 (1999), 146–52.

White, Melvin R. 'Thomas Wood Stevens: Creative Pioneer', *Educational Theatre Journal* 3, 4 (December 1951), 280–93.

Woods, A. 'Reporting Performance Research', *Theatre Survey* 6 (1989), 171–6.

Worthen, W. B. 'Staging "Shakespeare": Acting, Authority and the Rhetoric of Performance', in James C. Bulman (ed.), *Shakespeare, Theory and Performance* (London: Routledge, 1996), pp. 12–28.

 'Reconstructing the Globe, Constructing Ourselves', in *Shakespeare and the Globe: Shakespeare Survey* 52 (1999), 33–45.

 Shakespeare and the Force of Modern Performance (Cambridge University Press, 2003).

Wright, George T. *Shakespeare's Metrical Art* (Berkeley: University of California Press, 1988).

INTERVIEWS

Interviews were conducted by the editors with members of Shakespeare's Globe creative team on the following dates:

Yolanda Vasquez, Actor and Globe Education Practitioner – 2 February 2007

Keith McGowan, Musician – 9 February 2007

Paul Chahidi, Actor and Globe Education Practitioner – 16 February 2007
Mark Rylance, Artistic Director 1996–2005 – 17 April 2007
Patrick Spottiswoode, Director, Globe Education 1984–currently – 18 May 2007
Dominic Dromgoole, Artistic Director 2006–currently – 24 May 2007
William Lyons, Musician – 12 June 2007
Christie Carson also interviewed the following members of the Education department on 12 June 2007:
Chris Stafford, Projects and Development Manager
Jo Elworthy, Southwark Community Projects Manager
Kieron Kirkland, Southwark Community Projects Co-ordinator

INDEX